Palgrave Studies in Adaptation and Visual Culture

Series Editors
Julie Grossman
Le Moyne College
Syracuse, NY, USA

R. Barton Palmer
Clemson University
Clemson, SC, USA

This new series addresses how adaptation functions as a principal mode of text production in visual culture. What makes the series distinctive is its focus on visual culture as both targets and sources for adaptations, and a vision to include media forms beyond film and television such as videogames, mobile applications, interactive fiction and film, print and nonprint media, and the avant-garde. As such, the series will contribute to an expansive understanding of adaptation as a central, but only one, form of a larger phenomenon within visual culture. Adaptations are texts that are not singular but complexly multiple, connecting them to other pervasive plural forms: sequels, series, genres, trilogies, authorial oeuvres, appropriations, remakes, reboots, cycles and franchises. This series especially welcomes studies that, in some form, treat the connection between adaptation and these other forms of multiplicity. We also welcome proposals that focus on aspects of theory that are relevant to the importance of adaptation as connected to various forms of visual culture.

Advisory Board
Sarah Cardwell, University of Kent, UK
Deborah Cartmell, De Montfort University, UK
Timothy Corrigan, University of Pennsylvania, US
Lars Ellestrom, Linnaeus University, Sweden
Kamilla Elliott, Lancaster University, UK
Christine Geraghty, University of Glasgow, UK
Helen Hanson, University of Exeter, UK
Linda Hutcheon, University of Toronto, Canada
Glenn Jellenik, University of Central Arkansas, US
Thomas Leitch, University of Delaware, US
Brian McFarlane, Monash University, Australia
Simone Murray, Monash University, Australia
James Naremore, Indiana University, US
Kate Newell, Savannah College of Art and Design, US
Laurence Raw, Baskent University, Turkey
Robert Stam, New York University, US
Constantine Verevis, Monash University, Australia
Imelda Whelehan, University of Tasmania, Australia
Shannon Wells-Lassagne, Universite de Bretagne Sud, France

More information about this series at
http://www.palgrave.com/gp/series/14654

Yvonne Griggs

Adaptable TV

Rewiring the Text

Yvonne Griggs
University of New England
Armidale, NSW, Australia

Palgrave Studies in Adaptation and Visual Culture
ISBN 978-3-319-77530-2   ISBN 978-3-319-77531-9 (eBook)
https://doi.org/10.1007/978-3-319-77531-9

Library of Congress Control Number: 2018943631

© The Editor(s) (if applicable) and The Author(s) 2018
This work is subject to copyright. All rights are solely and exclusively licensed by the Publisher, whether the whole or part of the material is concerned, specifically the rights of translation, reprinting, reuse of illustrations, recitation, broadcasting, reproduction on microfilms or in any other physical way, and transmission or information storage and retrieval, electronic adaptation, computer software, or by similar or dissimilar methodology now known or hereafter developed.
The use of general descriptive names, registered names, trademarks, service marks, etc. in this publication does not imply, even in the absence of a specific statement, that such names are exempt from the relevant protective laws and regulations and therefore free for general use.
The publisher, the authors, and the editors are safe to assume that the advice and information in this book are believed to be true and accurate at the date of publication. Neither the publisher nor the authors or the editors give a warranty, express or implied, with respect to the material contained herein or for any errors or omissions that may have been made. The publisher remains neutral with regard to jurisdictional claims in published maps and institutional affiliations.

Cover image: © Łukasz Szczepanski/Alamy Stock Photo
Cover design: Akihiro Nakayama

Printed on acid-free paper

This Palgrave Macmillan imprint is published by the registered company Springer International Publishing AG part of Springer Nature
The registered company address is: Gewerbestrasse 11, 6330 Cham, Switzerland

For Laura and Sarah, always…

Acknowledgements

I would like to express my thanks to those whose support for this project has ensured its journey to completion: my editor Lina Aboujieb for her endless patience, series editors Julie Grossmann and R. Barton Palmer for giving me the opportunity to contribute to the Adaptation and Visual Culture series, and the University of New England for granting me study leave, without which completion of this monograph would have been 'mission impossible'. I'd also like to thank the various anonymous reviewers who, through their incisive critiques of the manuscript throughout the writing process, enabled me to see things more clearly. A final word of thanks must go to my ever supportive family: to Rob, Laura and Sarah without whom not a single word could have been written.

Contents

1 Introduction   1

2 *Penny Dreadful*: The Neo-Victorian 'Made-for-TV' Series   13

3 *Fargo*: To Be Continued...   67

4 *Orange Is the New Black* as 'Living Text': From Memoir to TV Series   105

5 *The Night Of*: A Remake 'Original'   151

Afterword: One More 'Turn'....   195

Index   199

CHAPTER 1

Introduction

Every facet of the TV industry is adapting in this contemporary era of media convergence, from the ways in which shows are transmitted and consumed to the changing nature of the relationship between networks and the audiences they court. The cultural kudos of the medium as a purveyor of quality drama, in what has come to be termed the current 'golden age' of TV, characterised by the increased involvement of creatives from a seemingly more prestigious film industry who are lured by the greater control offered within the industrial terrain of TV production and by the time-rich potentialities of TV seriality, is also changing. Part of this increasing kudos can be attributed to the emergence of a more innovative and boundary-pushing approach to the adaptation of pre-existing stories within the unique context of TV's long-form serial narrative. TV is a medium which is historically and industrially primed to view the art of adaptation as profitable industry practice: it embraces the recycling of narrative forms as an established mode of TV production. The recent unprecedented rise in adapted TV scripted drama commissioned by an ever-expanding number of media outlets, from seasoned cable channels like HBO and rivals FX or Showtime to new streaming providers like Netflix and Hulu, serves as a clear indicator of the industry's ongoing investment in adaptive practices. Scholarship that focuses on TV remakes, reboots, prequels and sequels as established adaptive modes is similarly on the rise and *Adaptable TV: Rewiring the Text* builds on this scholarly interest. However, instead of concentrating on the traditional aforementioned types of adaption, this study explores

© The Author(s) 2018
Y. Griggs, *Adaptable TV*, Palgrave Studies in Adaptation and Visual Culture, https://doi.org/10.1007/978-3-319-77531-9_1

experimental adaptive practices that are currently generating a body of prestige serial drama within an ever-evolving TV landscape.

I argue that these serialised TV reconceptualisation of existing narratives serve as a provocation: they posit a reassessment of our understanding of adaptation as a cultural, theoretical and creative process by inviting us to rethink questions of authorship and ownership of narrative and to take into account both the impact of media-specific industrial production contexts, and of sociocultural influences at play in the reconfiguration of pre-loved stories. My aim, with particular reference to the serial narrative form, is to contextualise the process of adaptation within the parameters of TV production and consumption by employing an analytical matrix which applies not only a theoretical approach that examines the affinities between an adapted text and its prior source or sources, but one that explores the paratextual discourse that surrounds them. As a means to interrogating these processes at work in the reconfiguration of narratives to the serialised TV format, I employ a range of case study texts, all of which offer something new to adaptations discourse. The study opens with a focus on two experimental serial adaptations, *Penny Dreadful* (Showtime 2014–2016) and *Fargo* (FX 2104–); the analytical focus then shifts to the more traditional yet equally ground-breaking *Orange is the New Black* (Netflix 2103–) and *The Night Of* (HBO 2016). The selected series are products of a contemporary American TV industry committed to the production of serial narratives adapted from other forms, and all share a preoccupation with branding and authorship. However, the synergies of each are counter-balanced by their points of difference: each series employs a different serialised format and a different approach to the reconfiguration of the precursor text or texts, and the media outlets that produce and disseminate them are notably diverse as are the audiences they attract.

Writing back in 2007, Creeber and Hills predict a 'radical transformation' of the 'economic and cultural worlds of television' in terms of TV production, distribution and consumption (1–2). Having moved from what Ellis terms the 'scarcity' of TV product that characterises the TVI phase of the medium's evolution to the TVII period which marks its greater 'availability', the current TVIII era is all about 'choice' (Ellis cited in Creeber and Hills 1).[1] The 'choice' factor has revolutionised

---

[1] Jason Mittell defines these three distinct eras within an American context as: the classic network era of the mid-1940s to 1980s (ABC, CBS, NBC); the satellite, cable and the VCR

television in ways that have shifted beyond those anticipated by Creeber and Hills. In this contemporary era of convergence, De Fino argues that current changes to the TV landscape are in the main a response to the 'legacy' provided by American cable channel HBO; by adopting a creative approach to programme content and to programme delivery 'in a medium notoriously averse to risk', HBO has found ways to generate a niche audience for its product (3), providing other cable channel competitors like Showtime, FX, AMC, Bravo, Pivot and TLC with an alternative industry model that has since facilitated TV's emergence as 'the pre-eminent narrative medium of our time' (7), for a new type of 'boutique audience' that traditionally did not engage in TV viewing (Mittell Narrative Complexity 31). However, it is the recent arrival of streaming providers like Netflix and Hulu as generators of 'original content' that has further enhanced the dominance of the TV medium as a purveyor of quality risk-taking drama in this digital age. Having evolved from their origins as video streaming libraries back in 2007, streaming outlets of this kind are challenging the long-held position of more established and prestigious cable channels like HBO, and this increased competition leads to further 'choice' for consumers in terms of not only what to watch but when and how. While HBO may be attributed with 'revolutionizing TV aesthetics and narrative structures' streaming outlets like Netflix and Hulu are at the forefront of equally revolutionary changes to the way programmes are currently released and consumed (Jenner 261), giving streaming providers the capacity to build 'even smaller "niche" audiences' who have the capacity to control their own viewing, to access whole seasons on demand, and to engage with 'increasingly complex narrative structures' (269–270). These changes in release patterns introduce what Mittell sees as a potential destabilisation of the serial form: to 'for[go]' the traditional 'gap-filled serial broadcast experience' works contrary to the norms TV consumption (Complex Poetics 41), and the ways in which we engage with stories before, during and after release are similarly disrupted by that change in consumption habits. Kustritz echoes Mittell's observations noting that both the 'function of seriality in the absence of fixed instalments' and the increased 'dispersion of

multi-channel era of the 1990s; and the current era of media convergence (TV and American Culture 11).

potential story elements across a diverse collection of media platforms and technologies' have the potential to further de-stabilise fixed notions of seriality (M/C). But with destabilisation comes opportunity—opportunity to expand the narrative boundaries of the serial form, taking it into evermore complex adaptive realms as the case studies focused on here demonstrate. In the interim, what we continue to consider scripted serial drama remains central to the re-evaluation of TV as a medium, and with serial drama's increased capacity for narrative complexity comes the capacity for writers and producers to develop evermore complex serialised long-form narratives, the visual quality of which equates with that of cinema due to today's advanced digital technologies.

In this postmillennial TV climate, TV's 'evaluative stock' has risen, affording it a kudos comparable to historically more prestigious modes of creative expression like the novel, theatre or cinema (Mittell Complex Poetics 37); moreover, this 'change in perception' of the medium's 'legitimacy' enhances its appeal to creatives working in other fields (31). As the rising number of successful TV series of varying types testifies, TV is no longer deemed the fall-back option for creatives working in the field of narrative adaptation. For the adapter working with densely layered narratives of pre-existing texts, contemporary TV seriality lends itself to a more labyrinthine unravelling of and/or potential expansion of existing story worlds within a TV production context that is less rigid and less time-constrained than its cinematic or theatrical counterpart. Since the 1990s, the long-form narrative has become what Innocenti and Pescatore term the 'canonical form of new TV seriality', its shape evolving from the 'multilinear' and 'complex' series of the nineties to include a range of series types that in recent times has also embraced the return of the anthologised series, a format once considered 'antiquated' and cost prohibitive (3). Instead of providing continuity of plot or character, the anthology series foregrounds its stylistic and thematic points of continuity across seasons, allowing for the emergence of seasonally discrete storylines that are nevertheless part of a unified whole; in much the same way, anthologised TV series adapted from prior texts can connect with that prior text at the level of style aesthetic and thematic preoccupation rather than narrative and character as demonstrated by the anthologised TV series, *Fargo*. Furthermore, the narratological boundaries of TV seriality are constantly shifting, presenting 'continuously expanding diegetic worlds within a single series', some of which are 'vast and detailed hyper-diegetic worlds' that are made visible only from time to time across a season or seasons (8). Each of the adaptive exemplars explored in this study envisions diegetic worlds that go beyond the confines of the precursor texts they adapt, and one notable consequence of increased competition in the field of scripted drama is an upsurge in the number of serial narratives that have their origins in prior texts: whether transitioning from stage, film, novel, comic book, biography or memoir, or in the guise of national remake, pre-loved stories are finding increased traction within a TV medium that is acutely aware of the financial advantages of harnessing an existing fan-base. In *Penny Dreadful* series creator John Logan harnesses fandoms that attach to nineteenth-century canonical texts appropriated at the level of story and archetype, *and* canonical twentieth-century cinematic horror texts appropriated in terms of their style aesthetic. Through these narrative and stylistic strategies, Logan draws in each pre-existing fan-base yet he also creates a diegesis that ventures beyond both, taking his new audience into the hyper-diegetic realms of a demi-monde of his own creation. In Noah Hawley's TV series, *Fargo*, the world envisioned by the Coen brothers in their film is extended across a timeline continuum that shifts back and forth across the series' anthologised seasons, expanding and destabilising the Fargo story world in ways that elongate its narrative reach and longevity. In a seven-season serial treatment of Piper Kerman's prison memoir, series creator Jenji Kohan extends the source text's limited diegesis beyond both the spatial and temporal confines of the correctional facility, giving the viewer access to social worlds and experiences that have brought inmates to their current impasse. Though *The Night Of* retains many of the generic markers of its precursor text, as a remake locating to a different geographical and cultural locale, its story world's transition to an American national context is an inevitable and essential feature of its successful appropriation. The adaptive possibilities are endless given the narrative freedoms of seriality, especially within contemporary TV's diverse and highly competitive production climate.

Regardless of the kinds of expansions that take place, what emerges as a *shared* trait of these TV series in general is their capacity to connect to the texts they are seen to adapt *and* to a body of intertexts that continue to circulate all four series and the texts they reference. The TV series should be read not as a single text presented on a single screen but as a product that has its genesis in an array of textual sites (Mittell Complex Poetics 7); the TV series *adaptation* is wedded in particular to an intertextual web of generic predecessors that inform its inception and its ongoing reception—an intertextual web that is further amplified by the body of generic intertexts already affiliated with the narrative that it is adapting, and this forms a major strand of enquiry across all four case study texts. However, TV genres are not of a 'timeless essence'; rather, they shift in response to 'changing cultural practices': their meaning, argues Mittell, is located 'beyond the text' itself within a set of 'complex interrelations' defined by 'texts, audiences and historical contexts' (Mittell A Cultural Approach 7), all of which form part of the transitional process at work in the adaptation of narrative as the case study texts explored here demonstrate. *Penny Dreadful* is a series which is a particularly rich and complex generic hybrid that draws from the generic gene pool of a range of historical periods, encompassing the gothic novel, sensationalist penny dreadful pulp fiction, the nineteenth-century literary canon, canonical horror cinema of the 1930s and Hammer horror films from the 1960 and 1970s, as well as contemporary horror TV series like *American Horror Story* and a body of neo-Victorian novels and screen texts. Genres have an important role to play in the 'interpretive process' but within the industrial practices of TV production what emerge as equally influential signifiers of meaning are the paratexts that circulate TV series, *especially* those adapted from prior texts: like genre, paratexts 'provi[de] an initial context and reading strategy for the text' that influences our perception and reception of the series (Gray Show Sold 36). In the realms of adaptation, paratextuality is a central facet of intertextuality. Paratexts scaffold serial adaptations before, during and after release, becoming an organic part of the series and its identity as a whole. That discourse encompasses: the role of generic markers, considered here in relation to the historical and industrial context of their usage; notions of authorial authenticity and the role of the TV auteur within a highly collaborative TV production environment; and the influence of TV branding, marketing and ongoing social interactions with reviewers and fans alike. To this end, my research is in part dependent upon interviews with not only those industry creatives involved in the production of serial adaptations but with those instrumental in its dissemination.

Though 'secondary' to the TV product they reference, paratexts have, according to Gray, 'primary power' over audience consumption (TV Previews 33), and for the adaptation, paratexts of various types can wield a significant influence over the relationship established between it and the text or texts being adapted. If, as Gray infers, the paratext is 'the first outpost of interpretation', and viewer expectation is 'managed' by the hype that surrounds the series, its identity as an adaptation of a prior text can be directed, creating an atmosphere receptive to its reading as something that has a close connection to an earlier narrative, or as a product that has a different kind of televisual identity. Branding and marketing within the TV industry have substantial influence in this respect. The way in which the text is first received by the increasingly influential TV reviewer, whose commentary can both shape audience perception and influence the connections established between the series, its forerunners and other texts that circulate it, is a similarly significant factor (Lotz, On TV Crit 21). *Fargo* is marketed by FX as a product that foregrounds its affiliation with the cultural capital of the work of the Coen brothers as Indie auteurs, yet *Penny Dreadful's* connection with the canonical literature it appropriates is treated as secondary to its affiliation with the horror genre, while *The Night Of's* identity as a remake is afforded little traction in its marketing and reception, this 'limited' series emerging instead as a prestige HBO product representative of the HBO brand. In these media convergent times, the ongoing paratextual discourse surrounding any series during its often extended seasonal roll-out is also maintained by fans and by the media outlets who continue to scaffold reception through evermore creative and divergent marketing means as evidenced by the highly successful and innovative strategies employed by Netflix in their handling of *Orange is the New Black* across not only the first five seasons but its pending seasons six and seven, its multiepisode release pattern making sustained fan interaction even more complex and potentially problematic.

Hutcheon notes that 'by their very existence' adaptations 'remind us there is no such thing as an autonomous text' penned by an 'original genius' (111). Yet debates about authorship and ownership of narrative continue to permeate the practice of adaptation, especially when a prior text is being revisioned for the screen. Stam's concerns about the predominantly negative language employed in the discourse surrounding adaptations in general and film adaptations in particular (54), finds less traction in the discourse surrounding the TV serial adaptation; in the paratextually rich environs of TV production, the relationship between prior texts and serial adaptations is invariably debated as a point of interest rather than as a moralistic battle site of contested ownership. Elitist assumptions of creative dominion of the kind that have come to define the film industry, where authorial authority has historically been ascribed to the director–auteur, have historically held hold no sway in a TV landscape characterised by its inherently collaborative working practices. In contrast to the 'director-centred model' of cinema production, TV functions in the main as 'a producer's medium' (Mittell Narrative Complexity 31), the showrunner taking the creative lead and ensuring a series' 'distinctive visual sensibility' across its various seasons (Mittell Complex Poetics 90). But in an era in which cable channels and streaming outlets vie for aesthetic distinction investment in prestige branding is no longer the sole domain of HBO, and the increasingly foregrounded role of the showrunner is a clear indication that where once television production was driven by a spirit of collaboration, it is now fuelled by a brand-led pursuit of an authorial integrity that works contrary to the collaborative traditions of TV authorship.

The current quest for quality brand identity by an ever-increasing number of cable channels and streaming providers is marked by the emergence of the showrunner as 'TV auteur' (Newman and Levine 2012; Mittell Complex Poetics; Chalaby 2015), and as several of the serialised adaptations explored in this study demonstrate, this recent trend towards a more singular mode of authorship complicates the relationship between series and prior text, posing further questions about authorial attribution. Where once attribution of authorship was seen as out of place in the context of TV production (Mittell Complex Poetics 95), notions of authorial integrity are now part of its cultural currency. In part a consequence of the influx of film creatives into TV production, and in part a reflection of the cinematic quality sought and attained within TV's contemporary industrial environs, the rise of the TV auteur in an American context marks a shift away from its revered Writers' Room model and towards the more centralised control of the showrunner who is not only involved on all facets of drafting and production but is often sole writer of a serial drama in a manner more commonly associated with UK TV writing models. Of the four case studies explored here, only Jenji Kohan emerges as a showrunner whose series evolves from and is sustained within the collaborative working practices of the Writers' Room. Bevan and O'Meara note that televisual serial storytelling has been 'historically dismissed and marginalized as lowbrow and feminine' until the recent the emergence of 'notions of the industrial role of the "showrunner" and the critical concept of "quality television"' (M/C). To a certain extent, the kudos afforded by attribution of authorship can be deemed a positive, even if it sets up a circular discourse that returns debate to romantic and elitist assumptions of 'originality'.

However, these study texts also illustrate the myriad ways in which adaptations can present innovative pathways to the revisioning of pre-loved narratives that afford a *shared* authorship. *Fargo* serves as a prime example of the creative possibilities presented by the newly inscribed stewardship of the TV auteur: as adapter and creator of the series, Hawley introduces his own 'distinctive visual sensibility' across all three seasons of this anthologised series, weaving interconnected nodes of cinematic expression that are both a continuation of the Coen brothers' experimental use of cinematic language *and* a deviation from their norm.

If, as Palmer claims, 'all texts are fragments...await[ing] gestures of continuation' (76), adaptation constitutes an evolutionary rather than an interventionist act that entails one more 'turn in an ongoing dialogical process' (Stam 81). Within the wider storytelling parameters of TV serialisation, would-be adapters are at liberty to explore and expand upon textual 'fragments' on a continuum that has the capacity to play out across multiple seasons ad infinitum. Since the advent of television broadcasting, TV producers have exploited the commercial potential of serialised adaptations of nineteenth-century literature: costume drama renditions of canonical texts abound, particularly within a British broadcasting context (Cardwell). However, a TV series like *Penny Dreadful* represents a shift away from that costume drama tradition, producing instead an intertextually complex metafiction that draws upon a vast array of literature, predominantly from the Victorian era. Building on the contemporary popularity of neo-Victorian literature, the series revisions a Victorian past through adaptation and appropriation of not only specific literary texts from the nineteenth century but of genres of popular appeal during the Victorian period. It is what I term neo-Victorian made-for-TV adaptation, created specifically for TV consumption: it is an adaptation of sorts and yet it is also a neo-Victorian point of *origin*. Characterised by its intertextual complexity and by its capacity to appropriate a particular auteur style aesthetic over and above adaptation of narrative content, the TV anthology series, *Fargo*, extends the existing story universe of the Coen brothers 1996 film, shifting narrative boundaries and adding new layers to the Fargo mythology within a much wider referential framework. Through the subtle spinning of complex webs of intertextual connectivity across each of its discrete seasons, it establishes a dialogue with the body of cinematic texts produced by these feted Indie auteurs. However, while it expands the existing Fargo story world for its newly acquired TV audience in a way that harnesses its cult film fan following, like *Penny Dreadful*, *Fargo* the TV series also operates in a self-referential, metatextual manner, its own original narratives becoming points of prequel and sequel across its three seasons thus far. *Orange is the New Black* is a multi-season series that, similarly, moves beyond the contained storyline of the prison memoir it adapts. Kohan constructs an ever-evolving fictional universe in which the memoir's 'truths' become secondary to the stories of the many different types of incarcerated women within America's prison system. By creating for them emotively charged melodramatic backstories that are strategically positioned and often revisited throughout the seasons, Kohan sustains audience interest in an open-ended fictitious story world across years rather than the fifteen-month time span of the prison memoir. *The Night Of*, in a similar fashion, demonstrates the adaptation's capacity to eclipse its origins; though ostensibly a remake of the first season of an anthologised British series, this American series emerges as a prestige HBO product with a higher televisual profile than the text it adapts, bringing matters of creative ownership within the realms of TV production into sharp focus. The intriguing nuances of the relationship between each of these TV adaptations and the texts they appropriate form the basis for this timely study of the contemporary emergence of the more experimental serialised TV adaptation.

Works Cited

Bevan, Alex, and Radha O'Meara. "Transmedia Theory's Author Discourse and Its Limitations." *M/C Journal* 21.1 (2018). Web. 10 Feb. 2018.

Cardwell, Sarah. *Adaptation Revisited: Television and the Classic Novel*. Manchester: Manchester University Press, 2002. Print.

Chalaby, Jean K. "Drama Without Drama: The Late Rise of Scripted TV Formats." *Television & New Media* 17.1 (2015): 1–18. Print.

Creeber, Glen, and Matt Hills. "Editorial: TV III." *New Review of Film and Television Studies* 5.1 (2007): 1–4. Print.

De Fino, Dean. *The HBO Effect*. London and New York: Bloomsbury Academic, 2014. Print.

Gray, Jonathan. *Show Sold Separately: Promos, Spoilers and Other Media Paratexts*. London and New York: New York University Press, 2010. Print.

———. "TV Previews and the Meaning of Hype." *International Journal of Cultural Studies* 11.1 (2008): 33–49. Print.

Hutcheon, Linda. *A Theory of Adaptation*. London: Routledge, 2006. Print.

Innocenti, Veronica, and Guglielmo Pescatore. "Changing Series: Narrative Models and the Role of the Viewer in Contemporary Television Seriality." *Between* 4.8 (2014): 1–15. Print.
Jenner, Mareike. "Is This TVIV? On Netflix, TVIII and Binge-Watching." *New Media and Society* 18.2 (2016): 257–273. Print.
Kustritz, Anne. "Transmedia Serial Narration:Crossroads of Media, Story and Time." *M/C Journal* 21.1 (2018). Web. 10 Feb. 2018.
Lotz, Amanda D. "On 'TV Criticism': The Pursuit of the Critical Examination of a Popular Art." *Popular Communication: The International Journal of Media and Culture* 6.1 (2008): 20–36. Web. 1 Nov. 2016.
Mittell, Jason. *Complex TV: The Poetics of Contemporary Television Storytelling*. New York and London: New York University Press, 2015. Print.
———. *Television and American Culture*. New York and Oxford: Oxford University Press, 2010. Print.
———. "Narrative Complexity in Contemporary American Television." *The Velvet Light Trap* 58 (2006): 29–40. Print.
———. "A Cultural Approach to Television Genre Theory." *Cinema Journal* 40.3 (2001): 3–24.
Newman, Michael Z, and Elana Levine. *Legitimating Television Media Convergence and Cultural Studies*. New York and Abingdon: Routledge, 2012. Print.
Palmer, R. Barton "Continuation, Adaptation Studies, and the Never-Finished Text." *Adaptation in Visual Culture: Images, Texts, and Their Multiple Worlds*. Eds. Julie Grossman and R. Barton Palmer. Houndsmill: Palgrave Macmillan, 2017. 73–100. Print.
Stam, Robert. "Beyond Fidelity: The Dialogics of Adaptation." *Film Adaptation*. Ed. James Naremore. New Brunswick: Rutgers University Press, 2000. 54–78. Print.

Screenography

TV

Fargo (2014-, US: FX).
Orange is the New Black (2103-, US: Netflix).
Penny Dreadful (2014–2016, US: SHOWTIME).
The Night Of (2016, US: HBO).

Film

Fargo. Dirs. Joel and Ethan Coen. 1996.

CHAPTER 2

Penny Dreadful: The Neo-Victorian 'Made-for-TV' Series

2.1 Introduction

Penny Dreadful (2014–2016) is an exemplary neo-Victorian TV series that heralds the arrival of a new kind of costume drama. Unlike the traditional, fidelity-driven 'classic' adaptations that dominated film and television screens pre-millennium, it taps into current audience desire for a more playful, less reverential adaptive treatment of canonical literature from the long nineteenth century. It is not yet another version of a canonical narrative taken from an earlier literary period: in its appropriation of Mary Shelley's *Frankenstein, or the Modern Myth of Prometheus* (1818), Oscar Wilde's *The Picture of Dorian Gray* (1891) and Bram Stoker's *Dracula* (1897), it is neither defined by its relationship with this body of texts nor the medium in which it is produced. The series adheres to certain conventions of period costume and set, but it takes an irreverent and decidedly cinematic approach to its storytelling; by exploiting its narrative's sensationalist horror elements rather than its heritage credentials, it breaches the boundaries of our perception of canonical tales, exploring instead their transgressive potentialities. It takes TV costume drama serialisation into the darker realms of Gothic TV horror, positioning itself beyond the conventional norms of both. The screen adaptation of Victorian realist narratives and their early nineteenth-century counterparts has been the subject of copious academic enquiry for decades and a dense body of existing scholarship already informs that particular debate (Cardwell, Giddings and Sheen, Elliott, McFarlane, Leitch, Klein and Parker, Wagner et al.). There is also an established body of academic criticism related to the study of neo-Victorian fiction (Bowler, Cox, Gutleben, Heilmann, Kaplan, Kohlke, Onega, Llewellyn, Mitchell, Poore et al.) and its subsequent adaptation to film and television. My aim here is to expand the field of academic enquiry by exploring the adaptive processes at work in the production of the neo-Victorian TV series created specifically for TV consumption.

2.2 Establishing a Generic Framework

Within the contemporary production climate of the TV industry, genre is, according to Mittell, as much connected to 'changing cultural practices' as to the so-called timeless essence of any particular genre (A Cultural Approach, 6–7). *Penny Dreadful* is an incestuous TV hybrid that crosses the borders of period costume drama, Gothic TV and TV horror: it shares an affinity with the kind of serialised costume drama adaptations of the nineteenth-century canon that have served as a trademark of quality prestige television since the early days of TV broadcasting, but it also takes its audience into new generic territory. Its period costume drama identity forms one part of a 'discursive cluster' (11) that is equally reliant upon the ever-evolving generic markers of Gothic TV and TV horror; it presents instead as part of the emerging genre of neo-Victorian TV—a genre that engages with 'period' in very different ways.

Through its affiliation with narratives from the long nineteenth century, the series positions itself in relation to the history and traditions associated with the TV costume drama and the adaptation of literary texts, periods and characters (both fictitious and historical); it continues to operate within certain generic conventions of the TV costume drama. However, it subverts expectation on every level, from its adaptive treatment of a host of pre-existing texts to its style aesthetic and its on-screen realisation of the Victorian period. It remains in dialogue with yet it is not defined by its relationship to its antecedents. The neo-Victorian text has a particular affinity with the processes involved in acts of adaptation and appropriation. Heilmann and Llewellyn see the adaptive act as a 'fundamental part of neo-Victorianism', in which the adapter enters into a process of 'self-conscious' engagement with the literature and cultural mores of the Victorian era, reinterpreting both for consumption by a contemporary audience (244). As with all writers of neo-Victorian narratives, series creator John Logan is engaged in acts that process a Victorian past in ways that go beyond the nostalgic recreation of an historical moment—beyond the kind of 'nostalgic yearning for a previous age' (Bowler and Cox 4) that is synonymous with period costume drama. *Penny Dreadful* is what Bowler and Cox would term a 'polyphonic text': one that 'illuminat[es] perspectives on its antecedents' yet 'generates a radically innovative and arguably "original" work' (8). If, as Heilmann and Llewellyn contend, the neo-Victorian text is characterised by its 'palimpsestuous' nature and its capacity to simultaneously inscribe a past narrative (170), then *Penny Dreadful* may be deemed an exemplary 'polyphonic' neo-Victorian text, written first and foremost as an original TV series.

2.2.1   From Period Costume Drama to Neo-Victorian TV Series

Popular neo-Victorian texts, both in print and on screen, seek what Kaplan refers to as a 'self-conscious *re-writing*' of the Victorian past (my italics)—one that explores stories which have been withheld, stories dealing in 'suppressed histories of gender and sexuality, race and empire' and which are then represented within a contemporary frame of reference (Kaplan 3–10). *Penny Dreadful* is a neo-Victorian text that is inherently and purposefully engaged in acts of adaptation and appropriation—of history and our perceptions thereof, offering up the kind of '*[re]-interpretation, [re]-discovery, and [re]-vision*' of Victoriana seen by Heilmann and Llewellyn as central to neo-Victorian revisionism (4). Unlike TV series which adapt existing neo-Victorian novels,[1] *Penny Dreadful* functions as a TV series that, as with film counterparts like Jane Campion's *The Piano* (1993) and Sandra Goldbacher's *The Governess* (1998), explores a Victorian past in which unspoken taboos and unnamed anxieties are foregrounded within a made-for-screen context. In their very 'newness', such neo-Victorian screen texts are themselves the neo-Victorian point of origin; they go beyond the potentialities of adaptive revisioning of existing text, beyond the 'safe' ground of classic adaptation. They are nomadic in nature, 'roam[ing]', as Imelda Whelehan astutely notes, 'across eras and genres in fantastic and dangerous liaisons' (289). *Penny Dreadful* is the consummate neo-Victorian nomad: it takes canonical narratives

---

[1] *Fingersmith* (2005), *The Crimson Petal and the White* (2011), *Alias Grace* (2017).

from across the long nineteenth century, earlier mythologies from across the globe and cinematic 're-interpretations' of both to present a neo-Victorian vision of London within the generic markers of TV period costume drama, Gothic TV and TV horror.

The parameters of what can and cannot be deemed 'neo-Victorian' have expanded of late; once considered the realm of 'high art' only, now other media forms, TV included, are being defined as 'neo-Victorian', and 'critical resistance towards the "popular" within neo-Victorianism' is on the wane (Cox 102). Logan engages in the 'self-conscious rewriting' of a range of texts, from the 'high art' canonical literature of the nineteenth century to the sensationalist penny dreadfuls of the Victorian era and from the populist horror narratives of cinema to popular mythologies that span both time and place. It is a story universe that evolves beyond the parameters of the canonical texts it references, its narrative momentum governed not by known outcomes but by a newly conceived story arc of Logan's imagining—a story arc that 'abandons' unconditionally 'the safe ground of classic adaptation' for 'something altogether riskier and more inventive' (Kaplan 119). Like neo-Victorian literature in general, *Penny Dreadful* assumes an identity that remains in dialogue with yet is distinct from both the histories it reinscribes and the texts produced and consumed in the Victorian period. For Logan, the Victorian period is a 'highly specialized era' with not only a 'cool visual' on which to build but points of cultural connection ripe for narrative expansion. It is a period that, notes Logan, is reminiscent of our contemporary world: both are on the 'cusp' of a new modernity infused with the fear, 'dissonance' and 'the excitement' of 'uncharted waters' (Logan quoted in Radish, web interview). He parallels, for example, our contemporary preoccupation with the Victorian era to *its* preoccupation with Egyptology, sought in an effort to understand 'where we belong in society' (Logan in Gosling 53), and this desire to belong becomes a prominent theme across the three-season story arc. Logan inscribes many aspects of Victoriana and its London landmarks in his *Penny Dreadful*; however, its identity as a neo-Victorian text dictates a revisionist approach to the content he adapts, whether related to period or literary and cinematic canon. Though set in the Victorian period and thus positioning itself as a text that recreates the historical moment, *Penny Dreadful* engages in a playful reordering of historical and literary 'truth': Sir Malcolm's quest to 'discover' the source of the Nile, for example, is already an outdated one since the Nile was 'discovered' back in 1858, and Logan's temporal realignment of Mary Shelley's *Frankenstein* is indicative of his irreverential treatment of period detail and the literary canon. Like Coppola's *Dracula*, the series functions as a neo-Victorian screen text that 'reflects an awareness of the difficulties of knowing the past' (Cordell 8). Foregrounding the technologies of Victoriana, from photography to magic lantern shows Logan, like Goldbacher (*The Governess*), posits a preoccupation with the difficulties of recapturing the indelible essence of the past—particularly a Victorian past which, argues Mitchell, 'only exists in our re-creations of it' (37). For Logan, this Victorian past serves as a cultural intertext that may be shaped and adapted to meet the needs of his own narrative experiment.

Broadcaster reliance upon period costume drama adaptations has been well documented, as has the fidelity-driven treatment such adaptations invariably employ from the 1950s through to the late 1990s (Cardwell Lit. on Screen 181). Cardwell argues that adaptations produced throughout this extended period, and historically by UK production companies for UK distribution first and foremost, are retrospectively viewed as 'staid and unimaginative', conservative in their ideology and generically formulaic, conforming to a set of prescribed conventions readily associated with the heritage fare of cinema (182–183). Produced by American cable channel Showtime in partnership with UK subscription channel Sky Atlantic, *Penny Dreadful* is a series that positions itself within a more global context from the outset but it remains, in part, connected to the legacy of its costume drama predecessors. Like its heritage cinema counterpart (Higson 109–129), the TV costume drama of this earlier broadcast era is overtly preoccupied with its period 'look', attaining fidelity to the 'source' text's surface details rather than its textual politics. Engaged in the visual recreation of period detail, these pre-1990s 'faithful', dialogue-driven, studio-based adaptations actively sought what, within a parallel American context, Laird and West term a 'distancing cordon sanitaire from not only other TV shows but also mass entertainment in general' (308). It is a genre that has become synonymous with 'polite, traditional values' that 'cultivate a culturally hegemonic "heritage Britishness"' (Regis 143)—a 'Britishness' that remains an indelible part of its DNA, regardless of the country of its production.

Within the context of American TV production and consumption of nineteenth-century period costume drama, America has historically functioned as the sycophantic 'poor relation'. Since 1970, when Masterpiece Theatre was introduced by the American broadcaster PBS as a platform dedicated to the release of imported British period costume dramas, their very 'Britishness' has been embraced wholeheartedly. Masterpiece Theatre was established as a portal for British period drama and has become a byword for a certain type of quality costume drama that appeals to a niche American audience. Traditionally regarded as the purveyor of safe, conservative drama, much of which consists of serial adaptations of the nineteenth-century realist novel, Masterpiece Theatre functions, notes Knox, as 'pejorative shorthand' for a kind of 'Anglophiliac elitism' (31), and is often viewed by its critics as a pedlar of 'cultural exclusivism' (41). Despite the remit of a national public broadcaster like PBS, it's Masterpiece Theatre programming is inevitably marked by a conspicuous absence of national representation. Though rebranded as 'Masterpiece' in 2008 in a move designed to dilute what has essentially been seen as its anglocentric and elitist identity, and to widen its remit to include contemporary drama and mystery drama, it remains to a marked extent a vehicle for British imports, even when those imports are co-produced. Free from the constraints of mainstream broadcasting Showtime's, *Penny Dreadful* marks a departure from this legacy and from the more conservative tropes of the period costume drama set in nineteenth-century England.

The TV period costume drama set in the nineteenth century and produced in and for an America audience has revolved in the main around frontier narratives rather than adaptations of the nineteenth-century realist novel. Conservative, long-running Western series like *Bonanza* (1959–1973), *High Chaparral* (1967–1971), *The Little House on the Prairie* (1974–1983) or *Dr Quinn, Medicine Woman* (1993–1998) have in recent years been replaced by more violent and controversial frontier narratives such as *Deadwood* (2004–2006) and *Godless* (2017–), or upcoming series like the Coen brothers' *The Ballad of Buster Scruggs*. Produced by cable and streaming networks like HBO (*Deadwood*) and Netflix (*Godless, the Ballad of Buster Scruggs*), these latter series operate outside the constraints of mainstream broadcasting protocols; they are culturally distanced from the 'polite' and conservative fare of both British costume dramas and from their earlier American Western period drama counterparts despite a shared temporal, geographical and historical framework. *Penny Dreadful* adheres to the visual splendour of the period costume drama so readily associated with British TV drama and its narrative unfolds in turn of the century London in Seasons One and Two; however, it is a series that also connects with these American frontier narratives. The presence of gun-slinging American Ethan Chandler affords Logan the narrative opportunity to widen the parameters of the story world into an American period context, and during the course of the series' three-season story arc, the story world shifts in its closing season to a violent American frontier period setting that operates outside the geographical and cultural norms of nineteenth-century period costume drama, investing the series with a very different period edge—one that aligns it in part with grittier contemporary US frontier narratives.

Just as the content and treatment of the Western TV series have undergone change in recent years, Cardwell notes a distinct shift in visual and performative aesthetic in 1990s serialised TV costume drama (Adaptation Revisited 34). This shift signals a move to a more self-consciously artistic treatment of narrative within screen space in the post-1990s TV landscape. In contemporary costume drama adaptation, 'visual style' is no longer deemed 'secondary to dialogue' (314) and its period detail is about much more than a nostalgic nod to an earlier historical period. The current TV landscape is awash with serialised period dramas set in the nineteenth and early twentieth century; TV series like *Ripper Street* (2012–), *Peaky Blinders* (2013–), *The Knick* (2014–), *Penny Dreadful*, *Jonathan Strange and Mr. Norrell* (2015–), *The Frankenstein Chronicles* (2015–), *Dickensian* (2015) and *Taboo* (2017–) step outside the conventional parameters of the period costume drama but with the exception of series like *The Knick* and *Penny Dreadful*, most are still produced by production companies associated with British broadcasters. From the early days of television broadcasting, British broadcasters have harnessed the cultural kudos and the commercial potential of the literary canon by producing, on the whole, fidelity-driven serialised adaptations of the nineteenth-century novel, and most contemporary serialised adaptations of canonical literature continue in this tradition. However, TV series that break with the kind of 'faithful' treatment of canonical texts in more than their visualisation of the period are on the rise. Though not the first to do so (TV film *Moll Flanders*, 1996, and TV series *Desperate Romantics*, 2006, serve as innovative TV forerunners), a TV series like *Penny Dreadful* represents a very different approach to period drama that operates outside the conventional bounds of TV costume drama both pre- and post-1990s, but it pushes the boundaries of the genre even further into new televisual territory. Through its affiliation with narratives from the long nineteenth century, it positions itself in relation to the history and traditions associated with the TV costume drama and the adaptation of literary texts, periods and characters (both fictitious and historical); it continues to operate within the anticipated generic tropes of the TV costume drama; and yet it subverts expectation on every level. Like several other contemporary period series (*Peaky Blinders, The Knick, Taboo*), it aspires to and attains a cinematic quality in its on-screen realisation of a particular period. The lensing of the fantastical elements in a series like *Jonathan Strange and Mr. Norrell* or of the supernatural elements embedded in *Taboo* serves to illustrate how the content and treatment of nineteenth-century period drama is changing.

There is also a notable trend towards the production of intertextually dense meta-fictions that breach the traditional norms of fidelity-driven adaptation of nineteenth-century literature at the level of narrative. Meta-fictions like *Penny Dreadful, The Frankenstein Chronicles* and *Dickensian* are what Palmer and Klein term 'multiplicities': texts which 'invite viewers to appreciate the *new* in the context of the *familiar* and already approved, sanctioning readings that criss-cross textual borders' (1, my italics). In *Dickensian*, an 'adaptation' that takes an innovative approach to 'familiar' narratives from the Dickens' canon, series creator Tony Jordan brings together characters and narrative threads from a range of Dickens' works and places them within the geographical backdrop of the decidedly 'Dickensian' London enshrined in Dickens' fiction. *The Frankenstein Chronicles* is a similarly innovative reworking of a known narrative from the long nineteenth century; taking its lead from Shelley's text, it recreates the novel's familiar 'monster' as one more readily assimilated with contemporary notions of the serial killer. But the monstrous nature of his actions is also aligned with those of Shelley's creator, Victor Frankenstein: like Frankenstein, the killer stitches together the various body parts of his innocent victims. *Penny Dreadful* is an assimilation of not one but three nineteenth-century canonical texts, all of which are employed in the service of Logan's newly created narrative. However, while *Dickensian* recreates the London of Dickens' invention—a London synonymous in mainstream culture with picture postcard olde worlde, cobbled London streets of the kind constructed in the BBC's series marketing materials—series like *Penny Dreadful, The Frankenstein Chronicles* and *Ripper Street* employ a dark and murky style aesthetic. Like the latter series, the plot of *Dickensian* is in part a detective narrative but rather than employing a similarly gritty approach to the generic tropes of Victorian detective fiction, Jordan plays to the series' identity as a costume drama that deals in a 'nostalgic return' to a 'collectively imagined past' (Mitchell 4). Filmed within the structural confines of a purposely constructed warehouse rather than on location, the series signals a self-conscious and purposeful return to the staged set 'look' of TV costume drama of the pre-1990s. Conroy notes there is 'something annoyingly old-fashioned', even 'claustrophobic', about the series with its 'tight, foggy wooden set[s]', especially in an era when period dramas have become so 'lavish', its set-bound 'look' prompting critic Jasper Rees to label it 'Eastenders in top hats and mobcaps'. As with the BBC's *Cranford* (2007), there is an 'absence of visually seductive shots' of the type anticipated in post-1990s costume drama (Louttit, Cranford 39). Unlike *Penny Dreadful* or *The Frankenstein Chronicles*, *Dickensian* remains for many reviewers a 'polite' costume drama synonymous with the kind of 'culturally hegemonic "heritage Britishness"' noted by Regis as symptomatic of the costume drama format (143), its initial 2015 Christmas scheduling, positioning it as part of a tradition of moralistic costume drama fare wheeled out during the festive season.

Though not employed as the mainstay of its narrative trajectory, *Penny Dreadful's* affiliation with the detective genre forms an essential part of its generic hybridity. The detective genre, which has its roots in the sensation novel and the Gothic, emerged as a distinct genre of mainstream popularity that flourished during the Victorian era (Allan 3). And as with the penny dreadful and the sensation novel, its content was regarded as morally questionable, and its narratives initially connected with 'moral degeneracy' by the middle- to upper-class Victorian (Pittard 107). Located in an increasingly urbanised London at the end of the nineteenth century, the series reflects the detective genre's preoccupation with what Allan terms the 'fragmented and inchoate metropolis' in which 'contemporaneous issues related to identity, urbanisation and gender' abound (Allan 4), making it a genre that lends itself to the kinds of preoccupations that characterise neo-Victorian texts in general and Logan's *Penny Dreadful* in particular. Furthermore, the style aesthetic employed by Logan in his revisioning of a nineteenth-century London aligns with the kind of 'sensory overload of modernity' noted by Christopher Pittard as a 'precondition' of the detective genre (110) rather than the style aesthetic of the costume drama, and like *The Frankenstein Chronicles* and *Ripper Street*, it engages on some level in the detection of a serial killer. The detection of crime does not provide *Penny Dreadful's* narrative mainframe but Inspector Galsworthy emerges as a dogged tracker of criminal prey and his tireless pursuit of Ethan

Chandler, whose connection to the myths surrounding Jack the Ripper remains one of its mysteries, forms an intrinsic part of the evolving *Penny Dreadful* narrative that takes Galsworthy and Chandler far beyond the geographical confines of Victorian London to the 'Wild West' of America in Season Three.

The contemporary popularity of the Victorian era in particular and of the neo-Victorian fictions it has inspired serve as the building blocks for a revisioning of a Victorian London through adaptation and appropriation of both specific canonical texts and mythologies that continue to circulate Western culture, and a host of populist screen adaptations that have come to inform our perception of those texts and the mythologies they re-inscribe. Like *The Frankenstein Chronicles* and *Ripper Street*, the series is filmed on location in Ireland, with the city of Dublin providing an architecture more reminiscent of Victorian London than contemporary London. Through Showtime's official ongoing blogs, delivered by various industry professionals involved in the series' production, including series creator John Logan, the audience is encouraged to engage at the level of process; as viewers we are made aware of the very constructed nature of this narrative, its 'period London', its character constructs and so on. Unlike the fixed Director's Commentary which is now an anticipated part of any DVD box set release, the production blog functions as a paratext that constantly builds on viewer engagement with not only the series' narrative trajectory and its characters but with the very constructed nature of this story world, undercutting any notion of the period realism that is traditionally a feature of classic costume drama adaptations of realist novels of the long nineteenth century. Logan's narrative is set in a vision of Victorian London built, argues Louttit on a 'Victorian Gothic image of the city' that has been 'plunder[ed] from London's "pop culture archives"' (Redux 3): it foregrounds popular and populist sites and pursuits, placing the sensationalist and unspoken, from penny dreadfuls, Vaudevillian theatre, House of Horror Waxworks, and magic lantern shows, to opium dens, séances, photographic pornography, rat baiting dens and the haunts of resurrectionists, adding to the mix a visualisation of London's underbelly. The anticipated costume drama flourishes of gentlemen's clubs, grand London mansions, and costume balls are retained but the splendour of the architecture, the period detail and the lavish costuming that traditionally characterises the genre is superseded by the series' horror tropes. Sir Malcolm's London mansion becomes his fortress, Sembene his only servant, and at Ferdinand Lyle's social gathering, it is the séance rather than the ball that takes narrative precedence (2.1). Logan also creates macabre ballroom scenes that subvert the tropes of the period costume ball in both this episode and the closing episode of Season Two, taking the narrative into the fantastical realms of the horror genre. Shot from Vanessa Ives' point of view, the visual splendour of the moment takes a very different and macabre turn as the room and Ferdinand's oblivious dancing guests are engulfed by a bloody downpour (2.1); and against a dimly lit backdrop, the sole dancing figures of Lily Frankenstein and Dorian Gray are similarly soaked in blood during the closing moments of Season Two (2.8).

Television production lends itself to an inherently malleable and proactive approach to the adaptation of stories that continue to fascinate us, leading to a creative interplay between genres, existing texts, new storylines and the body of ideas that circulate both old and new. Logan produces a story which transcends the timeworn fidelity debate that continues to haunt the scholarly field of adaptation studies by engaging in an incestuous intermingling of canonical and populist texts within a hybrid confection of high brow (costume drama) and low brow (horror) genres. Using the framework of his new story to bring together characters that share not story but a host of disturbing preoccupations, he maps out a relationship between a body of texts that continue to speak to the cultural anxieties of contemporary times. Initially drawn only to Frankenstein's narrative, Logan soon discovered 'the joy' of bringing into his story world characters from *Dracula* and *The Picture of Dorian Gray*, both of which are narratives he sees as 'thematically linked' to Frankenstein 'in terms of alienation' and 'the need for love' (Logan in Gosling 122). These texts share the same Gothic DNA, the same crossover appeals to both a populist and a literary readership, but Logan extends the parameters of his newly mapped universe to include sensationalist narratives of the penny dreadful variety and with enduringly popular narratives of shape-shifting werewolves. However, in this series it is the story of newly created protagonist, Vanessa Ives, that takes precedence; characters, storylines and thematic preoccupations appropriated from precursor texts are all employed in the service of her narrative trajectory.

2.2.2 Neo-Victorian Gothic Meets TV Horror

Like costume dramas, Gothic TV narratives are often adapted from pre-existing literature (both canonical and populist) set in the long nineteenth and early twentieth century and a decorous approach to the telling of Gothic tales is an established norm: historically, they are bound by the same broadcasting constraints as the TV costume drama. However, Helen Wheatley aptly terms it '"feel-bad" heritage TV' of a kind that rejects costume drama's bourgeois affiliations: it 'remov[es] the surety of the past as a haven or site of nostalgia' (49–51), and embraces instead a 'distinctly post-modern form' (Ledwon 260). Characterised by a 'fundamental resistance to boundaries', it is an 'unstable' genre that embraces 'multiplicity' (Ledwon 261) and intertextuality. TV Gothic's propensity for cinematic experimentation dates back to its early days: unlike its costume drama counterpart, Gothic TV has always sought new ways to represent the uncanny and the supernatural on screen, no matter how constrained by broadcasting regulations (Wheatley 68, Ledwon 172). But despite its historical claim to more experimental credentials, as a genre Gothic TV has remained mindful of the old adage 'less is more' (Wheatley 51), while contemporary Gothic TV series like *Penny Dreadful* take a very different approach to the visualisation of on-screen horror. For series executive producer Sam Mendes, *Penny Dreadful* is 'an attempt to finally take Gothic horror seriously again' (Mendes in Gosling 10–11), by operating through visceral shock and horror rather than the subtleties of traditional TV Gothic. Logan exploits the creative licence afforded by the series' cable TV release platform, visualising levels of violence and gore that are on a par with adult-rated horror cinema, and employing the emotive excess associated with horror: guilt, shame and secrets abound. With its blood-fuelled vampire showdowns and the killing rampages of a bestial shape-shifting werewolf, its ghostly visitations, poltergeist mayhem and acts of demonic possession visualised on screen in graphic detail, this is a series that 'rende[rs] visible' what Kolkhe and Gutleben argue traditionally belongs to the realms of the imagination (1): the 'less is more' approach of early Gothic TV producers finds no traction here. Instead, Logan aligns his style aesthetic with that of populist cinematic horror. Yet through his exploration of character and relationships, the psychological complexities of the canonical texts remain part of *Penny Dreadful's* narrative fabric, even as it presents as a new kind of neo-Victorian Gothic horror TV. In addition to this, the supernatural elements of the Penny Dreadful story world tap into the fantasy genre—a genre which is currently universally popular (Jowett and Abbott 224).

Penny Dreadful is inevitably affiliated with the tropes of TV costume drama but it is its overriding identity as Gothic horror in general and neo-Victorian Gothic horror in particular that is central to its engagement with the canonical texts it appropriates. Kolkhe and Gutleben see neo-Victorian texts as '*quintessentially Gothic*' narratives that are invariably engaged in 'constant reactivation of the Gothic', the two genres 'doomed to converge if not merge' due to a 'predestined' and 'revivalist' compulsion (3–4 Neo-Victorian Gothic). *Penny Dreadful* is a TV series that revives and reactivates Gothic tropes as a means to exploring the anxieties that connect the late nineteenth century with those of our contemporary era. It serves as an exemplary Gothic text that has the 'contradictory' capacity that Kolkhe and Gutleben afford the Gothic: 'realism and romance, anachronism and nostalgic reiteration, thrilling spectacle and post-modern self-abjection, ethical didacticism and sheer *fun*' (43). It also engages with what Kolkhe identifies as the genre's prerequisite tropes, from mediums and séances to ghostly manifestations and possession, aligning those anticipated markers of the genre with the neo-Victorian Gothic's propensity for presenting both the darker side of nineteenth-century existence and often a 'sensationalized world of desire' in which 'sexual fantasy might be gratified' (Kolkhe 345). From the outset, Vanessa Ives is constructed as a woman possessed: she first enters the narrative as a disembodied voice, uttering an indecipherable incantation as the opening black screen space widens out into a shot of a strikingly bare room that holds a makeshift altar and female figure bent in prayer. Reminiscent of the opening moments of Jack Clayton's classic gothic adaptation, *The Innocents*, the scene slowly evolves to a moment of clarity as the camera shifts to a side-on close-up of a distraught face, eyes closed, lips moving and hands clasped in prayer; and just as the unnatural bird song that infiltrates the black frame in Clayton's film fills his audience with a sense of foreboding, the presence of a spider crawling over the crucifix of the makeshift altar signals the incongruity of the moment—an incongruity that is amplified as the camera tracks the spider's progress across the crucifix and down to the arm of the woman, her fears shown in close-up as the non-diegetic sound of a Gregorian chant builds to a point at which a deep female voice speaks out of frame, declaring 'Soon child, soon. I'm hungry', before an animalistic growl dominates the soundtrack; at that moment, the camera edits to a close-up of the female's shoulders, still bent in prayer, suggesting some kind of monstrous presence lurks behind her.

By the end of the first two episodes of Season One, this female figure has not only been involved in a showdown with vampires, but has taken part in a séance during which her possession is made manifest, Sir

Malcolm Murray's dead children, Peter and Mina, speaking through her, before she exits to fulfil a compulsion to have sex with the first male she can find. The six-minute séance sequence is particularly graphic: it presents the startling image of Vanessa Ives' bodily transformation from very controlled and detached vessel for the communication of messages from those on the 'other side' to the beast-like image of a raging, levitated and contorted body. Both the vampire showdown and the séance sequence cross the boundaries of the Gothic into the realms of the neo-Gothic and supernatural fantasy; like the penny dreadfuls from which the series takes its title, it presents from the outset sensational plot points that take the series into new generic territory, building on yet extending the parameters of the Gothic genre within a televisual context. By the end of the second episode, the audience is left in doubt that Vanessa Ives is going to be embroiled in an epic battle between good and evil—a battle that, if lost, will result in the destruction of humankind. When asked to decipher the hieroglyphics tattooed onto the section of skin Sir Malcolm presents to him, Egyptologist Ferdinand Lyle advises that the god Amun-Ra is in pursuit of Vanessa's soul since he believes her to be his reincarnated consort, Amunet, with whom he must reunite in order to hold dominion over all.

There are also numerous scenes throughout the series that foreground a 'sensationalized world of desire' fuelled by 'sexual fantasy' of the type Kolkhe sees as characteristic of the neo-Victorian Gothic (Kolkhe 1 Sexsation). Logan explores gratification of sexual fantasy through his appropriation of *The Picture of Dorian Gray* by adopting a neo-Victorian approach to Oscar Wilde's veiled treatment of sexual difference, highlighting the hidden undercurrents of Victorian attitudes towards sex by bringing to the fore Dorian's sexual curiosity, his bi-sexuality and his voyeuristic leanings. The homoerotic properties of both Wilde's novella and Stoker's *Dracula* are brought into Logan's story universe as a means to foregrounding matters related to gender and sexuality—concerns related to 'wider disquisitions on empire, social freedom, and individual choice' that are characteristic of neo-Victorian texts (Whelehan 275). Dorian Gray is lensed as a figure whose every sexual desire plays out on screen, from the graphic yet mechanically asexual orgy scenes that involve women bound together on a crucifix as they engage in sexual acts with men and with each other, to scenes that present his own sexual encounters with men, women and transsexuals. The orgy scene, orchestrated by Dorian, serves as a prelude to his violent bisexual encounter with Ethan Chandler at the end of the aptly titled Demimonde (4.1).

Using the research of historian Matthew Sweet as his period touchstone (Logan DVD video production blog, Season One), Logan recreates the underbelly of the Victorian period alongside the wealth of its exclusive gentlemen's clubs and the London mansions of Sir Malcolm and Dorian Gray. Gray acts as a catalyst for the exploration of all things considered taboo yet often avidly pursued by his fellow Victorians: his presence in rat baiting dens, his pornographic photo shoots and his lavish orgies, all of which are realised on screen in graphic detail, are of a kind that do not fit with our expectations of TV period drama and classic serial TV adaptations in particular. His overt voyeurism and his sexual experimentation with Ethan Chandler and transgendered Angelique echo the homoeroticism of both Stoker's Dracula and Wilde's Dorian; his sexual encounters with women, including Brona Croft (alias Lily Frankenstein) and Vanessa Ives, position him as one who has an insatiable sexual curiosity and a desire to seek out new experiences as a means to reinvigorating his eternal existence. However, even though Dorian is, attests Logan, a character of Faustian proportions, in league with the devil (Logan in Gosling 108), in this story he is not constructed as the 'ultimate playboy' of Wilde's text; in *Penny Dreadful*, he is a more 'aloof' individual, 'alienated from his own affections' and 'filled with the sadness of a character who will never die' (Logan in Gosling 109). In many ways, he functions as a foil to Vanessa Ives: where Dorian embraces immortality and the consequent evils attached to that choice, Vanessa ultimately embraces death and a return to religious grace.

The canonical texts Logan chooses to appropriate are exemplars of the Gothic, but it is in his treatment of the female characters in particular that Logan *exceeds* the anticipated boundaries of the genre, even as the binary opposites that characterise it—good versus evil, life versus death, light versus dark—are at play in both the series' central storyline and in its character constructs. Shelley's *Frankenstein* and Stoker's *Dracula* provide points of literary connection with the Gothic genre and Logan builds this into the mainframe of his new story arc, bringing the same pressing matters of life and death, good and evil, and a host of ethical conundrums into the narrative through the introduction of Victor Frankenstein as one of Sir Malcolm's newly formed band of vampire hunters, and Mina as the daughter who has transitioned to the dark side to join the vampires he now pursues. But as with Stoker's seminal text and Coppola's film adaptation thereof, *Penny Dreadful* explores the 'cultural anxieties regarding women's selfhood' (Rocha 31) in a Victorian and, by inference, a contemporary context that explores the genre in new and innovative ways. There is no pre-existing canonical nineteenth-century text from which Logan can tease out the construction of his female protagonist. Vanessa Ives is no trembling Gothic heroine: rather, she is a woman whose 'monstrous yearnings... for liberation... personifies what it is to be a "monster" tormented and cursed' for being 'strong, powerful and liberated at a time when women couldn't be' (Logan in Gosling 123).

Vanessa Ives' demonic possession and her affinity with witchcraft and the occult as well as her 'madness' and sexual agency position her instead as the feared female 'Other' of the horror genre in which women's 'uncontrollable bodies' are invariably the focus of fear and the site of 'monstrous eruptions' (Submarnian 109–110). Her on-screen bodily transformations in Séance (2.1) align her from the opening moments of the series with the horror genre's exploration of anxieties surrounding the female body, taking us beyond the boundaries of the Gothic. But part of Logan's agenda is to explore the ways in which the Victorian woman is 'quite literally corseted and constrained... by the societal, social, sexual conventions of the day' (Logan in Gosling 122), and during the course of the series three-season story arc, he ventriloquises a very different kind of Victorian woman. He subverts Victorian expectations of the 'angel in the house', of the 'fallen woman' and the heroine of early Gothic literature. It is Vanessa who stops the male vampire leader with her gaze in the pilot episode's vampire action sequence, and Vanessa who has sought to seduce Mina's fiancé, setting in motion the storyline that shapes Season One; and just as Logan's Mina chooses to embrace the danger and eroticism of her vampire existence rather than return to the domestic confines of hearth and home, Vanessa is complicit in her own demise. When 'the Devil spoke', she listened; when 'God didn't answer [her], another did' (1.5).

Mina and Vanessa are constructed as sensual, sexually experienced women, and their sexual knowledge and selfhood are aligned with a freedom of choice afforded to the Victorian woman only in neo-Victorian texts. Vanessa's sexual quest at the end of episode two is but one of her disturbing sexual encounters. Her desire to find a closeness with Mina through the seduction of Mina's fiancé in the episode titled 'Closer than Sisters' (5.1) marks a point of sexual desire that, towards the end of the episode, has degenerated into an act of possession as, along with Vanessa's bewildered mother, we witness a naked and possessed Vanessa during a violent act of sexual intercourse with the devil. There are further moments of sexual fantasy in this episode, with the devil trying to seduce her in the guise of Sir Malcolm who suggests her seduction of Mina's fiancé was a purposeful choice she made, stating 'Hell, you sought it out and fucked it' because 'you've always been drawn to the ocean, to the dark whisper... the mirror behind the glass eyes'; ultimately, argues the devil, she chose to 'liste[n]' to the darkness. In tune with Victorian moral standards and the emerging field of psychology in this era, Vanessa's sexual proclivities are diagnosed within the framework of the narrative as female hysteria—a 'psycho-sexual' disorder according to her psychiatrist—and are treated by an horrific barrage of experimental cures. She is connected to the 'transgressive women' of the Gothic sensationalist novel, to 'women who do not conform to the Victorian ideals of feminine governance, especially in its governance of female sexuality' (Mitchell 133), but Logan takes his female protagonist into new narrative territory by setting up the disturbing juxtaposition of his transgressive Vanessa and the Victorian ideal of womanhood, particularly in the closing and opening scenes of episodes 6 and 7 of Season One. At the end of 'What Death Can Join Together' (6.1), her supernatural powers are made manifest as she levitates, circling slowly in mid-air; at the start of 'Possession' (7.1), she lies prone on the couch in the mode of many a heroine of the Victorian novel but her unsettling and lengthy disquisition on the position of women in Victorian society is just as disquieting as her earlier display of supernatural power:

> To be beautiful is to be almost dead. The lassitude of the perfect woman. The languish of ease. The obeseiance...spirit drowned. Anaemic. Pale as stone and weak as a kitten.

In repose as in her uncanny act of levitation, Vanessa challenges societal norms: her sleepy body language echoes the seminal Gothic image of the female at the centre of Fuseli's 'The Nightmare' but her language brings into sharp focus the 'almost dead' nature of such repose in both literal and metaphorical form. Through Vanessa, Logan builds on this critique of Victorian values and its reverence of passive femininity when, for example, she questions 'the brisk trade' in photographs of dead women whose 'corpses are improved with cosmetics and then posed in postures of abject surrender' to produce Victorian pornography. Similarly, while Stoker's Mina is restored to family at the close of the narrative, this Mina, like the Mina of Coppola's film (*Bram Stoker's Dracula*, 1992), chooses her seductive allegiance with her vampire master over and above any return to the fold and to her father. Mina's choice and the choices of Logan's protagonist Vanessa speak of a different kind of sexually charged neo-Victorian construct of womanhood. But in *Penny Dreadful*, Mina's story is always secondary: it serves as a foil to that of the show's newly created female protagonist, Mina functioning here as bait to ensnare her former friend. The most compelling plot conundrum emerges at the end of Season One with the question posed by the priest whose advice Vanessa seeks. He points out that being 'touched by the demon' confers a uniqueness—a 'kind of glory' that she may not wish to relinquish; his question—'Do you really want to be normal?'—provides the narrative momentum for the rest of the series as Seasons Two and Three revolve around Vanessa's search for the answer (8.1).

In this neo-Victorian TV series, Logan also brings to the fore silenced voices of dispossessed and non-conformist females of different social standing; but for all of these women—from Vanessa Ives, Mina Murray, Evelyn Poole (alias Madame Kali) and the witches of her coven to Cutwife Joan Clayton and Lily Frankenstein (alias Brona Croft)—there are no 'safe rebellions' of the kind Asscheid sees as characteristic of the women who populate neo-Victorian fiction (Asscheid cited in Primorac 7). 'Safe rebellions' are replaced by daring acts of female resistance that take the narrative beyond the generic parameters of the Gothic *and* the neo-Victorian, and into the realms of fantasy and horror. Prostitute Brona Croft is reborn as Lily, Frankenstein's 'bride', and from her moment of rebirth, she is constructed as yet another female figure who exists outside the parameters of Victorian expectations and values. She is, argues Green, not the politicised New Woman of fin de siècle England but the 'Gothic New Woman' who rails against the former's placard waving tactics, advocating instead a route to female empowerment that is accomplished 'By craft. By stealth. By poison. By the throat…quietly slit in the dead of night (Lily Frankenstein 3.3)'. Primorac deems Logan's depiction of female empowerment flawed and inherently conservative: constructed as women who are 'possessed' (Vanessa Ives); 'vamped' (Mina Murray); 'or hell bent on criminal and immoral mayhem' (witches, Nightcomers, Lily Frankenstein), they remain seemingly bound by the patriarchal 'Victorian dichotomy' between 'angel and fallen woman', the Nightcomers—and by inference Mina Murray—'symbolic of female submission' (150–151). But *Penny Dreadful* is a narrative that roams beyond the anticipated parameters of the neo-Victorian Gothic and into the realms of supernatural fantasy where the rules of narrative engagement are fuelled by a more extreme and sensationalistic set of generic markers that pay little heed to the kind of feminist politics Primorac feels is lacking in this series. Even so, Logan is able to engage in complex explorations of the position of the women who populate his story world without compromising their fantastical identity as women possessed and capable of wreaking 'mayhem'.

Lily transforms from the seeming innocent who quietly protests against the discomfort of being trussed up in corsetry (2.4) to the vagina-dentata of the horror genre (Creed 6). Logan adds further complications that see the Frankenstein story evolve beyond its existing borders by introducing a riff on the Pygmalion myth, taking it to new and violent extremes that fit his story universe and his exploration of feminist issues across the series. Frankenstein is instrumental in the creation of his 'perfect' woman: his relationship with Lily echoes the timeworn sentiments of the Pygmalion myth of male dominance as he seeks to mould her, clothing her in corsets and gowns of his choosing, and awkwardly drilling her in social etiquette. The scene in which Lily is placed on a pseudo pedestal as Frankenstein hems her gown presents visual echoes of the many paintings and sculptures of Pygmalion and Galatea (2.2) but unlike Galatea, Lily's resistance to male control becomes an intrinsic part of her story. At first couched as a polite resistance against male control, her protestations about the discomfort of her corsetry speak to her later emergence as a woman who not only rejects all attempts to contain her, but who becomes a man-hating mass murderer set to avenge all wronged women. In graphic moments of sexual violence across Seasons Two and Three, Lily leads her band of female avengers in a bloody quest to replace the male Master Race with her own female collective. 'Never again', she declares, 'will I kneel to any man. Now they shall kneel to me' (3.2). She emerges as a much more empowered female creature than those of the 1930s Universal and later Hammer bride narratives from which she evolves. It is Lily who presents as the most violent of Frankenstein's creations; she and John Clare are, she argues 'the conquerors', destined 'to rule' (2.8) but where Lily seeks a universal revenge against *man*kind Clare's quest is of a more personal nature.

However, despite her physical powers and her single-minded revenge quest, in a chilling return to their unequal power status at the close of the final season, Lily is ultimately tamed by her male creator who reasserts his dominance over her, and by inference all women. Having captured Lily and taken her to Bedlam, in an act presented to her as a kindness designed to reinstate her 'serenity', Frankenstein and Dr. Jekyll seek to 'take away' her 'anger and pain and replace them with something much better' (3.8). But Braid argues that Lily redefines their attempts to make her into 'a proper woman', to 'normalize' her behaviour, as an act of patriarchal control, designed to return her to the preordained status of 'an offering! A whore resurrected to be given to [Frankenstein's] Creature' (3.8): the interventions of Jekyll and Frankenstein, through the 'obliteration of [Lily's] past', are seen to deny not only her freedom but her agency (237). It is this capacity to retain even the most minute recollection of a past that is not controlled by their 'maker' that ensures the humanity of both Lily and John Clare. Despite their affiliation with the feared female 'Other' Vanessa and Lily, like all of Logan's 'monsters', retain their humanity; the latter's hatred is eventually revealed as a consequence of the death of her child, while Vanessa, always on 'the cusp of dark and light', vacillates throughout between the extremes of 'angel and demon' (Logan in Gosling 124), choosing ultimately to reject evil in the closing moments of the final season.

The series continues to expand the parameters of the genre and to examine polar extremes by exploring in close detail the Gothic's preoccupation with marginality and 'otherness', in all of its 'manifold shapes and monstrous misshapes' (Kolkhe and Gutleben Neo-Victorian Gothic 4). Logan is interested in examining what he terms 'the monster within' (Logan in Gosling 6): he constructs a dysfunctional 'monstrous family' of sorts peopled by characters, some known to us from other stories, others newly created to form the main narrative thrust of the series and all of whom are grappling with monsters both literal and metaphorical in Victorian London and the demimonde. Newly created characters like Sembene and Sir Malcolm are emblematic of the marginalised, though their 'otherness' is of a more conventional type. Sir Malcolm chooses to position himself outside the realms of the 'polite' upper-class society to which he belongs; Sembene is the consummate exotic and mysterious outsider, the lone servant in Sir Malcolm's fortress-like London mansion. Both belong to the dysfunctional 'family' that Sir Malcolm gathers about him in order to fulfil his quest to atone for his own 'monstrous' parenting, and Logan's preoccupation with notions of 'monstrous' parenting forms a story thread that also connects with newly constructed characters like Vanessa Ives and Ethan Chandler who, like Frankenstein and his creations, have troubled relationships with parents.

However, Logan's revisioning of characters from the canonical texts he appropriates is more complex and nuanced. Victor Frankenstein is not the overtly villainous creator realised through Peter Cushing's star performance in the Hammer series, and his creatures are far more layered and complicated as are the relationships between them and their creator. Nor is his story confined to his relationship with his creatures—creatures who are also intimately involved with other characters from the new storyline. Logan's Frankenstein emerges as a socially and emotionally inept individual, driven initially, like Shelley's Frankenstein, by the sole desire to create life beyond death; yet in this series, he is increasingly drawn into a more emotionally complex relationship with the creatures he births. The first creature to enter the narrative does not align with either our expectations of the 'monster' Frankenstein traditionally creates or the anticipated relationship between creator and creature. In the role of nurturing parent, Frankenstein helps the self-named Proteus come to terms with his new existence, building a bond that steps outside the bounds of earlier Frankenstein narratives as part of Logan's ongoing exploration of father/child relationships. But what takes centre frame in the first episode and across Season One's story arc is his flawed relationship with his first creature who reappears in episode two in a dramatic scene more akin to the body horror of mainstream cinema than lush period drama. At this point, Logan leaves us in no doubt that this younger Dr. Frankenstein, placed in a different era and a different locale to that of Shelley's Frankenstein, is the creator of the monster we already know. Frankenstein's narrative continues to evolve across the three-season story arc, delivering more multilayered character studies of both Frankenstein and his creatures than can be found in other iterations, and providing both prequel and sequel to their stories. He emerges as a conflicted 'father' whose 'love' of his offspring is conditional and complex, his love for his 'daughter', Lily, manifesting as monstrous incestuous desire.

The bond between *Penny Dreadful's* newly created protagonist, Vanessa Ives and the very human yet conflicted poetry-devouring 'monster', self-named John Clare, also evolves over three seasons. Their relationship foregrounds the philosophical conundrum that drives Logan's neo-Victorian narrative throughout: how do we deal with the most monstrous of monsters—the one that lies within all of us? In an homage to cinema's similar attempts to explore the humanity of so-called monsters, Logan's John Clare, like Ridley Scott's Roy Batty in *Blade Runner*

(1982), forces his audience to see beyond his monstrous self. Episode three of Season One opens with a flashback to Frankenstein's childhood before cutting intermittently to the earlier moment when his creature destroys Proteus; the episode is dominated by over twelve minutes of dialogue between Frankenstein and his creature, the latter delivering astonishing, poetically charged speeches that attest to Logan's theatrical pedigree and serve to introduce further neo-Victorian gothic themes of the series related to the burden of immortality and what Kolkhe and Gutleben describe as the genre's preoccupation with 'post-modern self-abjection' (43): an abjection directly addressed in one of the many eloquent speeches delivered by self-named 'monster' John Clare who challenges Frankenstein's dominion over creation, arguing, 'I am not a creation of the antique pastoral world. I am modernity personified' (3.1). In an earlier, eloquent disquisition on matters of mortality and ever-lasting life, Clare forces both his creator and his audience to question the morality of and motivation behind Frankenstein's actions stating, 'Surely this was not the Protean man you had envisioned? …This was not the Golden Triumph over mortality—the lyrical Adonis of whom Shelley wrote?'; rather, he concludes 'This was an abomination' (2.1).

In Logan's story world, the creatures, though still of monstrous strength and capable of monstrous actions, are less clearly identifiable as monsters. They are provided with backstory, motivational drivers that produce monsters capable of evoking an emotional response from Logan's contemporary audience. Throughout the series run, the creature's capacity to remember becomes a central concern, leading in the final season to his reunion with his former family and a telling moment of past recognition in which his former relationship with the show's protagonist, Vanessa Ives, emerges as a thread that seamlessly connects this iconic literary figure with Logan's newly created character across a three-season story arc that, by the end of the series, sees John Clare's 'monstrous shape' superseded by his humanity. Ethan Chandler serves as yet another complex and conflicted 'monster' who, like Vanessa Ives and John Clare, resists the evil he is aware lurks within. From the outset, he is plagued by fears of his 'otherness' and of his culpability in acts of bloody violence that are narratively aligned with the bloody acts of the infamous Jack the Ripper. He is one of several males in the narrative who are plagued by self-doubt, whose 'fragmented identities' subvert the 'Victorian masculine ideal' of the 'self-composed man' (Rocha 33).

Logan also brings into the narrative frame the populist werewolf myth, presenting Ethan Chandler as a figure who, despite his compassion for others, from prostitute Brona Croft and the conflicted Vanessa Ives to vampire child Fenton, must deal with the literal as well as the figurative monster within during the course of the series three-season run. Introduced as a carefree gunslinger performing in a travelling Wild West show, Chandler's mythology is tied up with flawed yet legendary constructs of the 'Wild West'—constructs that are slowly undermined as the series moves into its third season and more of the reality of his experiences as a hunter of indigenous Americans during the early days of settlement is revealed. His story is also connected to other urban myths that circulate the Victorian period: the mythologised violence of Jack the Ripper becomes intertwined with his own bloody deeds, and both are enshrined for public consumption in penny dreadfuls of the Victorian period. The global nature of the werewolf myth is further exploited by Logan when the story draws to its Season Three denouement as shape shifter stories of Victorian England merge with those of native American Indian mythology, melding together different religious beliefs (Christian, Egyptian, Native American Indian, occult) and different creation stories to form one plot that deals in the salvation of humankind as 'Lupus Dei' Ethan and his surrogate werewolf Indian father confound the prophesised apocalypse and save the world from imminent darkness. On one level, *Penny Dreadful's* shape-shifting Ethan Chandler is an homage to Stoker's Texan Quincey Morris, one of the Crew of Light in search of vampires in general and Dracula in particular, but Logan's werewolf builds on the Gothic novel, *Wagner the Wher-Wolf* (1847), written by penny dreadful writer George W. M. Reynolds, in which the werewolf is a good man who, like Chandler, ultimately resists the devil's attempts to corrupt him. Logan's appropriation of the myth also connects with Clemence Housman's *The Werewolf* (1896) which envisions instead a female werewolf. A number of interesting parallels can be drawn between Housman's werewolf, Logan's werewolf and his protagonist, Vanessa Ives. Housman's werewolf can only be destroyed through the sacrificial spilling of 'pure' blood but we see a complex intertextualisation of this werewolf tale in *Penny Dreadful*. Werewolf Ethan is not the one who must be sacrificed in order to save humanity from darkness; instead, he is the saviour of humanity, destined from the series outset to be the one who spills Vanessa's blood as he sacrifices her in order to defeat the dark side during Season Three's finalé. Like Wagner's werewolf, Vanessa

Ives wants to be good, and in the series' closing moments, she chooses death and 'Our Lord' over eternal life and evil, leading to the anticipated narrative closure that Logan has built into the story arc from its earliest moments. The werewolf myth presents Logan with the opportunity to explore a tale of shape-shifting bodies that lends itself to the same kinds of erotic bodily transformations found in *Dracula* and *Frankenstein* but it remains a legend that provides the kind of sensationalist storyline that is taken up more readily by mainstream media forms like the penny dreadful of the Victorian era, B Horror movies of the forties and beyond, and contemporary TV series. Designed to appeal to the show's film literate horror fan base, Ethan's bodily transformations into his werewolf self are depicted in graphic detail on-screen in a visual style reminiscent of the iconic wolf man of Universal's *The Wolf Man*. Plagued by fears of his own 'otherness' throughout Season One, his dramatic on-screen transformation into a werewolf in the closing moments of the final episode leaves the audience in no doubt as to the violent and bloody acts he is capable of, and at such sensationalistic moments, the series enters the realms of the horror genre, in a style more readily associated with the graphic visualisation of cinema than TV horror. At such moments, Chandler's dramatic bodily transformations make the unseen 'monster within' a tangible screen presence. However, the horror of his bodily transformations is counter-balanced by his innate humanity.

With its spectacular moments of werewolf shape shifting, levitating bodies and graphic on-screen violence, *Penny Dreadful* enters a generic dimension that exceeds the boundaries of both the period costume drama and the Gothic and is symptomatic of a contemporary repositioning of the Gothic in particular. Of late, the Gothic has according to Kolkhe and Gutleben 'permanently emerged from the crepuscular unconscious into the brightly lit mainstream', and is now being visualised in many facets of popular culture in 'a seeming frenzy of rendering visible what was once largely relegated to the imagination and the arts' (1). Where once Gothic TV was aligned with a predominantly pre-packaged female audience that sought its pleasures in heritage fare (Cherry 169–178), contemporary Gothic TV has a closer affinity with TV horror, from *The Walking Dead* (2010) and *American Horror Story* (2011–) to Showtime's reincarnation of David Lynch's *Twin Peaks* (2017) and Logan's *Penny Dreadful*. Even as it grounds itself within a backdrop of fin de siècle Victorian London, *Penny Dreadful's* identity as costume drama is constantly at odds with its established identity as

Gothic TV—an identity which ensures it transcends its own historical boundaries. The second episode of *Penny Dreadful* foregrounds a staple trope of costume drama, the costume ball, but the scene is swiftly undercut, shifting from traditional matters of social etiquette and the choreography of dance to focus on a staged séance in which Vanessa Ives channels the voices of the dead in a series of terrifying acts of bodily possession, before leaving in search of casual sex—a final transgressive act in a scene that explores a very different construct of femininity to both the anticipated costume drama heroine and her gothic counterpart. Kolkhe and Gutleben question the contemporary Gothic's capacity to explore and 'defend marginality' when that marginality has become 'not only trendy but run-of the-mill' (3), but it is the Gothic's capacity to 'adapt over time to radically different social and cultural matrices' that sets it apart (Akilli and Oz 24), and what is currently emerging is a Gothic hybrid that, in its on-screen visualisation, has more in common with the contemporary horror movie than with the understated Gothic television of earlier eras.

However, it is only in recent years that TV production companies have sought to exploit the generic potential of stories that, within a cinematic context, would be *promoted* as horror. Hills argues that the horror genre has historically been 'render[ed]..relatively invisible' within the history of TV production (111–112); it has been subsumed into other generic labels like Gothic TV, comedy horror of the *Addams Family* (1964–1966) and *The Munsters* (1964–1966) variety or teen horror dramas like *Buffy the Vampire Slayer* (1997–2003) and *The Vampire Diaries* (2009–). However, with the arrival of shows like *American Horror Story, Carnivale* (2003–2005), *True Blood* (2008–2014), *The Walking Dead, Wolf Creek* (2016–), *Dexter* (2006–2013), *Hannibal* (2013–2015), *Bates Motel* (2013–), *Rosemary's Baby* (2014), *Salem* (2014–), *The Exorcist* (2016–) and *Penny Dreadful*, produced by cable channels and streaming providers that operate beyond the moralistic constraints of TV broadcasting, TV is at last able to realise on the small screen narratives that embrace the content and visual excess of its cinematic counterpart. Jowett and Abbott refute Hills earlier claims that TV is a small screen medium which is not suited to the graphic visualisation of horror; such claims, they argue, no longer have credence within a twenty-first century context given the technologically advanced nature of today's TV industry (13). At this point in time, when the TV horror genre is no longer constrained by either technological incapacity or censorship of the kind that has historically dominated within the realms of broadcast TV, we are, McGrath argues, not only 'experiencing a "Golden Age of television"   but specifically of horror television' (2014). McGrath, like Hoppenstand (2), notes that the 'traditionally conservative' treatment of TV horror within an American context is on the wane, and both attribute this shift to FX's ground-breaking anthology series, *American Horror Story*. It is a series that illustrates TV horror's capacity to bridge the divide between what Jowett and Abbott claim are 'the boundaries between trash and art' (60) turning what was once a genre deemed to be in 'bad taste' or 'excessively violent' (2), into one that has aesthetic as well as a kinaesthetic audience appeal. Like *American Horror Story*, *Penny Dreadful* is a series that purposefully operates within the realms of both 'trash and art', appealing as much to a cult fantasy-horror fan base as to viewers interested in its more literary properties: it engages with 'high art' through its appropriation of canonical texts from the nineteenth century and through its affiliation with neo-Victorian revisionism but it is also a series that has its roots in sensationalist fiction and populist horror cinema. In the current TV landscape, with the advent of new viewing platforms and the emergence of cable TV networks that operate outside the constraints of mainstream broadcasting, the aesthetic and content-based limitations of TV programming are being eroded, particularly in the realms of more risk-taking genres such as TV horror and Gothic TV. While Kolkhe and Gutleben view the 'global consumption and commoditisation' of the Gothic as a negative (3), in an industry sense this is its attraction.

In the realms of cinema *and* TV, the horror genre remains difficult to define in any concrete terms; it operates within so many varying guises, from the supernatural and other worldly, to psychological horror, body horror or realist horror rooted in graphic acts of violence. The pilot episode of *Penny Dreadful* begins with an opening pre-credit sequence that foregrounds its affiliation with sensationalist mainstream horror before moving to the more subtle psychological horror of a protagonist plagued by the manifestation of a demon within. In a pre-credit sequence added to the script during production, a compendium of horror tropes is employed to create stylised horror moments that build to the mysterious murder of a mother and her child. The scene is initially characterised by dim lighting, tight framing, disorientating hand-held camera work and the naturalistic sounds of heavy breathing, creaking floorboards, the distant thrum of trains on the track; but we build to anticipated moments of horror, replete with blood-curdling screams and a tense musical score as both mother and child inexplicably disappear from view, the mother sucked out of a window in spectacular fashion, the investigating child left in black screen, her screams continuing out of frame. The opening positions the text as horror rather than costume drama from the outset and a similar pre-credit sequence is added to the script of the second episode in which the bloody murder of a young woman takes centre stage, the gory closing shot of her severed arm leaving the viewer in no doubt as to the series identity as horror fare. The series credit sequence again eschews the motifs of the costume drama in favour of a more cryptic approach to its period identity—one that disorientates the viewer through a series of fast edits that cut between images associated with familiar Gothic horror tropes (scorpions, spiders, tarot cards, carrion beetles, fangs, bats) and jarring images of china tea cups overflowing with blood, bleeding orchids, rotating crucifixes and fragmented body parts, bloodied hands holding medical instruments, all interspersed with random images of the main characters from the *Penny Dreadful* story world. A frenzied, melodramatic orchestral score accompanies this image overload, bathed in a blue ethereal light as they come in and out of focus. Within fifteen minutes, the emphasis in 'Night Work' (1.1) shifts to a vampire action showdown of the kind more readily associated with cinema's action genre and the graphic violence of horror cinema; the series' alignment with the gore of body horror is also affirmed by the end of this opening episode as Victor Frankenstein's first creation violently erupts through the ripped torso of Frankenstein's second creature. Logan presents a compendium of horror 'types' that surpass our expectations of Gothic TV in both content and televisual style as the subtleties of the latter are consumed by the visual excesses of cinematic horror more readily associated with the Hammer horror brand.

Logan's exploration of 'Otherness' and the dysfunctional 'family' connects it with the horror genre in general, and TV horror shares many generic traits with Gothic TV: 'home' as the site of horror prevails in numerous horror narratives, from *Bates Motel* to *American Horror Story* and *Rosemary's Baby*. The trope of the dysfunctional family is a central motif within Logan's series, from flawed biological families like that of Ethan Chandler, the Ives and the Murrays, to its constructed families like Sir Malcolm's makeshift vampire-hunting 'family', Frankenstein's mutated 'family' or Evelyn Poole's coven of witches. But it is its thematic preoccupation with the monster within that ensures the series is most clearly identifiable as *Gothic* Horror. It taps into the horror genre's traditional preoccupation with 'character-based... charismatic and engaging monsters' (Jowett and Abbott 201) by presenting complex and multilayered individuals who are battling personal demons on both a literal and a psychological plane. Frankenstein's Creature, for example, has since the early days of cinema presented as a character whose innate humanity demands our attention, and Logan monopolises on this, expanding across the time-rich potentialities of a three-season story arc the characterisation of this Creature, affording him narrative opportunities to explore his quest for acceptance and love through his relationships with others and through provision of a backstory that gives us a sense of the man he was before his 'monstrous' rebirth. Carroll argues that 'within the context of the horror genre, monsters are identified as impure and unclean' beings who evoke emotions of 'fear' and 'loathing', 'terror' and 'disgust' in others (54), and in *Penny Dreadful*, the self-named John Clare's monstrous appearance does indeed evoke the revulsion of some, from the actors he engages with in the theatre in Season One to the owners of the waxworks who would exploit him in Season Two. He is shown to be capable of acts of gross violence, but Logan complicates what Carroll identifies as the anticipated response to monstrosity by investing the character with an emotional register that he is denied in other iterations of the Frankenstein myth; moreover, the response of the series' female protagonist to John Clare and the intertwining of their past lives counteracts any initial feeling of 'fear' and 'disgust' directed towards him as the monster of Carroll's definition.

In keeping with the tropes of contemporary TV horror, Logan provides us with glimpses of the 'man-within-the monster' (Jowett and Abbott 221). But what is equally important here is Logan's capacity to explore contemporary TV horror's preoccupation with 'the monster-within-the man' (221): Ethan Chandler presents as a sensitive individual who constantly battles the monster within. And like many of the characters, from Victor Frankenstein and Sir Malcolm, to Vanessa Ives and Dorian Gray, all of whom may in some sense be construed at least in part as monstrous, he belies the outward appearance of monstrosity. Through the casting of star performers known for their physical appeal, from teen heart-throb Josh Hartnett and former Bond Timothy Dalton, to Eva Green, Billy Piper and musician-actor Reeve Carney, Logan underlines at a visual level the contradictions inherent in constructions of 'monstrosity'. The physically beautiful Mina Murray and Lily

Frankenstein are outwardly appealing characters, yet both are capable of monstrous acts of violence, while the outwardly monstrous John Clare is constantly seeking to cloak his 'disgusting' appearance by constructing a Gothic 'look' that, without success, aligns with the romance of his chosen name. For Logan, 'horror' is a complex concept, realised in a multifaceted manner in *Penny Dreadful*: he takes a Humanist approach, seeing horror as the 'quantif[ying]' of 'anxiety', as we 'tr[y] to name and understand those things we fear' (DVD production blog)—things associated with what he terms 'the monster within' (Logan in Gosling 6) rather than with either the outwardly monstrous or monstrous acts per se. It is in the main a show about outliers in search of themselves; it operates as 'a valorization of outsiderdom' that according to Poore is 'tailor-made to appeal to, and to create, dedicated fans' interested in matters of identity and 'transformation' (75–76). Like other TV horror shows, *Penny Dreadful* uses its time-rich seriality to extend our understanding of monstrosity, building on what Jowett and Abbott see as TV's capacity to 'exploit and challenge horror fans love of monsters' (221).

2.3 Logan as Textual Cartographer

Although an already established and highly successful screenplay writer of a wide range of classic Hollywood stories (*Gladiator*, 2000; *The Last Samurai*, 2003; *The Aviator*, 2004; *Hugo*, 2011; *Skyfall*, 2012) Logan, like many other film industry creatives in recent times, chooses to develop the complex story world of *Penny Dreadful* outside of the industrial and temporal constraints of the film industry, opting to work instead within a TV production context that provides the time to build and unravel dense and complex plotlines. Working outside the norms of the 'writer's room' model now so widely adopted as the dominant mode of collaborative story-writing in USA TV series production, he serves as sole scriptwriter as well as series creator, composing, orchestrating and extending the amalgamation of the plotlines, characters and relationships of existing and new narratives. Series directors on the show may change, with a two-episode pattern of directorial engagement established in Season One, but the script remains Logan's creation. He sees *Penny Dreadful* as his 'nineteenth century novel, each episode a chapter in [an] ongoing tale' that lends itself to the structural format of TV serialisation rather than the 90–180 minute film (Logan in Gosling 6).

Penny Dreadful maintains an incestuous relationship with the body of texts that circulate it, establishing 'an ever-expanding network of textual relations', rooted in stories both canonical and populist; it is, in Sanders terminology, an audacious act of 'appropriation', capable of 'encourag[ing] the ongoing evolving production of meaning' (2–3), and involved in what Stam defines as an 'endless process of recycling, transformation and mutation, with no clear point of origin' (66). However, though Logan is engaged in complex adaptive acts of 'transformation and mutation' of existing narratives, *his* narrative centres on 'a fictional story that [is] completely unknown to the audience' (Logan in Radish); the show's three-season story arc places Vanessa Ives, Sir Malcolm Murray and Ethan Chandler at the centre of its fictitious universe—a universe that goes beyond the horizons of its neo-Victorian landscape and the demimonde, into Africa and 'Wild West' USA in Season Three—with characters from other, well-known narratives sewn into the fabric of its newly created plotline. Logan is 'playing with familiar worlds' and with characters he and his fan base have known since childhood, but he also asserts his intention to explore them from a 'new perspective' (Logan in Radish): a perspective that presents the audience with mutated versions of the Frankenstein and Dracula myth, and that takes Wilde's Dorian Gray on to new narrative trajectories, all of which are connected across Logan's complex story world. He 'both [re]interpretat[es]and *then* [re]-creates', in acts of 'appropriation and salvaging' that extend the story world of prior texts within the narrative framework of his own fictional world (8 Hutcheon), 'salvaging' what will work for his new story by refashioning and 'reinterpreting' points of known narratives from three nineteenth-century canonical texts that are in their own right disturbing iterations of the Gothic; *Dracula*, *The Picture of Dorian Gray* and *Frankenstein or the Modern Prometheus* and their back catalogue of on-screen renditions are appropriated throughout the series run, while Dr. Jekyll of *The Strange Case of Dr. Jekyll and Mr. Hyde* becomes an additional 'bit' player in the final season and is indelibly connected to Ethan Chandler's werewolf persona.

Logan's approach encourages the kind of audience interaction noted by Hutcheon as central to the act of adaptation: one that invites a 'conceptual flipping back and forth', a proactive interplay between the familiar and the new (139). However, though Hutcheon notes that 'most theories of adaptation assume... story is the common denominator, the core of what is transposed across different media and genres' [10], in *Penny Dreadful* the existing narratives are integrated *into* Logan's narrative—a narrative that revolves first and foremost around his newly created protagonist, Vanessa Ives: for Logan, 'everything must triangulate around Vanessa Ives' and 'all of the characters ha[ve] to refract off her central story' (Logan in Gosling 89). Speaking at a ComiCon convention in 2014, at which his series is introduced by the panel presenter Catriona Wightman as an 'innovative mash-up', Logan claims to 'cherish the sacred text' but also acknowledges that he and his production team have no desire to 'recrea[te]' it. Instead, the aim is, he notes, both to 'align comfortably with mythology' and to 'break it completely' in accordance with 'what suits the story' (ComiCon 2014). Logan's choice of title speaks to this; by aligning his series with the sensationalist content and the populist appeal of the penny dreadful, he destabilises our perception of the 'high art' canonical narratives that infiltrate his story. Undercutting further the primacy and authority afforded to precursor texts by a temporal reordering of events, and by redefining the character traits and narrative trajectories of their protagonists, Logan adopts the kind of 'writerly approach' to adaptation advocated by Thomas Leitch: 'every text', argues Leitch, 'is itself an invitation to be rewritten' (16). Logan is engaged in acts of writerly reclamation and affirmation that add further layers to an already complex story universe, and this layering becomes an intrinsic part of the narrative *evolution* of the culturally loaded precursor texts he chooses to appropriate. The series and the texts it engages with are what Brian A. Rose terms 'cultural texts'—texts that evolve as they are adapted over time, 'permitting a redefinition of anxiety-provoking issues' (2). What remains central to the relationship between Logan's new story and those already known narratives are shared preoccupations that transcend the temporal and the cultural; its fin de siècle setting speaks not only to the Victorian era's anxieties—a fear of yet a desire to embrace technological and scientific advancement, a gnawing longing for but acknowledgement of the limitations of religious faith, a disturbing compulsion to explore new horizons—but also to those of our post-millennial scene. The anxieties that circulate the stories Logan 'borrows' from continue to evolve alongside the narratives.

By cross-pollinating old and new stories through the filter of these shared anxieties, Logan ensures *Penny Dreadful* is part of each precursor text's cultural evolution; it speaks to the Victorian period from which it takes inspiration but it is also in dialogue with the many screen adaptations that serve as further markers of each narrative's cultural journey, each period's contemporaneous angst. Literary figures like Dr. Frankenstein and his creature/s, Dorian Gray, Dracula and his somnambulant female vampires (and Dr. Jekyll in the final season) are iconographic signifiers of horror and anxiety that translate readily to a contemporary context. Logan builds on his audience's potential knowledge of the literary canon but he also builds on its knowledge of a body of cinematic adaptations from the Universal and Hammer horror studios. He embraces cinema's textual irreverence through similarly creative acts of assimilation and composition, producing an intertextually layered metafiction that draws together new and familiar story worlds in an unholy marriage between 'high' and 'low' art. The Greek myths of Prometheus referenced in the title of Mary Shelley's novel, the echoes of Narcissus found in *The Picture of Dorian Gray* and the many folkloric myths that are part of the narrative fabric of Bram Stoker's *Dracula* become part of an ever-evolving compendium of tales to which Logan also adds riffs on the Pygmalion myth, Egyptian creation stories of Amun-Ra and his consort Amunet, the biblical narrative of Satan's fall from grace, mythologised tales of werewolves and of the Wild West frontier. Furthermore, through a process of retrieval and reconstruction, *Penny Dreadful* taps into the Western viewer's knowledge of a body of myth that reinscribes notions of literal and metaphorical transformation and mutation at the level of narrative, characterisation and spectatorship; the act of mutation is visually realised on screen through moments of demonic possession, werewolf transformations, Nightcomer shape-shifting and the uncanny on-screen healing of wounds. The narrative's more metaphorical mutations are explored in the guise of warped 'coming of age' plotlines that see the 'monster' within each character vanquished and/or embraced. The show is also an intertextual compendium of literary references from Shakespearean allusion to the poetry of Milton, John Clare and the Romantics, all of which serve to elaborate on the myths and the thematic preoccupations it explores. As with other neo-Victorian screen texts like *The Piano* and *The Governess*, Logan's *Penny Dreadful* does not treat the appropriated stories and 'histories' of a bygone age as cultural artefacts; rather, as a consequence of their adaptive evolution in print and screen media forms, they remain a part of the new story's textual fabric.

This narratively complex series employs what Mittell terms 'complex serial poetics' in which 'a cumulative narrative' builds 'over time' (Complex Poetics 58). It is a narrative that 'foreground[ds] plot developmen[t]' (Narrative Complexity 36), and its relationships evolve *from* those plot developments. All three seasons are shaped by Vanessa Ives' narrative trajectory: Season One revolves around the quest to 'save' Mina Murray, and while presented as an act of atonement on the part of Vanessa and Sir Malcolm Murray, it also introduces the series' preoccupation with Vanessa's attempts to resist the lure of evil in Seasons Two and Three. It is, in the main, what Mittell labels a 'centrifugal narrative', its plot events 'pushing out across an expanding story world'; yet, it is also, in part, a 'centripetal narrative' propelled here by the psychology of its female protagonist whose 'thickness of backstory' takes us 'inwards to its narrative centre' (Complex Poetics 52–53). Throughout Season One of *Penny Dreadful*, the connection between Vanessa Ives and Ethan Chandler builds to a point of mutual trust whereby she is able to charge him to 'look into [her] eyes' and 'know' when the time has come to end her life (7.1); though at this stage in the story arc he chooses instead to save her through an act of exorcism, by the season finale and in accordance with the series linear logic, he knows there is no option but to make good his Season One promise in order not only to release her but to save the world from impending darkness. Though she remains an enigma of sorts throughout the series, she emerges as the character whose psychological mysteries and crises of faith provide both narrative depth and crucial plot points. Despite the show's appeal to a cult fan base (and that fan base's inevitable desire for a franchise-like continuation of the narrative), Logan is very clear on his directional intent. To take the story in its serial TV form into a fourth season would be to compromise the integrity of his protagonist and the story world he has created.

Points of connection between Vanessa Ives and characters from the texts Logan appropriates are intricate and varied yet all form part of the fabric of this original tale, and an additional 'thickness of backstory' is afforded some of the literary icons with whom the audience is already familiar. The father/child relationship between Frankenstein and his creatures is particularly complex, and much time is devoted to exploring the first creature's sensitivities as well as his rage, developing for the self-named John Clare an inverted 'coming of age' story that builds back to memories of his former life in Season Three. The significance of Dr. Victor Frankenstein's story within the series as a whole is established from the outset; however, as with the other stories *Penny Dreadful* appropriates, it is a story that is not dominated solely by its relationship with Shelley's novel—a novel that in the adaptive *histories* of the Frankenstein narrative is just 'one more version' and 'not necessarily the most influential one' (Garcia 224). Like all of the appropriated characters who people the *Penny Dreadful* universe Frankenstein's part in Logan's narrative services first and foremost its newly established characters. In this iteration of the Frankenstein tale, Frankenstein is recruited as one of a disparate band of vampire hunters whose mission is to 'save' Sir Malcolm Murray's daughter, Mina, who by virtue of her name and her predicament is indelibly linked to Bram stoker's *Dracula*. Logan actions both a temporal and a geographical shift away from the novel's eighteenth-century time frame and its various Northern Hemisphere locales, repositioning Frankenstein within a clearly delineated fin de siècle London of the 1890s, and creating a more complex study of Shelley's arch over-reacher. The 'omissions and additions, amplification and elaboration' characteristic of adaptations of the Frankenstein myth (Tropp 39) are also characteristic of Logan's adaptive approach to this story: earlier 'additions and omissions' made to the Frankenstein narrative by producers of both the Universal Studio films of the 1930s and the Hammer Horror films from 1957–1976 are sewn into *Penny Dreadful's* story world. Populist mainstream Frankenstein films of Universal's horror franchise (*Frankenstein*, 1931 and *The Bride of Frankenstein*, 1935) have since acquired iconic status as part of the cinematic canon. However, it is their populist appeal that Logan taps into here, building on our known perceptions of Boris Karloff's performance as Frankenstein's Creature in these seminal film texts and on the creation of the Creature's 'bride'. Logan also adapts and elaborates on the visual style aesthetic of the Hammer Frankenstein series (*The Curse of Frankenstein*, 1957; *The Revenge of Frankenstein*, 1958; *The Evil of Frankenstein*, 1964; *Frankenstein Created Woman*, 1967; *Frankenstein Must Be Destroyed*, 1969; and *Frankenstein and the Monster from Hell*, 1976) which, as with their Universal predecessors, have shifted from the populist domain of their time of release to attain contemporary canonical cinematic status. *Penny Dreadful* shares the visual richness and period treatment of the Hammer horror stable, and exudes a style more readily affiliated with cinematic horror than TV horror, both of the Hammer variety and more contemporaneous horror films characterised by an excess of bloody violence and gore. In yet another homage to early horror cinema, Logan references MGM's 1945 adaptation of Wilde's *The Picture of Dorian Gray*: when we are eventually afforded a glimpse of Dorian's portrait in Season Three, what we are presented with is almost a replica of the decrepit figure of the aged Dorian of MGM's earlier imagining.

However, Wilde's story has not been adapted to screen as often as the other canonical Gothic texts that form part of Logan's story world. It also operates on a more tangential level within that story world, but it adds another essential layer to the thematic preoccupations of the *Penny Dreadful* universe by amplifying its exploration of the appeal and the shortcomings of eternal life, and by underscoring the fin de siècle anxieties revolving around challenges to religious faith in Victorian England.

Logan's appropriation of aspects of the Frankenstein myth is intertwined with his borrowings from Bram Stoker's *Dracula*, a text which ostensibly provides a structural framework for the new narrative. *Penny Dreadful's* storyline builds from its opening atonement quest to Vanessa's ongoing battle against the lure of evil—an evil made corporeal by Season Three when Dracula appears as the quietly seductive Dr. Sweet, a museum curator whose capacity to appear in daylight and to be killed by means other than a stake through the heart breaks with the traditional lore of the vampire myth. This audacious rewrite of vampire mythology also includes the introduction in Season Three of a female vampire hunter, shifting the Dracula narrative into territory that intertextualises other contemporary female vampire slayers like Anna Valerius (*Van Helsing*, 2004) and Buffy Summers (*Buffy the Vampire Slayer*, 1997–2003). The dominant story, however, remains that of unconventional Vanessa Ives and here Dracula serves as the catalyst for her ultimate downfall rather than as protagonist of the tale. The early demise of Van Helsing, murdered by Frankenstein's first creature in episode 6 of Season One heralds a further daring textual intervention on the part of Logan. Stoker's novel functions as yet another text that transitions from the populist to the canonical on both page and screen. Though now considered a literary classic, *Dracula* was first received as 'entertaining thriller...the pulp fiction of its day both castigated and enjoyed for its ability to fascinate and absorb readers' (Bignell 116). It builds on folkloric myth and on already popular narratives like penny blood *Varney the Vampire Slayer*, and as with Hammer horror productions of the Frankenstein myth, there are many diverse, populist reworkings of *Dracula* by this iconic studio (*The Horror of Dracula*, 1958; *The Brides of Dracula*, 1960; *Dracula, Prince of Darkness*, 1966; *Dracula Has Risen from the Grave*, 1968; *The Scars of Dracula*, 1970; *Taste the Blood of Dracula*, 1970; *Dracula A.D. 1972*, 1972; *The Satanic Rites of Dracula*, 1973) that have of late acquired a canonical cinematic status, built around the star persona of Christopher Lee as the count. *Nosferatu*

(1922) and Todd Browning's *Dracula* (1931) also attest to the established canonical pedigree of the vampire narrative on screen. Vampire narratives on screen engage in 'a process of familiarization and defamiliarization' (Gelder 70), building on prior knowledge but also introducing narrative difference and new ways of visualising the iconic figure of the vampire. Aware that the vampire trope has been overworked in contemporary times, Logan is at pains to explore its potential in new ways, even as he is acutely mindful of the ways in which other vampire narratives, past and present, seep into his own (Gosling 40). The somnambulant vampire women of Season One owe much to the visual style of their Hammer horror predecessors (Logan in Gosling 47), but for his lead vampire Logan seeks and attains an original 'look'; in keeping with the show's 'ethos' his vampire is a lean, sleek, battle-scarred being covered in hieroglyphic tattoos, 'an actor in old-fashioned make-up' rather than an animated creation (40).

The werewolf myth is a further staple of horror films past and present; as with their adaptations of the Frankenstein myth and *Dracula*, Universal Studios (*The Wolf Man*, 1941) and Hammer (*The Curse of the Werewolf*, 1961) attach their style signature to the werewolf myth, forming yet another thread in the dense intertextual web that is *Penny Dreadful*. There is also an enduring history of werewolf narratives on TV, the werewolf traditionally appearing as one iconic figure among many if not as the sole protagonist of TV dramas involving 'monsters'. However, there has been a millennial upsurge in werewolf-related TV series, a first since the late 1980s (*Werewolf*, 1987–1988). In recent years, several werewolf narratives have emerged, from the early millennial show *Wolf Lake* (2001–2002) to *Wolfblood* (2012), *Bitten* (2014) and *Being Human* (2008–2013). But despite its on-screen popularity, the werewolf has not attained the literary canonical status of figures like Dracula and Frankenstein's creature. Though in part indebted to yet another Greek legend, Ovid's *Metamorphosis* in which King Lycaon is transformed into a wolf, werewolf mythology evolves from a host of populist literature that is itself a reworking of ancient stories of shape-shifting humans found in cultures across the globe. For American Logan, Ethan serves as 'our eyes into the story, an American [he] can follow in this alien landscape' (Logan in Gosling 20). The angry young man of the pilot script becomes a much more likeable character when translated to screen during production where he is instead introduced as a carefree 'Casanova' figure whose dialogue is peppered with humorous lines. But Ethan emerges as a troubled individual: one who, despite his American origins, shares the same Victorian anxieties related to matters of identity in a fin de siècle Victorian London (Akilli and Oz 22). While Logan chooses to build first and foremost on the long tradition of populist on-screen werewolf narratives, his werewolf's affiliation with cinematic Hydes is also written into the text. There are clear parallels to be drawn between the iconic screen werewolf and populist cinematic reconfigurations of Mr. Hyde, yet another canonical figure this time from Stevenson's novella, *The Strange Case of Dr. Jekyll and Mr. Hyde* (1886) which explores the metaphorical monster within. And as with Wilde's *The Picture of Dorian Gray* and Stoker's *Dracula*, it is a novel that engages with the fin de siècle anxieties of the Victorian age. Even though Jekyll's transformation to Hyde is couched in metaphorical rather than literal terms in Stevenson's novella, subsequent screen adaptations of the text have translated these transformations into literal visual spectacle that plays to the strengths of the cinematic medium, and it is these spectacular on-screen visualisations of transformation, alongside those that form part of the wider mythology of the screen werewolf, that inform Chandler's dramatic bodily transformations at crucial moments in *Penny Dreadful*, making the unseen 'monster within' a tangible screen presence.

2.4 The Paratextual Context of the *Penny Dreadful* Universe

As with other cable TV providers like HBO, AMC and FX, the Showtime network is now part of a post-millennial TV drama renaissance in which the creation of exclusive content forms an increasingly important part of network brand identity. Having emerged in the nineties as a network that sought distinction as a purveyor of sci-fi and queer drama (De Fino 13), Showtime is currently building a reputation as a provider of quality Horror TV with successful series like *Dexter* and *Penny Dreadful* being followed by the long-awaited continuation of David Lynch's *Twin Peaks* (ABC, 1990–1991) released in 2017. All three series push the boundaries of mainstream horror: *Dexter* (an adaptation of the 2004 novel *Darkly Dreaming Dexter*) positions us with a serial killer, while *Twin Peaks* and *Penny Dreadful* (2017) continue to breach the parameters of Gothic TV. Like *Dexter*, *Penny Dreadful* attracts a broad mainstream fan base, but as with its *Twin Peaks* forerunner, it also offers the cineliterate and readers of classic literature the opportunity to engage with the series in different ways[2]: the unravelling of both overt and covert allusions to other texts forms part of the show's complex game-playing identity—an identity knowingly courted by and exploited within an industry context.

TV texts exist within a 'network of power' (Lotz and Gray 39) , defined in industry terms by practices that extend beyond the series themselves to 'pre-coded' paratexts that continue to circulate them (Gray 33) . For Mittell, the 'active practices of fan involvement' are of central paratextual import (Complex Poetics 17); for Lotz, the critic plays a central role in the 'creation and circulation of cultural texts' like TV series (21), while Gray foregrounds the significance of marketing 'hype' as 'the first outpost of interpretation' (34). But regardless of the emphasis each is afforded, all constitute paratexts, whether in the form of reviewer discourse and fandoms, or more industrially controlled marketing strategies that shape audience perception of TV shows. A body of academic scholarship may also be deemed a paratext that influences reception and perception of a TV product with regard to its relationship with computer games, comic books, history, film, theatre, canonical literature or other TV programmes. Paratexts provide what Gray and Lotz term another meaningful 'subset of intertextuality', between the TV text and its surrounding material (134), and as such form a further adaptive dimension. *Penny Dreadful*, like all cultural products, is neither produced nor consumed in a cultural vacuum; it is a text that openly engages in the appropriation of stories from a vast array of existing sources, each with its own attendant paratexts related to history, film, classic literature and populist mythologies. Its paratextualities extend beyond the confines associated with the series to embrace other paratextualities, all of which prepare us for and have an impact on our reception of it to varying degrees, adding yet more layers of meaning to the paratexts it generates in its own right.

According to Showtime's vice president of digital marketing, Marcelo Guerra, the marketing strategy employed by the network targeted a relatively far-reaching audience—'fans of horror, classic literature and period dramas'—and the pre-release emphasis focused on foregrounding its 'pedigree and production values', all of which was documented on set by a dedicated digital producer and made accessible to fans via its website

---

[2] *Penny Dreadful* was voted 'best contemporary adaptation' by scholars in attendance at the International Association of Adaptation Studies conference in 2015.

prior to the series release of episode one (Guerra in Edelsburg). Its highend period drama look and its connections with canonical literature of the long nineteenth century align it with classical TV serialisation that attracts fans of costume drama. But Gray suggests that, even though classed as secondary paratexts, pre-release materials like billboards, bus stop adverts, radio/TV adverts and 'guerilla marketing' create industry 'hype' that has 'primary power' over our 'consumption' and reception of TV products (33). Billboards accompanying Season One play to *Penny Dreadful's* period drama aesthetic; they feature, in period costume, Vanessa Ives and Ethan Chandler, characters created by Logan for *his* story, setting up expectations of a tale that takes us into new narrative territory, and there are subtle hints of the female protagonist's unconventionality, the lace at her throat being interwoven with images of scorpions. Later, billboard releases bring Logan's other new creations, Sir Malcolm Murray and Sembene, into focus alongside the iconic figure of Victor Frankenstein, realised here as a much younger man, which again distorts our anticipated reception of a show in which the Frankenstein we are familiar with will appear. In a similar move, a third billboard design replaces Frankenstein with a young Dorian Gray whose anachronistic costuming infers a similar displacement and a similarly different approach to the configuration of literary figures already known to many potential viewers. The show's appropriation of classic nineteenth-century texts is acknowledged in billboards for Season One but such appropriations are not seen to overwhelm it. Season Two's billboards focus solely on Vanessa Ives or on Ethan Chandler whose journeys continue to provide the series' narrative momentum, foregrounding once more the new story that will play out on screen. However, in this instance, though both appear as solitary figures on separate billboard designs, each image is accompanied by a tagline ('No rest for the wicked') that foregrounds the show's identity as horror over and above its identity as serialised costume drama, and by Season Three billboards suggest the marketing strategy has moved firmly to exploitation of its identity as horror TV. The Season Three billboard is dominated by what at first glance appears to be a skull yet is on closer inspection a human form—that of Ethan Chandler—suggesting yet again that it is his narrative trajectory that will provide the final story arc of this three season series, and that the series revolves not around its appropriation of other texts but around Logan's new creation. In an intensive two-week campaign that ran prior to its premiere, Showtime employed an innovative 'guerilla marketing' tactic designed to foreground the show's identity as Gothic horror fare through the creation of interactive window displays in busy New York and Los Angeles shopping areas. These displays featured eerie Gothic tropes: silhouettes that followed passers-by, accompanied by fleeting glimpses of bats, spiders, wolves and horse-drawn carriages.

Despite *Penny Dreadful's* complex engagement with texts from the literary canon, Logan is, from the outset, writing for a fan base that is rooted in the popular domain for consumption by the 'genre fans' and 'Comic-Con geeks' with whom he identifies (Logan quoted Radish). The panel appearance of Logan and some of the lead performers from the series at the 2014 Comic-Con International Convention in its year of release also speaks volumes about how the series is positioned in industry terms: it takes its place at the convention alongside canonical sci-fi fantasy Comic-Con texts like *Star Wars, Dr. Who* and *Star Trek*, and other contemporary TV horror shows such as *The Walking Dead, Supernatural, Dexter and True Blood* as a TV series that courts a dedicated, proactive fan base within the populist domain—a strategy that at first seems at odds with the literary pedigree of some of the stories *Penny Dreadful* appropriates. A self-confessed comic book fan whose notion of the TV 'family' is informed by *Star Trek* rather than *The Brady Bunch*, Logan is forthright in his claims to fellow geekdom; he references Universal Studio's horror films as his source of inspiration and cites the early demise of Van Helsing as 'a provocation, fan to fan' rather than as an irreverential revision of Stoker's classic vampire narrative (Logan Comic-Con). To those familiar with Hammer horror films, the series' visual aesthetic references the Hammer brand, rebirthing earlier cinematic iterations of the various narratives it appropriates by building on a pre-existing horror fan base. Though it plays to its Gothic and its period strengths, it is the strengths that align the series with its cinematic horror forerunners and with its titular penny dreadful that are central to the marketing strategies employed by the Showtime network. The narrative also references Alan Moore's steam-punk mashup comic book series, *The League of Extraordinary Gentlemen*, in which a similarly disparate 'crew of light' is assembled, this time with Mina Murray at the helm. In Season Three, Logan introduces a female vampire hunter who serves as a further textual allusion to Moore's fantasy narrative and to its 2003 film adaptation.

Penny Dreadful aligns itself with the proactive ethos of Comic-Con fandoms and media convergence in which not only consumption *by* but creative engagement *of* fans is seen as intrinsic to its textual meaning (Jenkins 8). Rather than maintaining any kind of aesthetic distance afforded by affiliation with the cultural capital of the classic texts the series appropriates, Showtime employs a marketing strategy that plays to its populist identity, both in print and on screen, and its ongoing presence is ensured through its use of various social media platforms. The series has one of Showtime's 'most engaged fan communities' (Guerra in Edelsburg) and fan participation is encouraged as part of its marketing strategy via its official Showtime website where fans are dubbed 'Dreadfuls' as a means to both legitimising their entry into the Penny Dreadful universe and generating a fan community with a clear identity and loyalty to the series. The official website is replete with fan-centred activities and ongoing video production blogs of the kind more readily associated with DVD box set commentaries, and fan traffic is also given a space via social media platforms. Its dedicated Facebook page and Twitter account (#Dreadfuls) emerge as the series 'top-performing platforms', where fans invariably refer to the series as horror TV with an 'innovative take on Gothic literature' (Guerra in Edelsburg). Building on its successful exploitation of social media during the first series run, Showtime created further social media hype before its release of Season Two, setting up a tarot card reading experience for its fans via Vine and Twitter, and a '100 Days of Penny Dreadful' campaign using Twitter and Storify, alongside a Season One recap using Victorian graphics on Facebook (Guerra in Edelsburg). Its financed campaigns, designed to maintain fan engagement beyond the confines of simply watching the series, entailed creation of YouTube videos that demonstrated how to achieve the 'look' of the various *Penny Dreadful* characters, and a Snapchat campaign related to Evelyn Poole's Season Two voodoo dolls (Guerra in Edelsburg) alongside the more traditional release of advertising in magazines, on billboards and via official season trailers. Merchandising also forms part of the series' ongoing presence: the usual array of posters, t-shirts and classic tie-ins to the literary texts abound. However, other forms of merchandising, less readily associated with period fare than with franchise cinema and TV shows like *Dr. Who* (Tarot cards, Victor Frankenstein notebooks, figurines, a glossy 'making-of' coffee table book), are part of the series' merchandising strategy. From the outset, Logan has proclaimed his desire to appeal to a mainstream fan base, to produce for them 'iconic figures…figures that you're going to want to buy an action figure of' (Logan in Radish) and has sanctioned

Penny Dreadful's expansion into other story worlds via the production of comic book prequels and sequels which, according to publishers Titan Comics, aim to 'captivate fans of horror, literature and *Penny Dreadful* alike' (press release) and which again attest to its positioning as populist fare with far-reaching audience appeal, much like the penny dreadfuls of the Victorian era from which the show takes its title.

Numerous fan-generated sites like the fanpop.com/clubs/penny-dreadful and the *Penny Dreadful* Wikia site provide outlets for further participatory engagement and debate of a kind that operates outside the purview of Showtime's marketing strategists; however, Showtime's active, interventionist approach to fandom, with its inception of the #Dreadfuls fan base, named and manoeuvred by them, signals a disturbance to the cultural norms of fandom's participatory ethos. If, as Scott argues, fandoms are traditionally seen to 'reinforce boundaries between "official" and "unauthorised" forms of narrative expansion' and participation (Mothership 44), then Showtime's attempts to generate and subsequently direct fan participation and allegiance serve to undermine fan engagement through the network's 'hierarch[ical] legitima[tion] of some fan practices' and the 'marginalizing [of] others' that operate outside the sphere of corporate control (Battle Star 327). Through both its legitimation and activation of a fan base that predominantly participates via the Showtime platform, what have historically been seen as 'unauthorised acts' of textual intervention are co-opted in the name of branding and corporate interests. The 'symbiotic relationship' between fans and producers is, argues Pearson, one that 'predates the digital age' (87) but increased transmedial visibility adds another dimension to that relationship and fandoms are at least in part left vulnerable to corporate takeover of their creative output. Nevertheless, in this age of media convergence, fans remain a powerful and ongoing part of the discourse surrounding any series through their engagement not only via dedicated fansites, commentaries on reviewer blogs and various websites that critique TV, but through self-generated reworkings of existing texts destined for online fan consumption. Through creation of fan videos uploaded to platforms like YouTube and Vimeo, today's TV audience can become part of what Mittell terms TV's 'operational aesthetic' by 'actively engag[ing] in story' (Complex Poetics 52–53). The adaptive process that has led to the creation of Logan's mashup TV series is itself reinscribed by online fans, known as 'vidders', in tribute fan videos (or fan vids) that serve as both acts of fan loyalty and a further means to ensuring its continued circulation within contemporary popular culture.

Just as the Victorians were consummate adapters (Hutcheon xi) so too are contemporary consumers of media product in this age of media convergence. Like the titular penny dreadful which 'ta[pped] into pre-existing story worlds with existing fandoms' (Poore 75), Logan's series 'taps into' and builds upon an existing fan base that engages in fan activities around televisual horror narratives, whether reworked as romance or as ongoing explorations of what constitutes a 'monster'. Through their engagement in what Leitch terms 'writerly' interaction with text (18–19), fans of the series are actively involved in acts of textual transformation, authoring new 'versions' and creating different spins on various aspects of the *Penny Dreadful* story world. Louttit notes that serial adaptations of period costume drama in general attract the attentions of female vidders interested predominantly in nineteenth-century adaptations of canonical texts, written by women, and with a central focus on heterosexual romance (Fan Videos 177). The majority of these reworkings, argues Louttit, rarely engage with the 'cultural' and 'architectural trappings' of period drama: their focus is on heterosexual romance and on the similarities rather than the differences between romance in a bygone era and romance in our own era (178). Due to its identity as Gothic horror TV, *Penny Dreadful* is immediately at odds with some of the tropes of the 'safe' costume dramas that are the mainstay of such a fan base, and it is the ultimate battle between good and evil that drives this narrative rather than romance. Yet, as with many of the TV mashups posted online, its 'vidders' are predominantly female, and despite the show's horror credentials, it is the romance angle that forms the main focus of *Penny Dreadful* inspired fan vids, the majority editing together scenes related to Vanessa Ives' romantic entanglements or dwelling on the poster-boy looks of Dorian Gray. Though in the series the romantic potential of the relationship between Vanessa Ives and Ethan Chandler is always qualified by the impossibility of any such union, in the online story world their romantic moments are adapted into a celebration of romance: 'Take Me to Church', 'Beautiful Crime (R.I.P.)', 'Dust to Dust' serve as prime examples of this kind of textual reconstruction. Similarly, and as may be anticipated given the star appeal of Eva Green and Reeve Carney, the 'romance' between Dorian and Vanessa is given far more emphasis by its vidders than by Logan and his production team ('Darkness Have a Name'). Creative revisions can totally subvert the sexual politics of the series in the name of romance: even the relationship between creator Victor Frankenstein and his creature, Lily Frankenstein, is in some instances reconfigured as an outright romance ('Every Breath You Take'). Like period drama vidders, *Penny Dreadful* vidders' reworkings are designed to bring story content closer to their own contemporary experience: they work through selective ordering of clips, often privileging the close-up, to produce what is most often a romantic emphasis but may also engage with the series overarching themes. In a clever sequence of edits in 'Darkness Have a Name', close-ups that linger on the beauty of Dorian and Vanessa are coupled with close-ups of flowers that here, as in the series, are emblematic of the brevity of beauty and the lure of the immortal. Just as selective editing is invariably employed by vidders as a visual storytelling strategy, purposeful choice of music is part of the vidders' art, and the series' orchestral score, composed by Abel Korzeniowski, is often replaced by populist songs which speak to a creative revisioning of the text. Song choice can simply add to an overriding thematic preoccupation as in the romanticised version of the Victor/Lily Frankenstein relationship presented in 'Every Breath You Take', but the most creative fan vidders engage in a process of selective editing that marries specific lines from contemporary song lyrics with specific moments from across all three seasons, seamlessly threading scenes together through the loaded language of the populist songs they employ to produce an irreverent homage to a series that is already an irreverent treatment of the nineteenth-century literary canon. 'Monster', as the title infers, employs this song to explore the series' exploration of monsters and the 'monstrous' through the use of edits that align specific moments and lines of dialogue with the lyrics: through the cipher of Dorian Gray, whose beautiful image is juxtaposed with the words, 'Monster, a monster, I've turned into a monster', Carroll's reading of monsters as inherently 'disgusting' and 'loathsome' is visually undermined, though fast edits to Dorian's portrait do serve to remind the viewer of the discrepancies between his interior and his exterior image, and his professed desire to 'fit in'.

As in other *Penny Dreadful* fan vids, the sexually explicit nature of the series is brought to the fore, the kind of sexual experimentation explored in the series once more setting it up as something very different from the staple costume drama adaptation. The most inventive of these irreverent fan vids engages not with *Penny Dreadful* as period drama romance but as horror fare, vidder attention again falling on Logan's protagonist, Vanessa Ives, whose possession becomes the narrative focus of numerous online mini-adaptations of the series ('Back Hand of God', 'You've Touched a Scorpion', 'Mother of Evil, Angel of God'). One such fan vid, 'The Devil Inside', foregrounds the series' less overt exploration of addiction, cutting between moments of obsessive behaviour involving Vanessa Ives and her possession, and Victor Frankenstein and his addiction to morphine, both of which, through strategically positioned inclusions of voice-over and dialogue from Sir Malcolm, Victor and Vanessa, and edits that are synchronised with lines of apt dialogue from the lyrics, suggest that the root cause of any addiction relates to the pain of personal experience. In the final moments of this fan vid, we are presented with Vanessa's dissection of the vampire as the refrain 'Devil inside, the devil inside, every single one of us, the devil inside' plays over an edit to the closing sequence in which childhood innocence is foregrounded; seen here playing on the beach, Vanessa and the Murray children are oblivious to the demons that will haunt their adult lives. *Penny Dreadful* fan vids that take a more direct focus on its horror elements are, nevertheless, often filtered through a romance angle of sorts, even if that romance is, contrary to costume drama expectation, constructed as sexually explicit and dangerous. In 'You've Touched a Scorpion', it is Vanessa's romantic liaisons with Dr. Sweet (alias Dracula) that shape the narrative, but through its many swift edits to visual tropes of the horror genre—from bats, scorpions, rats and bloody-mouthed wolves to images of naked, dangling corpses and Dracula's zombified creatures—its identity as Gothic horror overrides its romantic potentialities, the opening voice-over of Vanessa's female counsellor in Season Three pointing out that she is and always has been 'drawn to dark, complicated, impossible men'. Where fan vids that shift the generic focus from horror to romance employ popular contemporary songs, those that maintain *Penny Dreadful's* horror credentials tend to employ the emotionally charged soundtrack of the original series. As in 'You've Touched a Scorpion', the interventions in a fan vid like 'Back Hand of God' come instead through creative editing that relies on montage and the merging of images related to Vanessa's possession, amplified by intermittent voice-over, while 'Mother of Evil, Angel of God' presents a sequence of edits that constitute a ten-minute-long chaotic and fragmented nonlinear mini-story of possession, disrupted in part by a shift of focus to the romance of Dr Sweet and Vanessa at its mid-point. 'Thee and Me', one of the most violent and sexually explicit online fan vids, shifts the focus to the relationship between Dorian Gray and Lily Frankenstein whose 'romance' of sorts is fuelled by their shared immortality and their pursuit of supremacy. Vids created by female vidders Rhaeys (Thee and Me) and Forsaken

Witchery (Monster) serve to counteract Louttit's claim that '"slash" fan fiction identities' and interest in 'alternative sexual or romantic identities' (177 Fan Videos) have no presence in online female fandoms.

For many fans, however, the initial and often the only sustained engagement with discourse surrounding a series comes via reviews. Just as marketing strategies serve as influential paratexts that shape audience perception, reception and subsequent consumption, reviewer discourse surrounding any TV programme—at pre- and post-release stage—has a role to play (Lotz 21). The body of paratextual materials generated by the reviewing process becomes part of a series' ongoing frame of reference. The official Showtime trailer was first revealed at the Television Critics Association winter press tour in January 2014, ahead of its public release on Valentine's Day, the timing of which infers the underlying presence of romance within the narrative despite its dense Gothic atmosphere, and the sexual, bloody, supernatural nature of the trailer's edited content. It is referred to as a 'psycho-sexual horror/thriller' in much of the pre-release discourse. In its pre-show postings, *The Huffington Post* describes it first and foremost as a 'sexy horror drama' that is 'straight up terrifying', paying scant attention to its appropriation of iconic figures from canonical literature who are noted only in passing as 'some of literature's most terrifying characters'. Later posts play upon its literary pedigree highlighting its 'roots in thriller classic literature' and dubbing it a 'period piece set in a world of monsters' (Sperry) but neither the official trailer nor pre-release posts foreground to any marked extent its relationship to precursor texts; rather, its identity is established as horror hybrid from the outset. Reviewer discourse post-release teases out *Penny Dreadful's* relationship with canonical literature, its attention to period detail and the thematic intricacies that play out as the series unfolds: its 'literary bent' (O'Neill) is noted, and its high-end production values are acknowledged, Zoller referring to it as 'a handsomely produced …Oscar-baiting historical drama', but its capacity to recreate more than the period detail of the Victorian era, to 'conjure a time and place where excitement about new discoveries and fear of the dark and unknown were equally prominent in the public mind' (Genzlinger), also forms part of reviewer discourse, suggesting that, on release, the show attained status as a quality drama that exceeds the expectations of both serialised costume drama and mainstream horror fare. Logan's merging of figures from iconic literature with new creations is positively reviewed as a meaningful 'rethinking and reanimating of these old and new stories', as more than an act of 'pilfering', more than a series of reverential nods to canonical texts (Zoller). Its relationship with Alan Moore's *The League of Extraordinary Gentlemen* is also couched in positive terms by reviewers, both being seen to represent the 'mash-up as art form' (de Bruin-More). Another notable feature of industry discourse surrounding the series relates to its 'emotional complexity' with reviewer Maureen Ryan comparing it to other 'ambitious horror programs' like *Hannibal* and *American Horror Story* that create similar 'atmospheres of dread and suspense' and 'psychological intensity'.

Penny Dreadful's identity as horror TV is a constant and much more prominent topic of discussion than either its period setting or its appropriation of canonical literature, Cali citing the scene in Season Two, in which Madame Kali dismembers an infant, as 'one of the most horrific in TV history'. Reviewer discourse of film critics writing about film adaptation is traditionally characterised by a 'profoundly moralistic' approach that employs negative language: the process of adaptation is invariably described as an act of 'infidelity, betrayal, deformation, violation, vulgarization and desecration' (Stam 74). In contrast, as reviewer commentary surrounding *Penny Dreadful* infers, quality TV's relationship with transformative practices in this golden age of TV drama is couched in positive terms, devoid of elitist, moralistic evaluations; rather, *Penny Dreadful's* inventive appropriation of a vast body of narratives (both canonical and populist) already in circulation is cited as one of several successful storytelling strategies employed during the unraveling of the series' three-season story arc. It emerges as a highly original made for TV revisioning of canonical texts that has been created for populist consumption via mainstream media outlets. It constitutes part of what I argue is an emerging genre of Neo-Victorian TV: by taking creative liberties with a body of precursor texts, including existing screen adaptations, it pushes the established boundaries of adaptation of nineteenth-century literature, breaching the parameters of the story worlds being appropriated and creating a *different* story universe peopled by characters reconfigured in service to the narrative trajectory of his own neo-Victorian protagonist.

Works Cited

Abbott, Stacey, and Lorna Jowett. *TV Horror: Investigating the Dark Side of the Small Screen*. London and New York: I.B. Taurus, 2013. Print.

Akilli S., and S. Oz. "No More Let Life Divide: Victorian Metropolis Confluence in *Penny Dreadful*." *Critical Survey* 28.1 (2016): 15–29. Print.

Allan, Janice M. "Victorian Detective Fiction: Part 1 Introduction." *Clues* 25.1 (2006): 3–4. Print.
AllysonCalleigh. "Beautiful Crime (R.I.P.)." *YouTube*, 20 June 2016. Web. 21 Nov. 2016.
Bignell, Jonathan. "A Taste of the Gothic: Film and Television Versions of *Dracula*." *The Classic Novel from Page to Screen*. Eds. Robert Giddings and Erica Sheen. Manchester: Manchester University Press, 2000. 114–130. Print.
Blake Elite. "Darkness Have a Name." *YouTube*, 29 June 2014. Web. 10 Feb. 2015.
Bowler, Alexia L., and Jessica Cox, "Introduction to Adapting the Nineteenth Century: Revisiting, Revising and Rewriting the Past." *Neo-Victorian Studies* 2.2 (2009/2010): 1–17. Print.
Boyce, Charlotte, and Elodie Rousselot. "The Other Dickens: Neo-Victorian Appropriation and Adaptation." *Neo-Victorian Studies* 5.2 (2012): 1–11. Print.
Braid, Barbara. "The Frankenstein Meme: *Penny Dreadful* and *The Frankenstein Chronicles* as Adaptations." *Open Cultural Studies* 1.1 (2017): 232–243. Print.
Cali, Michael. "'Penny Dreadful' Creator John Logan on Witches, the Occult and 'the Horror of People.'" *The Washington Post*, 15 May 2015. Web. 20 June 2015.
Cardwell, Sarah. *Adaptation Revisited: Television and the Classic Novel*. Manchester: Manchester University Press, 2002. Print.
———. "Literature on the Small Screen: Television Adaptations." *Literature on Screen on Screen*. Eds. Deborah Cartmell and Imelda Whelehan. Cambridge: Cambridge University Press, 2007. 181–195. Print.
Carroll, Noel. "The Nature of Horror." *The Journal of Aesthetics and Art Criticism* 46.1 (1987): 51–59. Print.
Cherry, B. "Refusing to Refuse to Look: Female Viewers of the Horror Film." *The Horror Film Reader*. Ed. M Jancovich. London: Routledge, 2001. 169–178. Print.
Cordell, S. A. "Sex, Terror, and Bram Stoker's *Dracula*: Coppola's Reinvention of Film History." *Neo-Victorian Studies* 6.1 (2103): 1–21. Print.
Cox, Jessica. "Canonization and the Rise of Neo-Victorianism." *English* 66 (2017): 101–123. Print.
Creed, Barbara. *The Monstrous Feminine: Film, Feminism, Psychoanalysis*. London and New York: Routledge, 1993. Print.
De Bruin-Mole. "Monster Mashups and Popular Culture: *Penny Dreadful* Versus *The League of Extraordinary Gentlemen*." *Angels and Apes*, 26 Aug. 2015. Web. 20 June 2015.
De Fino, Dean. *The HBO Effect*. London and New York: Bloomsbury Academic, 2014. Print.

Edelsberg, Natan. "Why Fans Fell in Love with Showtime's *Penny Dreadful*: Interview with VP of Digital Marketing at Showtime Marcello Guerra." *The Drum*, 26 May 2015. Web. 30 June 2015.
Elliott, Kamilla. *Rethinking the Novel/Film Debate*. Cambridge: Cambridge University Press, 2003. Print.
FairyKingdom86. "Every Breath You Take." *YouTube*, 6 Aug. 2015. Web. 21 Nov. 2016.
Flicks and the City. "*Penny Dreadful* Comic-Con Panel." *YouTube*, 2014. Web. 5 Aug. 2014.
ForsakenWitchery. "Monster." *YouTube*, 7 July 2015. Web.
Garcia, Pedro Javier Pardo. "Beyond Adaptation: Frankenstein's Postmodern Progeny." *Books in Motion: Adaptation, Intertextuality, Authorship*. Ed. Mireia Aragay. Amsterdam and New York: Rodopi, 2005. 223–242. Print.
Gelder, Ken. *Reading the Vampire*. London: Routledge, 1994. Print.
Genzlinger, Neil. "Literary Help Sending a Shiver Down Your Spine: *Penny Dreadful*, Showtime's Supernatural Entry." *New York Times*, 9 May 2014. Television Review, 9 May 2014. Web. 30 June 2015.
Goodlad, L. "The Mad Men in the Attic: Seriality and Identity in the Narrative of Capitalist Globalization." *The Modern Language Quarterly* 73.2 (2012): 201–235. Print.
Giddings, Robert, and Erica Sheen. Eds. *The Classic Novel: From Page to Screen*. Manchester: Manchester University Press, 2000. Print.
Gosling, Sharon. *The Art and Making of Penny Dreadful: The Official Companion Book to the Showtime Series Created and Written by John Logan*. London: Titan Books, 2015. Print.
Gray, Jonathan. "TV Previews and the Meaning of Hype." *International Journal of Cultural Studies* 11.1 (2008): 33–49. Print.
Gray, Jonathan, and Amanda D. Lotz. *Television Studies*. Cambridge: Polity Press, 2012. Print.
Green, Stephanie. "Lily Frankenstein: The Gothic New Woman in Penny Dreadful." *Refractory: A Journal of Entertainment Media* 28 (2017). Web. 31 Aug. 2017.
Gutleben, Christian, and Marie-Luise Kohlke. *Neo-Victorian Gothic: Horror, Violence and Degeneration in the Re-imagined Nineteenth Century*. Amsterdam and New York: Rodopi, 2012. Print.
Gutleben, Christian, and Susana Onega. Eds. *Refracting the Canon in Contemporary British Literature and Film*. Amsterdam and New York: Rodopi, 2004. Print.
Higson, Andrew. "Representing the National Past: Nostalgia & Pastiche." *The Heritage Film: British Cinema and Thatcherism*. Ed. Lester Friedman. London: UCL Press, 1993. 109–129. Print.
Hills, Matt. *The Pleasures of Horror*. London: Continuum, 2005. Print.

Hoppenstand, Gary. "Editorial: The Horror of It All." *The Journal of Popular Culture* 45.1 (2012): 1–2. Print.
Housman, Clemence Annie. *The Were-Wolf* [1896]. *The Project Gutenberg eBook*, 2004. Web. 3 Jan. 2015.
Hutcheon, Linda. *A Theory of Adaptation*. London: Routledge, 2006. Print.
Jenkins, Henry. *Textual Poachers: Television Fans and Participatory Culture*. London: Routledge, 1992. Print.
Kaplan, Cora. *Victoriana: Histories, Fictions, Criticism*. Edinburgh: Edinburgh University Press, 2007. Print.
Katarine2007. "Back Hand of God." *YouTube*, 25 Jan. 2015. Web. 10 Feb. 2015.
Klein, Amanda Ann, and R. Barton Palmer. Eds. *Cycles, Sequels, Spin-Offs, Remakes and Reboots: Multiplicities in Film and Television*. Austin: University of Texas Press, 2016. Print.
Klein, Michael, and Gillian Parker. *The English Novel and the Movies*. New York: Ungar, 1981. Print.
Knox, Simone. "Masterpiece Theatre and British Drama Imports on US Television: Discourses of Tension." *Critical Studies in Television* 7.1 (2012): 29–48. Print.
Kohlke, Marie-Luise. "Sexsation: Literary Excursions into the Nineteenth Century Erotic." *Probing the Problematics: Sex and Sexuality*. Eds. Marie-Luise Kohlke and Luisa Orza. Oxford: Inter-Disciplinary Press, 2008. 345–356. eBook.
Ledwon, Lenora. "*Twin Peaks* and the TV Gothic." *Literature Film Quarterly* 21.4 (1993): 260–270. Print.
Lee, Alison, and Frederick D. King. "From Text, to Myth, to Meme: Penny Dreadful and Adaptation." *Victorian and Edwardian Cahiers* 82 (2015). Web. 10 Oct. 2016.
Leitch, Thomas. *Film Adaptation and its Discontents: From Gone with the Wind to the Passion of the Christ*. Baltimore: John Hopkins Press, 2007. Print.
Lex's Edits. "Take Me to Church." *YouTube*, 1 Dec. 2015. Web. 21 Nov. 2016.
Llewellyn, Mark. "What is Neo-Victorian Studies?" *Neo-Victorian Studies* 1.1 (2008): 164–185. Print.
Llewellyn, Mark, and Ann Heilmann. *Neo-Victorianism: The Victorians in the Twenty-First Century, 1999–2009*. Houndmills: Palgrave Macmillan, 2010.
Logan, John. *Penny Dreadful*. Shooting Script, Ep. 1 (1/11/12). *Scribd*. Web. 10 Jan. 2014.
———. "DVD Extras." *Penny Dreadful: The Complete Series*, 2017. DVD.
Lotz, Amanda D. "On 'TV Criticism': The Pursuit of the Critical Examination of a Popular Art." *Popular Communication* (Online Journal) 6.1 (2008): 20–36. Web. 1 Nov. 2016.

Louttit, Chris. "Victorian London Redux: Adopting the Gothic Metropolis." *Critical Survey* 28.1 (2016): 2–14. Print.
———. "Remixing Period Drama: The Fan Video and the Classic Novel Adaptation." *Adaptation* 6.2 (2013): 172–186. Print.
———. "Cranford, Popular Culture and the Politics of Adapting Period Drama for Television." *Adaptation* 2.1 (2009): 34–48. Print.
McFarlane, Brian. *Novel to Film: An Introduction to the Theory of Adaptation*. Oxford: Oxford University Press, 1996. Print.
McGrath, M. "The New Wave of Horror Television." *TN2 Magazine*, 12 Aug. 2014. Web. 17 Aug. 2015.
Miss1Vogue. "Mother of Evil, Angel of God." *YouTube*, 26 June 2016. Web. 21 Nov. 2016.
Mitchell, Kate. *History and Cultural Memory in Neo-Victorian Fiction: Victorian Afterimages*. London: Palgrave Macmillan, 2010. Print.
Mittell, Jason. *Complex TV: The Poetics of Contemporary Television Storytelling*. New York and London: New York University Press, 2015. Print.
———. "A Cultural Approach to Television Genre Theory." *Cinema Journal* 40.3 (2001): 3–24. Print.
———. "Narrative Complexity in Contemporary American Television." *The Velvet Light Trap* 58 (2006): 29–40. Print.
Moore, Alan, and Kevin O'Neill. *The League of Extraordinary Gentlemen*. ABC/Wildstorm/DC Comics, 1999. Print.
O'Neill, Phelim. "*Penny Dreadful* Is So Gory and So Great It'd Be a Crime Not to Watch." *The Guardian*, 4 May 2016. Print.
Pearson, Roberta. "Fandom in the Digitsl Era." *Popular Communication* 8.1 (2010): 84–95. Print.
PinkTardisFloyd. "Devil Inside." *YouTube*, 27 June 2014. Web. 10 Feb. 2015.
Pittard, Christopher. "From Sensation to the Strand." *A Companion to Crime Fiction*. Eds. Lee Horsley and Charles J. Rezepka. Chichester: Wiley Blackwell, 2010. 105–116. Print.
Poore, B. "The Transformed Beast: *Penny Dreadful*, Adaptation, and the Gothic." *Victoriographies* 6.1 (2016): 62–81. Print.
Primorac, Antonia. *Neo-Victorianism on Screen: Postfeminsim and Contemporary Adaptations of Victorian Women*. Houndmills: Palgrave Macmillan, 2018. Print.
Radish, Christina. "John Logan Talks *Penny Dreadful*, Exploring Sexuality, and Planning the Series Well into the Future." *Collider*, 18 Jan. 2014. Web. 24 Oct. 2016.
Rees, Jasper. "Charles Dickens Characters Assemble form All Corners in a Moreish Soap." *theartsdesk.com*. 27 Dec. 2015. Web. 3 Jan. 2016.

Regis, Amber. "Performance Anxiety and Costume Drama: Lesbian Sex on the BBC." *Television, Sex and Society: Analysing Contemporary Representations.* Eds. J. Aston, B. Glyn, and B. Johnson. London: Continuum, 2012. 137–150. Print.

Reynolds, George W. M. *Wagner the Wher-Wolf* [1846]. New York: Cosimo Classics, 2008. Print.

Rhaeys. "Thee and Me." *YouTube*, 11 Nov. 2017. Web. 19 Dec. 2017.

Rocha, Lauren. "Angel in the House, Devil in the City: Explorations of Gender in *Dracula* and *Penny Dreadful*." *Critical Survey* 28.1 (2016): 30–39. Print.

Rose, Brian A. *Jekyll and Hyde Adapted: Dramatizations of Cultural Anxiety.* Westport, CT: Greenwood, 1996. Print.

Ryan, Maureen. "'Penny Dreadful' Review: This Victorian Horror Show Is a Winner." *The Huffington Post*, 9 May 2014. Web. 3 Jan. 2016.

Rymer, James Malcolm. *Varney the Vampire Slayer, or the Feast of Blood* [1845–1847]. Camarillo: Zittaw Press, 2007. Print.

Sanders, Julie. *Adaptation and Appropriation.* London: Routledge, 2006. Print.

-sb-. "You've Touched a Scorpion." *YouTube*, 16 Oct. 2016. Web. 21 Nov. 2016.

Scott, Suzanne. "Who's Steering the Mothership? The Role of the Fanboy Auteur in Transmedia Storytelling." *The Participatory Cultures Handbook.* Eds. Aaron Delwiche and Jennifer Jacobs Henderson. London: Routledge, 2013. 43–52. Print.

———. "Battlestar Glactica: Fans and Ancillary Content." *How to Watch Television.* Eds. Jason Mittell and Ethan Thompson. London and New York: New York University Press, 2013, 320–329. Print.

Seitz Zoller, Matt. "Showtime's *Penny Dreadful* Is a Wonderful Surprise." Vulture, 11 May 2014. Web. 30 June 2015.

Shelley, Mary. *Frankenstein, or the Modern Myth of Prometheus* [1818]. Oxford: Oxford University Press, 2008.

Sperry, April. "If You Like 'American Horror Story,' Check Out 'Penny Dreadful.'" *The Huffington Post*, 24 Mar. 2014. Web. 30 June 2015.

Stam, Robert. "Beyond Fidelity: The Dialogics of Adaptation." *Film Adaptation.* Ed. James Naremore. London: Athlone, 2000. 54–76. Print.

Stoker, Bram. *Dracula* [1897]. Oxford: Oxford University Press, 2011. Print.

Stevenson, Robert Louis. *The Strange Case of Dr. Jekyll and Mr. Hyde* [1886]. Cirencester: Echo Library, 2005. Print.

Submarnian, Janani. "The Monstrous Makeover: *American Horror Story*, Femininity and Special Effects." *Critical Studies in Television* 8.3 (2103): 108–123. Print.

Tropp, Martin. "Recreating the Monster: Frankenstein and Film." *Nineteenth-Century Women at the Movies: Adapting Classic Women's Fiction to Film.* Ed. Barbara Tepa Lupack. Bowling Green, OH: Bowling Green State University, 1999. 23–77. Print.

Twilightx. "Dust to Dust." *YouTube*, 8 Sept. 2015. Web. 21 Nov. 2016.
Wagner, Geoffrey. *The Novel and the Cinema*. Rutherford, NJ: Fairleigh Dickinson University Press, 1975. Print.
West, Nancy, and Karen Laird. "Prequels, Sequels, and Pop Stars: Masterpiece Theatre and the New Culture of Classic Adaptations." *Literature Film Quarterly* 39.4 (2011): 306–322. Print.
Wheatley, Helen. *Gothic Television*. Manchester, NY: Manchester University Press, 2006. Print.
Whelehan, I. "Neo-Victorian Adaptations." *A Companion to Literature, Film and Adaptation*. Eds. Deborah Cartmell and Imelda Whelehan. Chichester: Wiley Blackwell, 2012. 272–292. Print.
Wightman, Catriona. "*Penny Dreadful's* Comic-Con 2014 Panel: As It Happened." *YouTube*, 25 July 2014. Web. 21 Aug. 2014.
Wilde, Oscar. *The Picture of Dorian Gray* [1891]. Oxford: Oxford University Press, 2006. Print.

Screenography

Television

American Horror Story (2011–, US: FX).
Bates Motel (2013–2017, US: A&E Network).
Being Human (2008–2013, UK: BBC).
Bitten (2014–2016, Canada: Space).
Boardwalk Empire (2010–2014, US: HBO).
Buffy the Vampire Slayer (1997–2003, US: WB).
Dickensian (2015, UK: BBC).
Carnivàle (2003–2005, US: HBO).
Cranford (2007, UK: BBC).
Dexter (2006–2013, US: SHOWTIME).
Dr. Who (1963–, UK: BBC).
Fingersmith (2005, UK: BBC).
Hannibal (2013–2015, US: NBC).
Peaky Blinders (2013–, UK: BBC).
Penny Dreadful (2014–2016, US/UK: Showtime/Sky).
Ripper Street (2012–2016, UK: BBC).
Rosemary's Baby (2014, US: NBC).
Salem (2014–, USA: WGN America).
Supernatural (2005–, US: WB).
Taboo (2017–, UK: BBC).
Teen Wolf (2011–2017, US: MTV).
The Addams Family (1964–1966, US: ABC).

The Crimson Petal and the White (2011, UK: BBC).
The Exorcist (2016–, US: Fox).
The Frankenstein Chronicles (2015–, UK: ITV).
The Knick (2014–2015, US: Cinemax).
The Munsters (1964–1966, US: CBS).
The Vampire Diaries (2009–2017, US: The CW).
The Walking Dead (2010–, US: AMC).
True Blood (2008–2014, US: HBO).
Werewolf (1987–1988, US: FOX).
Wolfblood (2012, UK: BBC).
Wolf Creek (2016–, Australia: STAN).
Wolf Lake (2001–2002, US: CBS).

Film

Blade Runner. Dir. Ridley Scott. 1982.
Taste the Blood of Dracula. Dir. Peter Sasdy. 1970.
Dracula. Dir. Todd Browning. 1931.
Dracula A.D. Dir. Alan Gibson. 1972.
Dracula, Prince of Darkness. Dir. Terence Fisher. 1966.
Dracula Has Risen from the Grave. Dir. Freddie Francis. 1968.
Frankenstein Created Woman. Dir. Terence Fisher. 1967.
Frankenstein Must be Destroyed. Dir. Terence Fisher. 1969.
Frankenstein and the Monster from Hell. Terence Fisher. 1976.
Frankenstein. Dir. James Whale. 1931.
Nosferatu. Dir. F. W. Murnau. 1922.
The Brides of Dracula. Dir. Terence Fisher. 1960.
The Bride of Frankenstein. Dir. James Whale. 1935.
The Curse of Frankenstein. Dir. Terence Fisher. 1957.
The Evil of Frankenstein. Dir. Freddie Francis. 1964.
The Horror of Dracula. Dir. Terence Fisher. 1958.
The Revenge of Frankenstein. Dir. Terence Fisher. 1958.
Scars of Dracula. Dir. Roy Ward Baker. 1970.
The Satanic Rites of Dracula. Dir. Alan Gibson. 1973.
The Curse of the Werewolf. Dir. Terence Fisher. 1961.
The Picture of Dorian Gray. Dir. Albert Lewin. 1945.
The Wolf Man. Dir. George Waggner. 1941.

CHAPTER 3

Fargo: To Be Continued…

3.1 Introduction

Much has already been written about the transition of successful television shows to cinema; both industries are acutely aware of the financial rewards and securities offered by the remake of a preloved story product, and both exploit the potential to capitalise on the representation of such narratives and the characters who people them. A similar if less frequent exchange has seen film texts of the franchised and the prestige auteur variety migrate to television screens but the current televisual climate is characterised by an unprecedented rise in the number of such adaptations.[1] Whether in the guise of remake, reboot, prequel or sequel, in this latest 'golden age' of TV drama, the transition of story from the narratively time poor production platform of film to the narratively time rich production climate of television is resulting in new and ever more inventive ways of exploiting the continuation of pre-existing story worlds in the guise of the long-form TV series. Characterised by its intertextual complexity and by its capacity to appropriate a particular auteur style aesthetic over and above adaptation of narrative content, Noah Hawley's TV anthology series, *Fargo*, extends the existing story universe of the

---

[1] *Terminator: The Sarah Connor Chronicles* (2008–), *Nikita* (2010–2013), *Mildred Pierce* (2011), *Hannibal* (2011–2013), *Bates Motel* (2013–2017), *12 Monkeys* (2015–), *Westworld* (2016), *Wolf Creek* (2016), *Legion* (2017–), *Taken* (2017–), *The Departed* (in production); *Shutter Island* (in production).

Coen brothers 1996 film, shifting narrative boundaries and adding new layers to the Fargo mythology.

The series is difficult to define in terms of adaptive 'type'. Though a remake of sorts, it retains neither narrative content—something Verevis sees as central to the remake (21)—nor characters from the Coen film that it continues to reference via its title, its location, its style aesthetic and its storytelling strategies. Instead, Hawley explores what Leitch terms the narrative 'gaps': gaps which represent potentially rich 'transactional moments rather than static qualities', (55) and *into* which Hawley, as series creator, writes a new narrative peopled by new characters. *Fargo*, as TV series, intersects with its similarly titled predecessor in particular but, through the subtle spinning of complex webs of intertextual connectivity across each of its discrete seasons, it is also in dialogue with the body of cinematic texts produced by the Coen brothers. This intertextually rich story world borrows from the prestige of the cinematic auteurs it constantly references; however, though a 'borrowing' of sorts, it functions instead as what Dudley Andrew terms a 'refraction' of a prior text—one that 'intersects' (67) with, evolves from, and is in dialogue with Coen stories across each of its anthologised seasons. Hawley takes an 'activist stance' to adaptation of the kind Stam deems 'less an attempted resuscitation' of a prior text than 'a turn in an ongoing dialogical process' (81), characterised in this instance by complex rather than mechanical interventions at the level of narrative, character, style aesthetic, theme and genre. Indeed if, as Palmer infers, 'all texts are fragments' that 'await gestures of continuation' (Continuation 76), this TV series may be read not as an adaptation of one precursor text but as a 'continuation' of numerous 'fragments' from the Coen's storytelling universe. While in part an homage to these filmmakers, it is nonetheless a work that generates its own identity, becoming a hypotext that perpetuates hypertexts of its own, Season Two serving as prequel to Season One; its 'beforeness' (Scahill 316) is self-referential. Season Three works as a further continuation of the film *and* prior seasons of *Fargo*, and neither Seasons One, Two or Three engage in repetition of existing story. Hawley shifts the narrative time frame back and forth across seasons from 2006 (Season One), to 1979 (Season Two), to 2010 (Season Three), expanding upon earlier thematic and generic preoccupations that continue to play out in what has by now become a mythically charged Fargo landscape characterised by its tone of 'midwestern Minnesota nice' (Hawley in Fienberg) , perpetuating and extending the Fargo fable beyond the more limited time frame of cinema.

Though there is little to denote the *need* for a resuscitation of the Coen's much lauded film, there are ways in which the *Fargo* series may be deemed more 'reboot' than 'remake': it not only generates new narratives and new characters but builds on an existing style signature initiating a series that, in reboot tradition, currently extends across three seasons, and which in its anthology format can continue to generate narratives within the Fargo story world ad infinitum. Nevertheless, the language employed to denote adaptive type is historically loaded with terms like 'remake' implying the secondary status of the resultant adaptation while, conversely, the term 'reboot' suggests the adapted text is in need of further revitalisation (Scahill 317). The *Fargo* series employs some of the iconic signs and signifiers of its cinematic counterpart, thus ensuring its identity as a show that is in close communion with the prestigious film text it references; through retention of the title alone, Hawley's *Fargo* reinscribes the status of the film it appropriates. In this remake, however, there is a total lack of character crossover, a much greater engagement with place and style than with the already known events of a former narrative, and a more complex intertextualisation of other stories from not only the signature works of the Coen brothers but from other adaptations generated in response to their 1996 film, providing the series with a much wider referential framework. In addition to the multitude of referential nods to a host of Coen films, each season foregrounds its relationship with a certain Coen film and particular film styles: Season One speaks to *No Country for Old Men* (2007) and Season Three is a style homage to *Inside Llewyn Davies* (2013), while Season Two shifts the adaptive parameters to encompass the style aesthetic of independent seventies cinema alongside the auteur signature of the Coen brothers.

3.2 From *Fargo* to *Fargo*: Redefining the Relationship

Both the remake and the reboot challenge our conventional understanding of authorial authenticity, none more so than Hawley's TV series: its relationship with its cinematic precursor and with the auteurs who constructed it operates on several complex levels, and during the course of the series' multi-season run, the adaptive positioning of each is subtly redefined. 'We are', states Hawley, 'just involved in a dialogue as writers with people who inspire us', and in this contemporary cultural climate, receptive as it is to the notion that 'nothing' is inherently 'sacred', he is able to 'interpret and reinterpret' existing story ideas with impunity: indeed, 'nothing [he's] doing is actually an adaptation of the Coen brothers' work on a certain level' according to Hawley (ATX). While he approaches each season by asking 'What would the Coens do?', merely to 'copy them' is not part of his creative agenda. What he hopes to achieve 'when the credits are rolling at the end of hour ten' of each season is 'that same feeling' of Coenesque quirkiness across the series as a whole (Hawley in Berkshire). *His* dialogic turn of the Fargo narrative is not an adaptation of the film per se but a 'singular vision' that employs their 'tone of voice' and encompasses their work as a whole (Hawley, ATX). From the outset, the FX network adopted a similar approach to that of their chosen show-runner: this had to be a series that did not involve any of the film's characters, especially its protagonist, Marge. Both were in agreement that it should not be a show that revolved around 'wholesome Midwesterners' of the Fargo variety depicted in 'outrageous situations season after season'; a 'Picket Fence' parody of the film was to be avoided at all costs (Hawley in Berkshire). One year after the film's release, a pilot episode for a TV series of *Fargo*, directed by Kathy Bates and starring Edie Falco as Marge, adopted this kind of 'picket fence' approach. Opening with a still pregnant Marge and her duck-painting husband Norm, whose exaggerated Midwestern accents and homely demeanour serve unwittingly to parody the characters they are meant to emulate, this 1997 pilot sets up a narrative template for the episodic solving of crimes on a weekly basis. Unlike the contemporary FX adaptation, this adaptation was not sanctioned by the Coen brothers and it failed to secure a series commission. Instead of presenting anything that resembles the 'kooky day-to-day adventures of Marge…with Marge tackling grim case after grim case', Hawley creates a season-long story arc across each season of this anthologised TV series (Hawley in Willmore). He chooses not to emphasise the film's 'iconic' Minnesota accents which have by now become a cultural 'caricature', employing instead a toned down regional accent that avoids any parodic or comedic intent (Hawley, Hollywood Reporter).

The increasingly popular anthologised series format adopted by Hawley affords opportunities not only to 'innova[te] every year' but to 'create a larger body of work' (Hawley, ATX). The contemporary anthologised series, consisting of an eight to ten episode 'stand-alone story', is characterised by its commitment to unifying features that ensure stylistic and thematic continuity from season to season rather than a continuity of plot or character (Garcia 7). Having already been involved in the successful production of *American Horror Story* (2011–), FX 'understood the paradigm' when Hawley pitched this format as the best way to realise the Fargo narrative in a televisual context (Hawley, Austin Film Festival); furthermore, they embraced his plans to write episodes of varying length, leaving him the creative freedom to pace the narrative according to story dictates rather than scheduling time frames, with episodes ranging from a running time of anywhere between 48 and 68 minutes (Hawley, Writer's Panel). Moreover, the anthology series is, argues Cary Fukunaga (series director, *True Detective* Season One (2014), a means to tell[ing] 'complete' and 'cinema-like stories' on television; Hawley concurs, labelling *Fargo* as 'not a television series' but a 'ten hour movie' (Hawley, Austin Film Festival), and this informs his overall approach both to narrative and to style aesthetic. Rather than produce a replica of the Coen brothers' film, Hawley adapts it into a number of discrete yet interconnected seasonal stories that challenge notions of textual singularity and redefine the relationship between precursor text and adaptation. His ambition is to reach a point in the narrative whereby regular viewers of the TV series may see the Coens' *film* 'as a great episode of "Fargo"', the 'movie now fit[ting] *into* a series' that presents in each season 'a separate true crime story from that region'(Hawley in Willmore). Both film and series are characterised by what Grossman terms 'elastextity', each in this instance becoming an 'indivisibly connected' part of one 'vastly stretched tarp or canvas' (Hideous 10) with 'permeable boundaries' that span an extensive Fargo universe (Grossman Fargos 194). But for some viewers, particularly those whose experience of the narrative comes first and foremost through familiarity with the TV series, it is the *film* that becomes yet another instalment in this anthologised Fargo story world.

The work of the Coen brothers is in itself a testimony to the art of appropriation and intertextuality. They are serial adapters who employ a similarly revisionist approach to the appropriation of existing narratives from literature and cinema, and their films in turn invite further recycling of the stories they choose to recalibrate. In some instances, they pay homage to the tone and preoccupations of detective fiction writers like James M Cain, Dashell Hammett, and Raymond Chandler (*Blood Simple*, 1984; *Millers Crossing*, 1990; *The Big Lebowski*, 1998; *The Man Who Wasn't There*, 2001); in others they are engaged in the reworking of mythology (*O Brother Where Art Thou*, 2000) or on occasion a closer reiteration of story (*No Country for Old Men*, 2007); and in all, they are referencing other movies as an integral part of a process of 'reinterpretation' (Robson 80). As adapters they reject the fidelity-driven model of adaptation which foregrounds the relationship between *one* source text and its adaptive offspring, favouring instead 'a wider circuitry of influences' and a 'broader arena of intertextual continuum' (Coughlin, Scope). Like Hawley's adaptation of *Fargo*, their films are characterised by their 'elastextity' and their capacity to become 'indivisibly connected' (Grossman Hideous 10) to prior texts while also attaining independent status. Their sanctioned yet 'hands-off' approach to Hawley's adaptation of *Fargo* speaks to their own ways of working with pre-existing material (Coens in Gill), leaving Hawley free to explore further 'gaps' and points of connection across the intertextually rich narratives that have already become part of the Coen brothers' cinematic oeuvre. Like the Coens, from whose body of films he borrows so liberally, Hawley finds new ways of re-presenting not only stories and their thematic preoccupations, but the generic and stylistic properties of pre-existing cultural artefacts shaping them, through the act of appropriation, into a unique signature art form within a televisual context.

3.3 Textual Continuities

Hawley's TV series is more continuation than adaptation. The relationship between series and film is not defined by the traditional transfer of plot points from one text to another: cardinal elements of narrative seen by McFarlane as central to the successful transition of source to adaptive offspring (13–14) have no traction within the story world of *Fargo*, the anthologised TV show, and none of the film's iconic characters transition here from cinema to TV screen. Instead, *Fargo* the TV series revolves around a number of textual continuities that establish its ongoing relationship with not only the film it references in its title but a wide range of films from the Coen brothers' cinematic oeuvre. These continuities operate at the level of story type and auteurial style signature, while both the significance of place and the mythical nature of storytelling provide ongoing points of thematic connection across the film, the series, its anthologised seasons, and the Coens' cinematic universe in general. It becomes a 'new fictional univers[e] with [its] own "mocroclimate"' (Romney cited in Grossman Fargos 195) yet, through these textual continuities, it remains in close communion with the work of the Coen brothers across each of its seasons.

Foregrounded by its opening intertitle as factual in nature and relating to events that happened in Minnesota in 1987, the events about to unfold in *Fargo* are constructed as 'truth' rather than fiction. Yet in this film such posturing is part of a game-playing strategy that serves to parody the 'true story' genre. As with other Coen films, it also critiques the noir genre, replacing in this instance the anticipated urban noir setting with a pastoral backwater characterised by brightly lit open spaces and associated with family values, noir's distanced lone detectives supplanted by the homely Marge Gunderson. While part of the narrative builds on two separate 'true' crimes, one related to fraud, the other to the 1986 murder of Helles Craft by her husband who then disposed of her body in a wood chipper, the Coens return in *Fargo* to their own fictional preoccupation with the kidnap plot—a plot that has already played out in *Blood Simple* (1984), *Raising Arizona* (1987), and *The Big Lebowski*—rather than any reported marital abduction scenario in 1987, Minnesota. The Coens employ 'true story' introductory intertitles found in films like the noir police procedural *He Walked by Night* (1948) as a means to framing story content as fact-based; Hawley adopts the same 'true crime' façade, each season presenting (in the same pastoral locale) a further iteration of a 'true crime' story that connects on some level with its cinematic predecessor in terms of the type of crime committed or the types of characters involved in those crimes. But as with the film, the *Fargo* series' 'true story' ploy is a parodic ruse: like the Coens, Hawley uses it as a means to exploring the nature of narrative truth and the power of storytelling.

For Hawley, story must always be 'character driven' (Hawley, Austin Film Festival). Throughout the *Fargo* series character 'types' from the film are maintained and each season is structured around a similar generic framework involving different incompetently executed crimes, but Hawley's ten hour stories go beyond the narrative scope of its 98 minute cinematic predecessor, presenting complex plotlines and more in-depth character studies across a broader storytelling canvas. Like the Coens, who wanted to 'shoot a crime film with characters away from the stereotypes of the [crime] genre' (Coens cited in Sherrir 12), Hawley presents flawed and ineffectual criminals alongside unassuming yet highly competent small town law enforcers whose tenacity is eventually rewarded. Season One's wife murderer and evolving arch schemer,

Lester Nygaard, is a mirror image of the Coen's emasculated and bungling Jerry Lundegaard, while officer Molly Solverson emerges as a younger version of the film's homely yet highly intuitive Chief, Marge Gunderson. A similar pattern is employed in subsequent seasons: accidental criminals Ed and Peggy Blumquist are on the run from both local mobsters and local law enforcers in Season Two, and the Stussy brothers are involved in a series of incompetently handled criminal acts that are being investigated by small town soon-to-be demoted police chief, Gloria Burgle, whose tenacity echoes that of Marge Gunderson and Molly Solverson, providing further continuities across the story worlds of series and film. However, Hawley changes the tenor of the professional criminal elements within his Fargo universe, and adds further layers to the relationships of those everyday Minnesotans at the centre of his narratives.

In all three seasons, there is a much more complex dynamic at work in the construction of both hitmen and their criminal bosses. The Coens' construction of criminal characters in *Fargo* is informed by their desire to undermine what they see as the generic 'Hollywood cliché of the bad guy as a super-professional' (Ethan Coen in Ciment and Niogret 118): hitmen Gaear Grimsrud and Carl Showalter are no more focused or competent than the ineffectual Lundegaard who hires them to abduct his wife in order to extract a ransom from his wealthy and overbearing father-in-law. But Hawley's Lorne Malvo (Season One), Mike Mulligan (Season Two), and V.M. Varga (Season Three) are highly intelligent criminals of a very different calibre, and the more traditional hitman pairings found in each season of the TV series, from Mr. Wrench and Mr. Numbers (Season One), to The Kitchen Brothers (Season Two) and Meemo and Yuri Gurka (Season Three), are skilled, efficient killers. For Hawley the construction of all such characters becomes a 'deeper philosophical exercise' that involves a continuation and in this instance an expansion of the 'metaphysical quality' that pervades so much of the Coen brothers' work (Hawley in Cohen). Season One's Lorne Malvo embodies the 'metaphysical quality' of 'elemental' … lone figures' like Anthony Chigurh from *No Country for Old Men*, attaining a similarly mythical, immortal quality—as one who has 'always been there, roaming the American terrain' (Hawley in Cohen). In Malvo, Hawley constructs a cynical, amoral observer motivated not by money but by the desire to manipulate the many gullible individuals who pepper the narrative, from the downtrodden Lester, to the impressionable Hess boys and the motel worker whom he goads into urinating in the petrol tank of his domineering employer. Few of the Coen brothers' characters incite audience empathy (Snee 220); however, unlike Showalter and Grimsrud, Malvo is a highly intelligent hitman with whom audiences collude against their better judgement. He is presented as a cross between the darkly mischievous malcontent of Jacobean drama, and a Satanic immortal who serves as the sin-inducing provocateur for downtrodden Lester, and who delivers sardonic culturally loaded lines like "I haven't had a piece of pie like that since the Garden of Eden" (9.1). Points of continuation are established with not only the metaphysical elements of the Coen brothers' body of work but *across* the various seasons of this anthologised series. Like Malvo, Season Two's Mike Milligan and Season Three's V.M. Varga, both of whom speak in metaphysical riddles, are presented as further elemental figures of a 'Faustian kind' (Hawley in Cohen), while Hanzee Dent emerges as the elemental 'loner' of Season Two *and* as Season One's re-invented Fargo mafia boss, Tripoli.

In general, the characters who people the films of the Coen brothers are invariably seen as potentially caricatured cyphers for the more conceptual ideas at work in their narratives rather than individuals with whom an audience can readily empathise and identify (Silverman, 32). Throughout the TV series Hawley builds on the darkly comedic potential of the Coens' often caricatured representational mode. Each season, for example, produces slow-witted law enforcers akin to the film's Officer Lou, and over the expansive timeframe of three ten episode seasons Hawley is able to construct an ensemble cast of caricatured types that expands the comedic potential of the narratives. From the 'intellectually challenged' personal trainer, Don Chumph, whose 'type' alludes to the Coen's Chad Feldheimer (*Burn After Reading*, 2008), to incompetent FBI agents Pepper and Budge of Season One or Season Two's failed entrepreneur Skip Sprang and Season Three's increasingly humiliated business man Sy Feltz (both of whom are connected to *Fargo*'s failing business man Jerry Lundegaard), Hawley creates characters with an affinity to those found throughout the Coens' story world. By taking the narrative beyond the scope of the titular *Fargo*, Hawley demonstrates the wider and more ambitious parameters of his work as an 'adapter'. From Season One's 'nagging housewife' stereotype, Pearl Nygaard, to Season Two's series of female caricatures ranging from predatory lesbian Constance Heck, to androgynous Judge Mundt or the vengeful

Widow Hess, Hawley presents amusing yet disquieting images of women matched by similarly damning critiques of ineffectual males.

However, like the Coens, Hawley is also conscious of the 'dangers' of comedic 'excess' (Joel Coen in Ciment and Niogret 112) when writing a narrative that purports to be a 'true story' grounded in reality rather than fantasy. The comedic potential of the Coens' narrative did not form part of the interpretive brief during the scripting process or in performance: 'the comedy' argues Ethan Coen, 'wouldn't have worked if it had been played as comedy rather than with sincerity' (Ethan Coen in Ciment and Niogret 113). The relationship between Marge and Norm is low key, understated, 'based on the unsaid' (Joel Coen in Ciment and Niogret 113), and this is a relationship that Hawley builds on, presenting similarly grounded partnerships, built on long-standing family values, between Vern and Ida Thurman, Molly Solverson and Gus Grimly (Season One), and Lou and Betsy Solverson (Season Two). Four generations of The Solversons are represented across Seasons One and Two, allowing Hawley the capacity to establish a more intimate relationship between audience and characters than can possibly be afforded within the time constraints of cinema. Tellingly, in the more contemporaneous climate of Season Three, those family values so central to the film and to Seasons One and Two of the TV series are under threat. Marge, Molly, Betsy and Ida represent 'women of a simpler world in a small town where everything made sense', but Season Three's Chief, Gloria Burgle, a single mother whose ex husband is now in a gay relationship, 'has a much harder edge' (Hawley in Fienberg). Like Marge, all of these women are constructed as morally good; however, the dubious morality of some of Hawley's other female characters takes the series' narratives beyond the story parameters of the film.

For Hawley, Frances McDormand's 'iconic performance' as Marge is one of the film's major strengths; it invests the narrative with a 'female identity' that is ripe for further exploration within the wider timeframe of an anthologised series, and the Season Two storyline in particular is dominated by strong female characters on a journey of late 1970s 'self-awareness' (Hawley in Casino). Characters like Peggy Blumquist and Simone Gerhardt who, in their own ways, challenge and confront the gender-based limitations placed on them as women living during the era of second wave feminism, are drawn alongside less vocal yet equally forthright matriarchs, Floyd Gerhardt and Betsy Solverson. Season Three's anti-hero, Nikki Swango, is presented as an equally strong and confrontational female, this time of the post-feminist generation. Her relationship with her probation officer, Ray Stussy, provides an unlikely yet convincing and endearing romance subplot, her gold-digger persona being subverted only in the closing episodes when it becomes clear that her blackmail of Varga is an act of retribution rather than avarice, her final quest being to avenge the murder of her lost love, Ray. Like Peggy Blumquist, she emerges as a complex, multi-layered character.

3.3.1   Mythical Continuities

A preoccupation with the ongoing potency of mythologies pervades the films of the Coens[2] and all three seasons of Hawley's *Fargo*. In the latter, reference to pre-existing mythologies sit alongside those generated *within* the newly evolving Fargo diegesis, ensuring a sense of continuity between film and anthologised TV series. Though not an adaptation per se, *Fargo* is yet another of the Coens' explorations of the mythical nature of all stories, whether fictional, factual, or the product of a creative merging of both. In a foreword to the published screenplay they detail their particular understanding of narrative 'truth'; examining their childhood responses to their grandmother's purportedly true yet decidedly unreliable stories, they highlight humankind's innate desire to consume stories, and to believe in the veracity of tales that, when recycled ad infinitum, attain a mythical status through a process of reiteration. Whether 'by virtue of [their] drama or [their] repetition' the stories related '[come] to feel mythic' (Coens vii), the stuff of fables worthy of ongoing appropriation. Their film has become a compelling fable in its own right, generating mythologies across various media platforms. The death of Japanese woman Takako Konishi became the stuff of urban legend when a version of her 'story', connected according to internet posts and news media hype to her search for buried treasure from the fictional Fargo story world emerged online in 2001. Both a film and a documentary short based on the events surrounding Konishi's death followed. *This is a True Story* (**2003**) sought to debunk the urban legend surrounding the death of Konichi, employing a factual re-enactment of events surrounding her demise but its 'truth' telling remains, in part, coloured by audience perception of and desire to 'believe' in the mythical properties invested in

---

[2] *O Brother Where Art Thou* (2000), for example, is a Coen brothers' film that appropriates Homer's *Odyssey* 36, an epic tale taken Greek mythology.

her story via its association with *Fargo* and with other fictional media-generated iterations thereof. Similarly, in the film *Kumiko, The Treasure Hunter* the Zellerman brothers use *Fargo* as 'a kind of conduit' for their appropriation and re-presentation of this urban legend, building a fiction around the truth of Konichi's death (David Zellerman in Caron)—a death which, post media hype, it transpires was a suicide in no way connected to a search for buried treasure. Both this film and the documentary add to the mythological potency of the Fargo story on which Hawley continues to build in his anthologised TV series by not only extending these established fables but by constructing new ones too.

The ransom money, buried by *Fargo* abductor Carl Showalter in an indistinguishable spot within a vast snow-laden landscape, and marked only by a diminutive red ice scraper, has a become distinctive part of *Fargo* mythology that provides narrative and visual continuity between film and TV series. The myth of buried treasure re-enters the Fargo story world through the visual signifier of the now iconic red scraper which is enshrined in a painting that adorns the office walls of wealthy supermarket king Stavros Milos in the early stages of Season One (2.1). Hawley builds on this visual cue in episode six through a flashback to a moment of Coenesque-like serendipity in which a younger Stavros, stranded on a snowy highway, stumbles across what is visually inferred to be Showalter's hastily buried 'treasure', its placement marked by a lone red scraper. A later episode, aptly titled 'Buridan's Ass', references a further fable that addresses the paradoxical nature of free will: Stavros, whose wealth appears to have been built upon this earlier fortuitous discovery, feels compelled to reverse his initial choice, and by returning the 'treasure' and the red marker to the snowbound highway, he reinscribes its mythical potential to enter future Fargo narratives in later seasons, attesting once more to the continuities at work in this reconfiguration of the Coen brothers' film.

Other myths generated *within* the newly evolving diegesis of this anthologised TV series span the various seasons, adding further layers of complexity and continuity to the Fargo fable. Season One references the Sioux Falls Massacre, a criminal event from the late 1970s that provides Season Two's climactic story arc and which, whether 'by virtue of its drama or its repetition' (Coens vii), has attained mythical status within the first season's diegesis. In Season Two Ed Solverson, the former season's diner owner and father of officer Molly Solverson, plays a much younger law enforcer who, investigating a series of murders at the local

Waffle Hut diner, is present at the resultant mass shoot out now alluded to as The Sioux Falls Massacre. This massacre and the criminal acts of Season Two's Ed and Peggy Blumquist are invested with further mythical potency through the on-screen introduction of an aside that literally enters the pages of *The History of True Crime in the Mid-west: 1825 to Present*, a book that references both in a story digression that once more parodies the nature of 'truth' by presenting fiction as recorded fact (9.2). This kind of crossover between 'true stories' and fiction becomes yet another stylistic act of continuation between film and TV series—one that is further reinforced by opening story asides in both Season Two and Season Three. Season Two opens with scenes from an old black and white movie titled *Massacre at Sioux Falls* as the camera pans across a field littered with the corpses of American soldiers and comes to rest on the image of a warrior-like indigenous chief surveying the mass slaughter. But what is initially couched as a fictitious on-screen depiction of an historical moment, invested with the mythical potency of 'Wild West' narratives habitually generated by the film industry, is then revealed to be a 1950s film set.

The precedent for narrative asides and digressions of this type is set by the Coens, and while Hawley 'plays into that "accept the mystery" philosophy that the Coens have built into their work' he also expands the 'nonsensical' elements within the wider scope of TV's long form narrative; what Hawley terms *Fargo*'s 'Mike Yanagita moments' form an essential part of the film's narrative identity (Hawley in Arnold). Even before narrative momentum is established, Season Three launches in its opening moments into yet another story aside with only tentative and highly circumspect connections to the main plotline—a plotline that has yet to be established. There are moments within this interrogation scene set in East Berlin prior to the fall of the wall that allude to Russian émigré Yuri Gurka; when, in 2010, Varga hit man Yuri Gurka enters the narrative the veiled inference is that he is the émigré, despite the fact that the timeframe makes this a 'nonsensical' impossibility of the kind so often sewn into the films of the Coen brothers. The crossover between truth and fiction and the latter's mythological potency is foregrounded once more in these opening moments, the East German officer declaring, "We're not here to tell stories, we're here to tell the truth" (3.1). Through such additions to the narrative, Hawley builds into the series moments of mythical continuity that provide a self-referential dimension, taking the narrative frame of reference beyond the parameters of the *Fargo* film and its adaptive offspring. Ed Blumquist's mythical status as The Butcher of Luvurne serves as a further example of myth-building so often generated through misinformation and exaggeration. In this instance the myth is initiated by Dodd Gerhardt as a diversionary tactic designed to redirect Ma Gerhardt's attention but, once unwittingly entangled in the crimes of this mobster family, unassuming Ed claims for himself that folkloric title as a means of self-preservation, even though he is more readily identifiable as the boulder-pushing Sisyphus referenced through both Noreen's constant reading of Camus' 'The Myth of Sisyphus' and its use as the title for episode three. Hawley introduces further layers of self-referential metatextuality that allude to the potency of mythical narratives by visually reinscribing the Sisyphus myth in Season Three, where the image of the boulder-pushing Sisyphus adorns the remaining stamp in a collection that has become the source of contention between brothers Ray and Emmit Stussy. Like the red marker painting that adorns the walls of Stavros's office in Season One, the stamp acquires iconic status and provides an ongoing intertextual allusion to the Season Two storyline, ensuring further continuities across the series' anthologised seasons.

Furthermore, in a Season Two allusion to the Coens' *The Man Who Wasn't There* (2001), Hawley generates an urban myth centred around UFOs, sightings of which were prevalent in the media during this season's late 1970s setting. For the Coen brothers, Ed Crane's sighting of a UFO on the eve of his execution is a conceit that has no impact on narrative momentum; instead it is emblematic of their tendency to include inexplicable narrative asides. Hawley builds on this UFO imagery within the cultural context of a post Watergate America fuelled by heightened paranoia, when sci-fi films like *Close Encounters of the Third Kind* (1977) and *Star Wars* (1977) were, he notes, 'very much in the zeitgeist' and nothing could be trusted, 'not even the skies' (Hawley in Casino). But in *Fargo* Season Two UFO sightings are more than a conceit; they are concretised on screen and have a direct impact on narrative momentum. The first UFO appearance in episode one results in the death of Rye Gerhardt as, distracted by its light post his Waffle Hut killing spree, he wanders out in front of Peggy Blumquist's car; the second on screen appearance of the UFO takes place in episode nine's climactic shoot out scene where it once more alters narrative outcomes by providing both the opportunity for Officer Lou Solverson to kill the distracted Bear Gerhardt, and a chance for Ed and Peggy to escape the police and hit man Hanzee

Dent. The era's cultural investment in this urban myth is further reinscribed through the mise en scène of the Rushmore Gas Station, the walls of which are adorned with UFO images and signs noting 'You are not alone' and 'The future is here. Keep your eyes to the sky' (8.2, 9.2); on finding the murdered gas station owner in the prelude to the Sioux Falls Massacre shoot out, Lou's attention is drawn to these signs and to a photograph of the gas station owner and his partner in which beams of unnatural light, of the kind that flooded the scene during Rye Gerhardt's UFO encounter, filter into the frame from above suggesting a similar encounter has occurred (9.2) and may happen again, as indeed it does by the end of this episode. The science fiction elements of Season Two find their way into the subsequent season, providing further narrative continuities; episode three of Season Three is dominated by a narrative aside that details the backstory of Thaddeus Mobley (alias Ennis Stussy) and his time as a writer of sci-fi pulp fiction back in the 1970s, before the narrative shifts into absurdist realms with the inclusion of a cartoon about a malfunctioning robot left to roam the universe.

Playful allusions to biblical mythologies that are integral to Seasons One and Two add yet more layers of mythical intertextuality to the series. Season One malcontent, Lorne Malvo, exploits the psychological potential of biblical stories of retribution as a means to emotionally bullying Stavros into parting with his money. In the dramatic and highly stylised closing moments of episode three Hawley merges biblical myth with stories that have attained a mythical status within popular culture (3.1). The story of Moses' origins and his slaying of the Egyptian (Exodus 2.5–2.12) is delivered in voiceover by Malvo across a sequence that builds from images of Lester and brother Chuck mid orgiastic shooting spree, to an incongruous shot of Fargo hitmen, Mr. Wrench and Mr. Numbers, huddled over a fire in a solitary wooden hut, before coming to rest on a close up of a concerned Stavros peering into his shaving mirror. The disturbing nature of what is about to unfold on screen as Stavros prepares to take a shower is signalled not only by the continuing voiceover narration and an increasingly intense instrumental score but by the visual echoes of iconic horror film images from Hitchcock's *Psycho* and de Palma's *Carrie* (1976). A shot of the showerhead as a naked and vulnerable Stavros enters screen space, his back to camera in a pose reminiscent of *Psycho*'s Marion Crane, serves to intertextualise the shower scene from Hitchcock's film (1960). The camera then moves into a close up shot of Stavros as, in a moment reminiscent of the prom queen scene from *Carrie*, the water turns into an increasingly dark and viscous red liquid pouring over his head and torso. Both create an image, manufactured by mischievious malcontent Malvo, that emasculates the initially assertive and arrogant Stavros, aligning him instead with constructs of female victimhood. As the episode draws to a close, the off screen screams of Stavros accompany a smiling Malvo who returns the King James bible from which he has been reading to the boot of his car, pointedly placing it on top of his copy of Stavros's autobiography, as if replacing that self-generated myth of empire building with one of Malvo's own warped creation. Hawley reinforces Malvo's manipulation of Stavros through the referencing of Old Testament revenge narratives (Exodus 10) in the subsequent episode in which a plague of locusts are released in Stavros's supermarket; the scene edits from the ensuing chaos in the store to the image of a smiling Malvo, sitting god-like on the roof above. Further Old Testament biblical allusions form part of the narrative fabric of Season Three; the Stussy brothers' feud mirrors that of Cain and Abel (Genesis 4) according to the bible-quoting V.M. Varga (4.3); and Paul Marrane, a character who is superfluous to narrative momentum yet central to the series' characteristic use of narrative asides is, by name and by virtue of his dialogue, synonymous with the Wandering Jew of thirteenth century biblical stories. In episode eight, in a bowling alley scene that borrows heavily from the Coens' *The Big Lebowski*, he functions as god-like protector and advisor of the season's anti-heroine Nikki Swango, delivering supernaturally charged messages to both Swango and hit man Yuri Gurka (8.3). In the final episode, when Swango seeks to fulfil her revenge quest by confronting Emmit Stussy, she delivers to him lines from Obidiah (1.4) first spoken to her in Hebrew during her encounter with Marrane, stating 'Thou thou exalt thyself as the eagle, and though thou set thy nest among the stars, thence will I bring thee down, saith the Lord,' claiming for herself a god-like power which is swiftly undermined by the random arrival of a state trooper.

Taking his lead from the film, Hawley continues to destabilise the myth of the Midwestern pastoral, presenting the region as one that aligns with the Coens' depiction of a 'darker, murkier and scarier' American Midwest 'than American mythologies have commonly allowed' (Sherrirr 22); however, he also explores the myth of the American dream, introducing narratives that revolve around the pursuit of a personalised version thereof. According to Ethan Coen characters in their films may 'embody those grand themes (the American dream)' but the brothers declare their decided lack of interest in American dream scenarios in general (Ethan Coen in Fuller). Any suggestion that the *Fargo* title references the mythical pioneering spirit of the Wells Fargo company is equally contested (Joel Cohen in Ciment and Niogret 110). Hawley, on the other hand, is keen to critique the concept of the American dream across each season thus far. In Season One, Lester Nygard realises his dream not through the archetypal American dream quest heroics of the solid work ethic but through a series of cunning and immoral acts that subvert the traditional tropes of the myth; his story arc maps his transformative rise from emasculated victim to successful Salesman of the Year but this chimera of an American dream, built on deception and cowardly acts, soon unravels and in a final narrative act of moral judgement that parodies the grand dream myth of transformation, Lester reverts to type and loses everything, including his life. Similarly, though Emmit Stussy is initially living the American dream as a consequence of his work ethic and business acumen, he too is guilty of underhand acts that ultimately bring about his demise; and even though Emmit's American dream lifestyle is momentarily re-established, he is executed by Swango's avenging angel, Mr. Wrench, in the season's closing moments.

In Season Two the myth of the American dream has a more integral thematic role in the narrative. The fable-like story of the rise to power of actor Ronald Reagan forms one such thematic thread; episode one begins on a film set where his presence is awaited, and his campaign trail in pursuit of selection as Republican leader and president becomes part of the narrative backdrop to the season, given occasional prominence in moments like the opening scenes of episode five when Reagan recounts in voiceover his humble origins as the son of a shoe salesman father (5.2). Reagan is emblematic of the traditional rags to riches fable at the heart of the American dream—one where the reality is more incredible than fiction—but, as in seasons one and two, the competing American dream scenarios of other more central characters are not realised by the season's close. Peggy Blumquist aspires to be 'the best self [she] can be', signing up for self-actualisation courses and compulsively amassing lifestyle magazines that present images of the life she wants to live beyond the parameters of her small town existence; Ed Blumquist's dream is to build an all American family and to purchase the local butcher's shop; and in true Coenesque fashion the dreams of both are made untenable due to a random yet life-changing act inadvertently brought about by a

UFO. Peggy continues to hold on to her dream, urging Ed to run away with her—away from what she sees as their restrictive Midwestern existence and into the Californian sunshine—but her pragmatic husband realises that the best they can hope for is to stay alive as the hunt for them escalates towards the season's close. Like Ed, the heroic characters, represented as law enforcers in all three seasons of the TV series and the film, aspire to a more attainable and normalised American dream centred around the concept of the 'happy family'; none of them seek to realise the 'grand themes' (Ethan Coen in Fuller 139) of the American dream, and as the narratives draw to a close the Solversons of seasons one and two are, like Marge and Norm Gunderson, depicted sharing everyday family moments, even if the negative projected outcomes for the Solversons of Season Two are already predicated by Season One.

3.3.2 Cultural and Geographical Continuities

Silverman argues that 'cinematic landscapes' are charged with 'the task of engaging our previous ideas about place' (33). The endless snowbound landscapes of North Dakota have become synonymous with the Fargo universe on screen: they form an intrinsic part of its ongoing mythology, the place name itself now heavily invested with imagery of 'desolate stretches of land' both 'dramatic and oppressive' (Joel Coen in Ciment and Niogret 116). From the Los Angeles of *The Big Lebowski* to the Hollywood of *Barton Fink* (1991) or *Fargo*, the Coens 'obsession with place' is a central tenet of their style of filmmaking (Silverman 32), signalling more than location and generic identity. Rather, it is an 'aesthetically' representational space that has the capacity to both 'augment events' within a narrative and to encourage a more 'contemplative gaze' (Roberts 367). The seemingly barren snowscapes of *Fargo* provide a visual continuity that goes beyond the simple transference of geographical location in all of the film's adaptive offspring, from *This is a True Story* and *Kumiko, the Treasure Hunter* to the anthologised TV series. In each, the viewer's 'contemplative gaze' is inevitably directed to these other textual landscapes, all of which envision not 'a neutral place of entertainment, or an objective documentation or mirror of the "real", but an ideologically charged cultural creation' (Jeff Hopkins cited in Silverman 34). Despite the Coens' desire to create a space that has 'no design', the end result of their search for a 'soul-deadening, flattened locatio[n]' results in the construction of a landscape that is redolent with mythical meaning. For Roberts 'landscape *is* the story, the memory, the meaning' (379); all things, he infers, stem from that.

The landscapes of *Fargo* the film and the anthologised TV series provide an epic backdrop for events that unfold across each story arc, and landscape, rather than plot or character, serves as the point of adaptive connection between the film and the adaptations that are in dialogue with it. The snowscapes of *Fargo* serve as the catalyst to events, many of its scenes playing out on snowbound highways, yet despite the title of film and TV series, neither are filmed in Fargo[3] and little of the action takes place in that titular town. Under Hawley's creative directive, Jeff Russo, composer of the series' musical score, creates a soundtrack that reflects a landscape which is 'cold' and 'stark', yet infused with emotion and melancholy; it serves to reinforce the landscape's 'Grimm's fairytale dichotomy,' its 'winter wonderland' quality but also to highlight its capacity to 'quickly turn into a nightmarish landscape', both 'soothing and unnerving at the same time' (Russo in Chagollan). Like the film, Season One's opening moments are dominated by the landscape. Russo's more dramatic orchestral version of Carter Burwell's *Fargo* soundtrack plays over a 48 seconds static wide angle shot of the snowy highway as a car approaches from the top left of the frame, accompanied by the film's 'true story' intertitles, its events set this time in Minnesota 2006. By affording the landscape such prominence in these opening moments and concluding this sequence with a shot that notes its retention of the Fargo title, Hawley ensures the series is aligned with its precursor text from the outset. The landscape purposely mirrors that of its cinematic predecessor and as in this instance reiterates some of its narrative plot points, but it also serves as the backdrop to newly generated narratives. Though the scale of *Fargo*'s cinematic landscape is reinscribed, the events and characters that enter Season One's narrative space in these early stages are very different. Hit-man, Lorne Malvo, is the first to enter story space on this same highway, his actions setting off a series of events that are central to the season's narrative momentum. Malvo is accompanied by an ominous unnatural red light that offers a stark visual contrast to the cold, barren surroundings, investing Malvo and the landscape he first appears in with the kind of 'mythic energy' that is a feature of the Coens' 'hyperreal landscapes' (Silverman 34). The bizarre, decidedly Coenesque image

---

[3] The snowscapes of *Fargo* were filmed in Eastern North Dakota, while all three seasons of the TV series were shot in Calgary, Alberta.

of a semi-naked man, escaping from the boot of Malvo's crashed car before hurtling off across the fields serves as an elongated, geographically significant prelude to the introduction of this season's downtrodden protagonist, Lester Nygaard and his fatalistic relationship with Malvo. Further echoes of the Fargo narrative are built into the season's plotline; in a visual reconstruction of the scene in which the film's Carl Showalter buries ransom money at the side of the snowy highway, Stavros Milos is shown both finding hidden money (3.1) and later replacing it (6.1) in what appears to be the same geographical location—a location that is by now imbued with mythical associations of buried treasure.

Landscape can function 'not merely as a setting provider' but as 'provocateur' for encounters that play out within it (Roberts 374). The highway itself is a recurring motif across all three seasons of the TV series; it is a tension-laden performative space on which many of the series' altercations take place, from the understated yet quietly menacing encounter between Malvo and Gus Grimwald in Season One and the similarly courteous exchanges between Sherriff Hank Larsson, Mike Milligan and the Kitchen Brothers in Season Two, to the more deadly moments of Season Three where, on seeking to avenge the death of Ray Stussy, it is Swango rather than Emmit Stussy who ends up dead, killed by a passing state trooper (10.3). The latter echoes in part a scene from *Fargo* in which the kidnappers are confronted by and kill a state trooper. But the most pointed homage to the film *and* to the cinematic style signature of regular Coens collaborator Roger Deakins' work on Andrew Dominik's *The Assassination of Jesse James by the Coward Robert Ford* (2007), comes at an earlier point in Season Three when the ambush of a prison bus by Varga's hit-men is witnessed by innocent by-passers who are then eliminated in much the same way as the innocent by-passers who witness the murder of the state trooper in the Coens' film (7.3) (Wrobleski in Chitwood). As the series progresses, it is the highway rather than the snowscapes that becomes the visual connector between the film and the various seasons. Hawley continues to build on the Coens' preoccupation with the geography of place and the cultural nuances of Midwestern America; however, though each of the anthologised seasons remains in dialogue with the film, an increasingly distinctive Fargo with its own identity emerges. The snowbound landscape, so central to the film's initial adaptation to a televisual story world, gives way to the autumnal colours of Season Two, while Season Three presents a visual amalgamation of both.

Though these landscapes establish an indelible point of continuation between film and TV show and provide a backdrop for the dark content of each crime story that ensues, it is the 'homey and exotic' Midwesterner tone noted by the Coens as a feature of this geographical locale (x *Fargo* screenplay) that remains the most prominent point of continuation across all three seasons of this anthologised series. Despite the epic nature of the landscape scenes *Fargo*, like *Blood Simple* (1984) and *Raising Arizona* (1987), is a film (and a TV series) 'set on a small scale' in a 'very specific geographical location' (Luhr 110). As with all of the Coens' crime stories each iteration of *Fargo* subverts generic expectations of the crime genre; both film and TV series present a contradictory white noir style aesthetic that plays out not in the dark urban centres of noir but in the light, open spaces of Brainerd, Bemidji, Luvurne and Eden Valley. And yet, as its various adaptive offspring attest, this small-town Midwestern pastoral landscape has the capacity to 'reach out "beyond the frame" of the diegetic world' it represents, serving as what Roberts terms a 'generic descriptor of a geographic region' with an 'embedded sense of place, locality or region' (371), replicated here in the TV series as Season One's Bemidji, Season Two's Luvurne and various small towns clustered around Eden Valley in Season Three.

Even the manner in which the cinematic landscape is shot becomes for the Coens an exercise in creating a 'flat Midwestern effect' in which 'land and sky… merge', each becoming 'indistinguishable' (Coens in Biskind 146 cited in Robson 147–148), and each stylistically emulated across the anthologised *Fargo* series. The 'specific Minnesota atmosphere was where the juice' of this narrative lay for the Coens (Ethan Coen in Fuller 139). The locale's distinctive Scandinavian heritage aligns the region with what Ethan Coen defines as an 'exoticism and strangeness' characterised by 'politeness and reservation', a 'refusal to show the least emotion', and a 'resistance to saying "No"' that provides the 'springs of the story' from which the 'conflict between that constant avoidance of all confrontations and the murders [are] gradually piling up' (Ethan Coen in Fuller 111).

In *Fargo*, Midwestern respectability, commonly termed 'Minnesota Nice', is more than a veneer; it is portrayed as a way of life that is in turn disrupted by external violent forces that enter the locale. Hawley seeks to mirror the Coens' portrayal of this region's 'stoic culture' where an 'inability to communicate' and to emote plays an integral part in the story world (Hawley in Willmore). His characters share more than their

Nordic surnames; they also act like those Midwesterners who people the Coens' story world. In Season Three, Hawley purposely explores this notion of 'Minnesota Nice and its heightened sense of community' within what he describes as an 'historically isolated' region (Hawley in Fienberg S3 Violence). The series aspires to a cinematic visual aesthetic that is less dependent upon dialogue-driven storytelling of the kind more readily associated with TV drama, but though Hawley avoids comedic or parodic exaggeration of the regional accents (Hawley, Hollywood Reporter) the speech patterns, mannerisms and cultural behaviours of the Midwesterners at the centre of the narratives remain important transition points between series and film. For the Coens the film's characteristic 'flat Midwestern effect', achieved 'through the dialogue and the rhythm of speech' was what proved 'interesting' about this script (Coens in Biskind 146 cited in Robson 147–148), and this interest in the dialect is retained in the series. Characters like Marge and Norm, Jerry and Jean speak in a distinctive manner and are symptomatic of a clearly recognisable Minnesotan mindset identified by Ethan Coen as being more akin to the understated behaviours of Japanese culture than America at large (Coen in Fuller 111). These characters, argues Silverman, 'function as part of the landscape from which they spring' (34). In a manner that emulates the Coens' reputation for 'critical exploration of particular cultures' (Coughlin, Senses), Hawley establishes a similar set of Midwestern cultural values as the moral and emotional touchstone for characters who, similarly, emerge from the cultural landscape of their origins However, within the more contemporaneous context of Season Three, Hawley explores the idea that the cultural values of 'Minnesota Nice itself are under threat'; the emotional exhibitionism of the era 'seems counter to the identity of that region', with every thought becoming a tweet, every image a Facebook posting (Hawley in Fienberg).

In addition to the larger scale location parallels between film and TV series there are numerous visual echoes at work across the various seasons that connect each narrative in this ever-evolving Fargo universe. References to parking lots abound, from their recurring appearance as the scene of ransom handovers in the film and Season One to their function as the centre of Emmit Stussy's car lot empire in Season Three—a car lot empire of the kind Jerry Lundegaard sought funding for and that prompted the doomed abduction plan. Images of small town police stations are an integral part of each Fargo's regional identity, though tellingly diminished in size to a corner of the local library by Season Three, while Season Two abduction scenes involving Dodd Gerhardt and his captors, the Blumquists, recall similar moments between the film's captor Gaear Grimsrud and the kidnapped Jean Lundegaard, both of which take place in lakeside cabins. On a wider scale other settings from the body of the Coens' work are intertextulaised across the various seasons. The woodland execution of Bernie Bernbaum in *Miller's Crossing* (1990) serves as a 'ghostly presence' (Geraghty 195) throughout Season Two's woodland execution scene in which Simone Gerhardt is shot by her uncle, Bear Gerhardt. The season's ultra-violent climactic shootout at the Sioux Falls Motel presents a similarly loaded 'shadowing' (195) of events that took place in the motel shootout from *No Country for Old Men*; and anxious altercations that take place in gas stations in Seasons Two and Three, with Hanzee Dent in role as a pseudo Anton Chigur, present further moments of stylistic, thematic and story-driven continuity across both film and seasons.

3.4 Stylistic Continuities and Detours

The term cinematic 'auteur' has, since its inception in the fifties, been employed as a means of assigning authorial kudos to film products, and even though the film industry, like its televisual screen counterpart, is one built around collaborative work practices, the mantle of authorship is overwhelmingly afforded to its directors. The Coens have long since acquired auteur status: their idiomatic style signature is evident across a body of work over more than thirty years. They are seen by some as highly successful 'postmodernist auteurs' (146 Newman) who have turned the practice of appropriation into an art form. In a place Newman terms 'Coen country', they create a cinematic 'universe where people talk and act in a way that exists only in their movies' (147). But most importantly, this is a 'country' distinguished by more than the distinctive nature of its content and its characters; the Coens' style aesthetic—a style aesthetic lauded and abhorred by critics and academics in equal measure—is unique. Film critic Pauline Kael views their films as 'merely pointless deconstructions or hybridizations' (cited in Palmer Coen 45); Julian Murphet decries the 'pronounced artificiality' of their cinematic style, a style signalled by an excessive use of conscious camerawork, montage sequences, and voiceovers that afford their films 'a distinctive tonal fetishism' (Murphet, The Conversation). However, while acknowledging the 'ostentatiously stylized' nature of their films, the Coens refute any notion of themselves as 'Hollywood auteurs': their work is characterised by ever-changing modes of presentation that highlight 'discontinuity' rather than the presence of a sustained authorial voice that can be mapped out across the body of their work (Palmer Coen 53). Certain construction processes are regularly foregrounded in their films: from the use of voice over in *Raising Arizona* and *The Man Who Wasn't There*, the direct address to camera employed in the opening moments of *Blood Simple* and the closing moments of *The Big Lebowski*, and the frequently flamboyant cinematography employed in films like *Millers Crossing* to the dream sequences of *The Big Lebowski*, definitive filming techniques that remind the audience of the constructed nature of the narrative and the characters who populate it abound. As with other notably idiosyncratic auteurs like Terrence Malick, David Lynch, Wes Anderson or Quentin Tarentino, certain stylistic flourishes remain indelibly linked to the films of the Coen brothers, and regardless of their denial of their own auteur status, theirs remains a decidedly individualised body of work with its own style signature. This style signature is one that Hawley appropriates and builds on; while he takes his lead from *Fargo*, the style aesthetic of the TV series as a whole draws upon a range of the Coens' films, creating across its three-season roll out thus far an equally eclectic and 'discontinuous' mix of contradistinctive yet recognisable stylistic flourishes.

The kind of self-conscious style signature that has come to epitomise a Coen brothers' film is purposely absent in some of their work. *Fargo* is a 'radically different', less stylised movie (Joel Coen in Luhr 112): it serves as an early example of the Coen brothers' capacity for stylistic 'discontinuity' (Palmer Coen 53), and has more in common with later films like *No Country for Old Men* (2007), *A Serious Man* (2009) and *True Grit* (2010) than the films that precede it. *Fargo's* cinematographer Roger Deakins, a regular collaborator on Coen brothers' films, claims the original intention was to make this a 'more observational' film, in the mode of social realist filmmakers 'like Ken Loach' (Deakins in The Playlist). A comparatively 'restrained' approach to the cinematography, devoid of the 'fast tracks and flowery camerawork' that dominate in prior films like *Blood Simple* and *Barton Fink* is employed here in pursuit of greater 'intimacy' (Deakins in Robson 76–77). Both the Coens and Deakins note that during shooting 'another form of stylization' emerged, with some of their signature tracking shots replacing their intended use of static camera at certain points (Joel Coen in Climent and Niogret 116) but the directorial 'presence' foregrounded so frequently in their films is conspicuously absent here.

It is replaced by an 'invisible stylization' that relies upon mise-en-scene rather than conscious camerawork and constructive editing (Palmer Coen 103). Hawley sees *Fargo*'s 'more objective' and 'classical' style of filmmaking as one of its strongest assets; citing *Fargo, No Country for Old Men* and *A Serious Man* as films that dictate his story-driven approach in Season One, he avoids the 'pyrotechniques of the camera' so often in evidence in Coen brothers' films (Hawley in Fienberg). Yet here, as in all three seasons, Hawley shifts the stylistic boundaries by introducing signature moments that appropriate the self-consciously crafted approach to visual storytelling found in their other, more flamboyant films too. His singular vision brings together elements of the Coen brothers' body of work across this anthologised TV series, producing the series' own distinctive style aesthetic—a style aesthetic that changes with each of its anthologised seasons.

Maintaining a connection with the Coens' style aesthetic during each season's transition from script to screen proves challenging. Hawley notes that 'it's one thing on the page to say you've got the voice' but to then 'emul[ate] two of the greatest filmmakers of all time' in terms of on-screen 'tone' is demanding (Hawley, ATX), especially given the change of directors inherent in a TV production context. Hawley establishes the series' narrative universe, writing all ten episodes of the first season prior to filming and, with the input of a small team of writers across seasons two and three, retains his involvement in the writing process throughout, taking on occasion a director's role too (2.2, 3.1). However, as series show runner, he also works with a team of regular collaborators who are responsible in part for the overall look and sound of this anthologised series. Jeff Russo, composer of the musical score of Hawley's recent series *Legion* and all three seasons of *Fargo*, has worked on both series alongside costume designer Carol Case and director of photography Dana Gonzalez who is similarly involved in both *Legion* and the majority of the TV series' episodes. As director of the pilot episode and the subsequent episode in Season One, Adam Bernstein was also instrumental in establishing the look that was to be sustained throughout this first season (Bernstein in Kaufman). Gonzalez points out that the 'visual rules' established at the start of the series 'keep it in [a] Coen world'—a world created to a marked extent by an overriding cinematic vision that its ever-changing directors *must* adhere to (Gonzalez in O'Falt). Craig Wrobleski, Gonzalez' fellow director of photography on both *Legion* and *Fargo*, claims 'the entire legacy' of the Coens and their cinematographer collaborator Roger Deakins provides 'a jumping off point for the aesthetics' of the show, an aesthetic that is 'honored' yet not 'slavish[ly] adhered to (Wrobleski in Chitwood).

While Hawley pays homage to that aesthetic throughout this anthologised TV series, he also constructs a definitive tonal look for each season inscribed by more than their shared location. Like the various films of the Coen brothers, the seasons are visually distinctive: still images from each, claims Hawley, are immediately identifiable as belonging to one particular season rather than another (Hawley in Yeoman). Season One combines a visual homage to both *Fargo* and *No Country for Old Men* (Gonzalez in O'Falt); the earthy tones of the latter and the 'distinctive color palette' of the former, with its dominant 'beige, blue and red hues' become central to the visualisation of Season One's Bemidji, with these seasonal colour palettes consciously employed in the minutiae of set design, costuming and props too (Bernstein in Kaufman). For Gonzalez Season One 'was more about [the] barren, frozen tundra' readily associated with the film whereas in Season Two wooded areas became the 'signature landscape' (Gonzalez in Hart). Set in the late 1970s, Season Two presents a very different 'retro' vibe indebted as much to the 'cinematic splendour' of '70s image-making' as to the films of the Coens, (Gonzalez in Hart). It is a 'period piece' infused with a Kodachromatic colour palette dominated by 'oranges, yellows and primary colors' in which Gonzalez attains its distinctive and vibrant look through the use of vintage lenses from the 1960s and 1970s and a conscious referencing of the work of 1970s street photographer William Eggleston, the 'godfather of color photography', (Gonzalez in Hart). Gonzalez' and Hawley's and shared vision for Season Three builds on the 'very distinctive look' of the Coen's *Inside Llewelyn Davies* (2013); in this season the colour blue is 'pull[ed] literally out of the image' as a means to emulating the kind of look and tone achieved in this 'winter film' (Hawley in Yeomans). The Fargo narrative returns to its winter landscape, yet Season Three is visually distinguishable from both the film and earlier seasons of the TV series due to subtle, style-conscious deviations of colour palette.

The cinematic style of the series is dictated first and foremost by the story and by the characters who populate it; as in the Coen brothers' *Fargo*, the stylisation is, on the whole, purposely 'invisible', and camera movement is dictated by narrative (Gonzalez in O'Falt). Across the series in general and Season One in particular, Hawley trusts the camera to 'tell the story' without 'drawing attention to it' (Hawley in Fienberg).

However, while cinematography is never allowed to 'overtake the story' (Wrobleski in Chitwood), stylistic flourishes of the kind associated with earlier Coen films are brought in to varying degrees in each season. There are, for instance, moments within Season One that, in service *to* the narrative, purposely foreground the constructed nature of the on screen image. An episode five flashback to the scene in which Malvo shoots Chief Thurman plays out first in real time and then in a slow motion replay, adding a cartoon-like quality to the scene as we track the trajectory of the bullets that both kill Thurman *and* are the root cause of Lester Nygaard's now festering wound. From a close up of the gun barrel, the focus seamlessly transitions to a tracking shot that follows the flight path of the magnified, shining bullets as they enter the body of Thurman where, on impact, they transform into blood-red orbs; focusing on the journey of one of these red orbs, the camera continues to track out, coming to rest on a static close up of Lester's upheld hand, at which point the camera speed is exaggerated and the entry wound's cartoonesque transition to suppurating sore plays out on screen, providing the audience with a visual explication of Lester's current predicament. Similarly, in some instances Hawley employs an overt cinematic means of adding further layers to our understanding of the characters involved in his stories. The contrast between Malvo's unassuming appearance and his capacity for acts of extreme violence, executed with terrifying efficiency, is visually and aurally realised in an extended two minute tracking shot of the exterior of the building he enters when seeking revenge on the Fargo mafia syndicate that has ordered his execution for the killing of their man, Sam Hess. The exterior shot tracks his movements within as the muffled sounds of gunshots and screams signal the mayhem that he is unleashing on the other side of the frame.

Other moments present camera-conscious homages to the films of the Coen brothers, some of fleeting duration like the mug shot sequence involving Season Three's anti-heroine Nikki Swango which, through a visual replication of the mug shot sequence involving *Raising Arizona's* H.I. McDonnough (1987), forges a further connection between this season and the Coen brothers' film by mirroring the romantic coupling of criminal (Swango and McDonnough) and government employee (probation officer, Ray Stussy and police officer, Ed). The series as a whole is peppered with visual and aural 'nods' to imagery and soundtracks associated with films from the Coen brothers' back catalogue, some as incidental as an allusion to *The Big Lebowski* via a sign noting the sale of the Dude's favourite cocktail, the White Russian, or through inclusion of songs from numerous films.[4] However, Gonzalez notes frequent instances in which a more extended referencing of what he terms 'the Coens brothers' precision-tooled cinematic universe' is employed; Season Two's woodland execution scene in which Bear Gerhardt shoots his neice, Simone, is 'by design' a reconstruction of *Miller's Crossing's* woodland execution of Bernie Bernbaum (Gonzalez in Hart). It employs the same aerial shots of woodland and the same melancholic tone, enhanced in the series by an a cappella rendition of 'Danny Boy', a song that features on the *Miller's Crossing* soundtrack. Played out in a bowling alley that is a visual replica of the closing scenes of *The Big Lebowski,* episode eight of Season Three presents yet another homage to the Coens' 'precision-tooled cinematic universe' and to the brothers' penchant for narrative asides, The Stranger replaced here by Paul Marrane whose philosophical conversations with Swango and Yuri Gurka create a narrative pause after the action-packed prison bus hijack sequence that spans the opening and closing moments of this episode and its predecessor. The hijack sequence provides a further intertextual allusion to the work of regular Coen brothers' collaborator Roger Deakins whose cinematography on *The Assassination of Jessie James by the Coward Robert Ford* (2007) is emulated here (Wrobleski in Chitwood). There are also several scenes in Season Two that intertextualise specific cinematic moments from *Fargo*. The macabre image of Ed Blumquist feeding Rye Gerhardt's body parts into the butcher's shop meat grinder in the presence of Officer Lou Solverson (2.2) presents a visual echo of the closing moments from *Fargo* in which Marge Gunderson finds Gaear Grimsrud feeding body parts into a wood chipper. Later lakeside cabin scenes are similarly haunted by disturbing images from *Fargo* (8.2): like the film's kidnap victim, Jean Lundegaard, captive Dodd Gerhardt is bound and hooded, and like the film's abductor Grimsrud, Peggy Blumquist's preoccupation with the TV set and her treatment of her victim aligns her increasingly amoral behaviour with that of her cinematic predecessor.

---

[4]'Danny Boy' (*Miller's Crossing*); 'Just dropped in, to See What Condition my Condition was in' and 'Run Through the Jungle' (*The Big Lebowski*); 'Let's find Each Other Tonight' (*Fargo*); 'Man of Constant Sorrow' and 'O Death' (*O Brother Where Art Thou*).

Although the cinematic language associated with the work of the Coens remains central to the ways in which the series relates its tales, Hawley's style signature becomes far more distinctive as the seasons progress. Wrobleski argues that the series' homages so 'beloved to audiences' already familiar with the work of the Coen brothers serve to 'put the audience back in that world', but more tellingly they are invited to revisit that world 'in a different way' (Wrobleski in Chitwood). A sense of the series' own metatextual reflexivity, denoted by more than its narrational connectivity and its consistent use of visual and aural homage, emerges by Seasons Two and Three, where stories within stories are related in a style conscious mode that foregrounds the constructed nature of the text. In the opening moments of Season Two's Episode 9 Hawley employs a complex narrational strategy to explore the constructed nature of 'truth' by presenting events surrounding the Sioux Falls Massacre and the role of the Blumquists in events leading up to that moment as an entry in a history text book titled *The History of True Crime in the Mid-West: 1825 to Present*. As the pages turn to reveal drawings of Peg and Ed Blumquist, a non-diegetic voiceover delivered by actor Martin Freeman, who stars as Season One's Lester Nygaard, relates the outcome of a tale that the audience is already familiar with from Season One, but has yet to see play out on screen in Season Two. This kind of metatextual referencing across seasons becomes part of the series' style signature. A similar strategy is employed in episode four of Season Three which opens with the voiceover of actor Billy Bob Thornton, Season One's Lorne Malvo; in a self-conscious manner that highlights the constructed nature of the narrative we are watching the voiceover aligns characters from this season's story world with specific musical instruments from Prokofiev's symphonic fairy tale, *Peter and the Wolf*. The inclusion of an extended six minute cartoon sequence based on a pulp science fiction novel, *The Planet WYH*, and written by the season's first murder victim, Ennis Stussy (alias writer Thaddeus Mobley), denotes the series increasingly experimental style aesthetic and highlights once again the ways in which stories are interconnected—to earlier seasons and to earlier Coen films, in this instance through the inclusion of UFO narratives.

Hawley introduces interconnected nodes of cinematic expression that are both a continuation of the Coen brothers' experimental use of cinematic language *and* a deviation from their norm. His own style signature evolves as the season's unfold. In Season Two Hawley moves away in part from the Coens' cinematic modus operandi, adopting a purposely style-conscious mode of storytelling dominated by split-screen techniques of the kind prevalent in cinema of the 1960s and 1970s. The cinematic 'language' employed here 'pre-dates the Coens' films'; Hawley names Sam Peckinpah's *The Getaway* (1972) and John Boorman's *Point Blank* (1967) as films which influence his approach (Hawley in Berkshire), and the 'old-school split-screen format' used in films like *The Boston Stranger* (1969) becomes part of this season's distinctive style signature (Gonzalez in Hart). The highly stylised split-screen cinematic 'language' often associated with filmmakers like Quentin Tarentino, Darren Aranofsky and Mike Figgis also resonates at an intertextual level. First employed in TV drama in *24* (2001–2010), the split-screen format offers a distinctive way to present a multi-stranded narrative on the small-screen. Gonzalez sees its use throughout Season Two as an effective means of 'tracking' its large ensemble cast across an epic story canvas of a different kind to that of the 'relatively spare' Season One (Gonzalez in Hart). Split-screen has several storytelling functions. In some instances it serves as a subtle form of storytelling shorthand, providing connections between characters. The Blumquists' very different outlook on life and on how to deal with their current dilemma is amplified through the frequent use of shared screen moments in which the physical division of screen space unites them in a common cause yet underscores their psychological and emotional distance. In other instances, it is employed as a means of creating tension through the simultaneous juxtaposition of a given scene from the perspective of various characters. When, for example, the Gerhardt clan descend upon the police station where Charlie Gerhardt is being held in custody, the screen is split into three, providing the viewer with unrestricted access to all parties involved in this highly charged dramatic scene: the top two halves of the frame set up Officer Lou Solverson and Charlie's father, Bear Gerhardt, as duelling adversaries in a western type showdown while the bottom of the frame reveals the overwhelming number of Gerhardts surrounding them (6.2). In the closing episode in which the Blumquists are on the run from the police and from Hanzee, interior and exterior shots of a chiller room they are hiding in are presented simultaneously in a split screen format that again builds tension without the intervention of edits from one scene to another: left of screen holds on the Blumquists while right of screen reveals the room's exterior and the impending arrival of Hanzee (10.2) Occasionally Hawley introduces a more complex use of split screen that cuts across different moments in time. When Hanzee enters the Waffle Hut to investigate the death of Rye Gerhardt, a split screen edit shows both the blood-stained table top where Judge Mundt fell and a flashback to that image at the moment of her death, cutting across beats and angles from the previous scene in order to display the inner workings of Hanzee's mind as he pieces together the events of that day (4.2).

The evolving style aesthetic of this anthologised series is indebted to both the Coens' idiosyncratic filmmaking and to the more 'invisible' mode of cinematic storytelling employed in films like *Fargo*; it serves as a continuation of each. One of the series most striking and consistent style homages to the Coens' work relates to its treatment of scenes dominated by dialogue. In this series, TV's characteristic dependence on dialogue as a means to delivering 'story' becomes secondary to a visual mode of narration more readily associated with cinema; Hawley cites *Breaking Bad* as the ground-breaking TV series that shifted the parameters by moving away from the 'dialogue dependence' of TV drama (Hawley, Austin Film Festival). Nevertheless, despite the series' visually cinematic qualities, the 'pyrotechniques of the camera' remain secondary to character and story, and each season's dialogue scenes form an essential component in the telling of each tale (Hawley in Fienberg). The Coens' film dialogue scenes are constructed with a view to creating intimacy between character and audience, shooting from 'inside the space of the conversation' (Zhou); foregoing the traditional mode of shooting on multiple long lens cameras to produce a dialogue scene that is then edited in post production, the Coens use instead just two cameras, positioned between the speakers to capture separate, single shots that place the viewer inside the moment. Coens' cinematographer Roger Deakins argues that this approach creates a 'sense of presence for the viewer', placing the audience 'right there with somebody…psychologically' (Deakins cited in Zhou). The Coens foreground not only the spoken dialogue but the non-spoken transactions taking place on screen through body language, loaded silence and mise en scène. They favour wide angle lenses that provide a visual environmental context for each speaker, and Hawley employs similar framing techniques; the overwhelmingly cluttered backdrop to conversations which take place between Ed and Peggy Blumquist in their home environment, for example, is indicative of Peggy's established obsessive behavioural profile. Hawley's conscious decision to employ the same filming techniques when approaching dialogue scenes throughout the series dictates the use of the wide angle lens and one or two cameras only, with close ups 'shot in a certain way'[5]; while some dialogue scenes are shot on two cameras, Gonzalez' primary aim as cinematographer is to make this is a 'one-camera show' (Gonzalez in O'Falt).

There are memorable dialogue moments in all three seasons in which the one camera filming approach dominates. The pivotal relationship between Season One's Lester Nygaard and Lorne Malvo is established in an extended seven minute dialogue-driven scene that employs in the main one static camera shot, and both characters are held in the frame throughout the sequence. Lester and Malvo, as patients awaiting treatment in a hospital Emergency Room, are placed side by side in a wide angled static shot of near perfect symmetry, the camera holding focus on them, while hospital routines play out around them (1.1). Like the Coen brothers, Hawley exploits the potential of non-verbal communication during this dialogue-driven moment. Immediately, the body language of each character amplifies their contrasting behaviours, Lester's restless movements indicative of his anxious personality while Malvo's disquieting immobility infers a more self-contained and controlled persona. When Malvo asks for a sip of Lester's drink the scene shifts to a series of alternating shots that place each of them in turn at the forefront of the frame, but Malvo remains the dominant figure, lurking out of focus at the edge of the frame or held in deep focus even as Lester is placed in the foreground of the shot. The camera then returns to the opening wide angle shot, placing both back in the frame before Malvo moves in to sit closer, his intense gaze holding on Lester's face throughout as the camera shifts to a tighter mid-shot that provides greater access to their facial expressions, and increased levels of intimacy for both the characters and the viewer who, as in the shooting of dialogue scenes in the films of the Coens', is placed 'right there', sharing in the 'psycholo[gy]' the moment (Deakins cited in Zhou). The tension increases when, on hearing how Sam Hess has belittled Lester, Malvo says 'I woulda killed that man'; his menacingly civilised demeanour and his courteous delivery are juxtaposed with the dark content of his dialogue as the camera slowly moves in and a percussive timpani note that becomes an ongoing aural signifier of Malvo's malign presence sounds. A further series of alternating side angled shots underscores the nervous body language of

---

[5]While the Coens use 27 and 32 mm lenses, Gonzalez employs a similar lens size of 21 mm or 29 mm lens for all close ups (Gonzalez in O'Falt).

Lester and the unflappable nature of Malvo as the scene builds to the point at which Malvo asks Lester 'Are you asking me to kill this man? (Pause). One word: Yes. Or No.' This Beckettesque seven minute sequence sets up the series' narrative momentum, establishes an ongoing relationship between its two very different villains, and through both their dialogue and their body language, constructs each as a particular 'type'. A similarly extended six minute dialogue scene occurs in Season Three when, after confessing to the murder of his brother Ray, Emmit Stussy is interrogated by Chief Gloria Burgle (9.3); both are held in a static wide angled shot for the majority of the sequence, their reflected images multiplied in the two way interrogation room mirror, presenting a visual allusion to film noir's preoccupation with mirrors and duplicity. When the camera shifts to focus on Emmit the audience is placed 'inside the conversation', sharing that intimate screen space with Emmit as he confesses all to Gloria Burgle; the confessional mode is amplified as the camera slowly moves in on Emmit as he recalls childhood memories that have led him to this point in time.

Like the Coens, Hawley uses the non-verbal moments inside his dialogue scenes but he also expands upon their non-verbal potential. Though he employs the Coens' cinematic treatment of dialogue scenes, Hawley also experiments with them, particularly in Season Two as cinematic treatment of the Blumquists' conversations demonstrate. On a bus ride home after faking a car accident, Peggy and Ed are placed side by side in a static medium shot that again employs almost perfect symmetry; though visually there is no sign of their dialogue, we hear their shared conversation in voiceovers that create a heightened sense of intimacy between the two of them at this moment in time (3.2). The scene employs the Coens' signature use of non-verbal dialogue, our vision focused directly on the body language of those placed centre frame, but Hawley's use of voiceovers introduces another level of psychological intimacy between both the characters and their audience. In contrast, a later dialogue scene involving the Blumquists, in which the season's characteristic split-screen format is employed, foregrounds the ever-increasing distance between them. In a scene that again plays out as they travel along, this time in a car while on the run from the police, Peg and Ed share a medium close up frame but the moment swiftly edits from one to the other before cutting to a split-screen that physically divides their on-screen image; in contrast to the earlier dialogue moment, in this instance, even though they speak directly to each other, there is no sense of shared intimacy, their responses suggesting instead that neither one of them is listening (8.2).

Hawley, however, is 'listening' and 'adapting' to changes in audience engagement with TV narratives: 'TV', argues Hawley, 'has [a] kind of "sophistication" now' (Hawley, Writers' Panel)—a sophistication that lends itself to complex intertextual game-playing of a type in evidence in the metatextually rich story world of the anthologised *Fargo* TV series. The compelling Fargo mythology initiated by the Coen brothers continues to find an audience but it too, notes Hawley, has to 'adapt' (Hawley in Fienberg). Though the series remains in close communion with the prestigious film text it references in particular and the Coen brothers' films in general, it attains its own distinctive identity, its own narrative momentum and visual aesthetic, and in so doing it affords the Fargo story an ongoing prominence and relevance within contemporary popular culture.

Works Cited

Andrew, Dudley. "Adaptation." *Film Adaptation*. Ed. James Naremore. New Brunswick: Rutgers UP, 2000. 28–37. Print.

Arnold, Ben. "*Fargo* Comes to Channel 4: 'This is not a TV series, it's a 10-hour Movie.'" *The Guardian* (Culture), 4 Dec. 2012. Print.

ATX Festival 2015. "To Adapt is to Evolve: James Hibberd (*Entertainment Weekly*) with Noah Hawley, Bryan Fuller, Graham Yost." *YouTube*, June 2015. Web. 10 Oct. 2015.

Austin Film Festival 2015. "On Story, *Fargo* and *True Detective*: Television Anthologies, with Noah Hawley and Cary Fukunaga." *YouTube*, 25 Apr. 2015. Web. Oct. 2015.

Berkshire, Geoff. "'Fargo' Showrunner Noah Hawley on Season 2 and Thinking Like a Coen Brother." *Variety*, 16 Sept. 2015. Web. 10 Oct. 2015.

Caron, Matthew. "This Gorgeous New Film Was Inspired By an Early Internet Legend About *Fargo*." *VICE*, 20 Mar. 2015. Web. 10 Oct. 2015.

Carter, Steven. "'Flare to White': *Fargo* and the Postmodern Turn." *Literature Film Quarterly* 27.4 (1999): 238–244. Print.

Casino, Khier. "'Fargo' Creator Noah Hawley Dishes on Season 2 and What's in Store for Season 3." *Daily News*, 16 Dec. 2015. Web. 20 Jan. 2016.

Chagollan, Steve. "'Fargo' Composer Jeff Russo Finds Strength in the Silence." *Variety*, 12 June 2014. Web. 10 Oct. 2015.

Chitwood, Adam. "'Fargo' and 'Legion' Cinematographer Craig Wrobleski on Coen Brothers' Nods, Noah Hawley, and More." *Collider*, 13 June 2017. Web. 30 June 2017.

Ciment, Michael, and Hubert Niogret. "Closer to Life Than the Conventions of Cinema." *The Coen Brothers: Interviews with Filmmakers*. Ed. William Rodney Allen. Mississippi: University Press of Mississippi, 2006. 109–118. Print.

Coen, Joel, and Ethan Coen. *Fargo Screenplay*. London and Boston: Faber and Faber, 1996. Print.

Cohen, Finn. "Noah Hawley on Season 3 of 'Fargo' and a 'Post-Truth World.'" *New York Times*, 21 June 2017. Web. 30 June 2017.

Coughlin, Paul. "The Mark of Cain: *Blood Simple* and *The Man Who Wasn't There*." *Scope* 3 (2005): 1–13. Print.

Coughlin, Paul. "Joel and Ethan Coen." *Senses of Cinema* Issue, 26 May 2003. Web. 10 Oct. 2015.

Fienberg, Daniel. "Noah Hawley Breaks Down Season 3 Violence and the Coen Brothers' Influences." *Hollywood Reporter*, 19 Apr. 2017. Web. 30 June 2017.

Fuller, Graham. "Do Not Miss *Fargo*: Interview with the Coens, March 1996." *Blood Siblings*. Ed. Paul A Woods. London: Plexus Publishing, 2000. 144–148. Print.

Garcia, Alberto N. "A Storytelling Machine: The Complexity and Revolution of Narrative Television." *Between* 6.11 (2016): 1–25. Print.

Geraghty, Christine. *Now a Major Motion Picture: Film Adaptations of Literature and Drama*. Maryland: Rowman, 2007. Print.

Gill, James. "The Coen Brothers on the Fargo TV Series: 'We're Just Not Very Interested.'" *Radio Times*, 22 Feb. 2016. Web. 30 June 2017.

Goodman, Tim. "Fargo: TV Review." *The Hollywood Reporter*, 4 Nov. 2016. Web. 30 June 2017.

Grossman, Julie. *Literature, Film and Their Hideous Progeny: Adaptation and ElasTEXTity*. Houndmills and New York: Palgrave Macmillan, 2015. Print.

———. "Fargos." *Adaptation in Visual Culture: Images, Texts, and Their Multiple Worlds*. Eds. Julie Grossman and R. Barton Palmer. Houndmills: Palgrave Macmillan, 2018. 193–212. Print.

Hart, Hugh. "Cinematographer Found that Retro Vibe in Light and Color for 'Fargo.'" *Los Angeles Times*, 23 June 2016. Web. 30 June 2016.

Hawley, Noah. "'Fargo' Boss Reveals What Ethan Coen Really Thought About the Pilot." *The Hollywood Reporter*, 5 Dec. 2014. Web. 15 Jan. 2016.

Hawley, Noah. *Fargo*. The Littlefield Company, MGM, FX Network. Production Draft of Script for Episode 1 (3 Apr. 2013). Air date 15 Apr. 2014.

Innocenti, Veronica, and Pascatore, Guglielmo. "Changing Series: Narrative Models and the Role of the Viewer in Contemporary Television Seriality." *Between* 4.8 (2014): 1–15. Print.

Jess-Cooke, Carolyn, and Constantine Verevis. Eds. *Second Takes: Critical Approaches to the Film Sequel*. Albany, NY: SUNY Press, 2010. Print.

Kaufman, Debra. "'Fargo' on FX: Returning to the Scene of the Coen Brothers' Crime(s)." *Creative Planet Network*, 18 Apr. 2014. Web. 30 June 2016.

Klein, Amanda Ann, and R. Barton Palmer. Eds. *Cycles, Sequels, Spin-Offs, Remakes, and Reboots*. Austin: University of Texas Press, 2016. Print.

Leitch, Thomas. "Mind the Gaps." *Adaptation in Visual Culture: Images, Texts, and Their Multiple Worlds*. Eds. Julie Grossman and R. Barton Palmer. London: Palgrave Macmillan, 2017. 53–72. Print.

Luhr, William G. Ed. *The Coen Brothers' Fargo*. Cambridge: Cambridge University Press, 2004. Print.

———. "Fargo: Far Returned from the Stereotypes of..." *The Coen Brothers' Fargo*. Ed. William G. Luhr. Cambridge: Cambridge University Press, 2004. 92–108. Print.

McFarlane, Brian. *Novel to Film: An Introduction to the Theory of Adaptation*. Oxford: Clarendon Press, 1996. Print.

Murphet, Julian. "O Coens What Art Thou? Auteurism in Today's Hollywood." *The Conversation*, 12 May 2014. Web. 15 Jan. 2016.

Newman, Michael Z. *Indie: An American Film Culture*. New York: Columbia University Press, 2011. Print.

O'Falt, Chris. "The Coen Brothers Rules: 4 Filmmaking Practices That Give 'Fargo' its Cinematic Consistency." *IndieWire*, 15 June 2017. Web. 5 Aug. 2017.

Palmer, R. Barton. *Joel and Ethan Coen*. Urbana and Chicago: University of Illinois Press, 2004. Print.

———. "Continuation, Adaptation Studies, and the Never-Finished Text." *Adaptation in Visual Culture: Images, Texts, and Their Multiple Worlds*. Eds. Julie Grossman and R. Barton Palmer. Houndmills: Palgrave Macmillan, 2017. 73–100. Print.

Roberts, Les. "Landscapes in the Frame: Exploring the Hinterlands of the British Procedural Drama." *New Review of Film and Television Studies* 14.3 (2016): 364–385. Print.

Robson, Eddie. "From *Hudsucker Proxy* to *Fargo*: A Different Concept, a Different Kind of Film." *Postscript: Essays in Film and the Humanities* 27.2 (2008): 72–82. Print.

Scahill, Andrew. "Serialized Killers: Prebooting Horror in *Bates Motel* and *Hannibal*." *Cycles, Sequels, Spin-Offs, Remakes, and Reboots*. Eds. Amanda Klein and R. Barton Palmer. Austin: University of Texas Press, 2016. 316–334. Print.

Sherrirr, "*Fargo* in Context: the Middle of Nowhere?" *The Coen Brothers' Fargo*. Ed. William G. Luhr. Cambridge: Cambridge University Press, 2004. 10–32. Print.

Silverman, Jonathan. "Up Close and Distant: The Coen Brothers' Sense of Place." *Journal of American Studies Association of Texas* 38 (2007): 31–38. Print.

Snee, Brian J. "Soft-Boiled Cinema: Joel and Ethan Coens' Neo-Classical Neo-Noirs." *Literature Film Quarterly* 37.3 (2009): 212–223. Print.

Stam, Robert. "Beyond Fidelity: The Dialogics of Adaptation." *Film Adaptation*. Ed. James Naremore. New Brunswick: Rutgers UP, 2000. 54–78. Print.

The Playlist Staff. "The Essentials: The 15 Best-Shot Roger Deakins Films." *The Playlist*, 7 Sep. 2015. Web. 20 Jan 2016.
The Writer's Panel, *Variety*. "A Night in the Writers' Room: Drama Panel with Brian Lowry." *YouTube*, 13 June 2013. Web. Oct. 2015.
Verevis, Constantine. *Film Remakes*. Edinburgh: Edinburgh University Press, 2006. Print.
Ward, Sarah. "Movies Making Myths: *Kumiko, the Treasure Hunter*." *Metro Magazine* 184 (2015): 61–64. Print.
Willmore, Alison. "Why There's No Marge in FX's 'Fargo' Series, and What Made Billy Bob Thornton Believe That Television Is Now 'Where It's at.'" *IndieWire*, 16 Jan. 2014. Web. 20 Jan. 2016.
Yeoman, Kevin. "How *Fargo* Season 3 Found its Distinct Look." *Screen Rant*, 19 Apr. 2017. Web. 5 Aug. 2017.
Zhou, Tony. "Joel & Ethan Coen- Shot/Reverse Shot." *Vimeo*, 2015. Web. Oct. 2015.

Screenography

TV
12 Monkeys (2015–, US: Syfy).
American Horror Story (2011–, US: FX).
Bates Motel (2013–2017, US: A & E).
Fargo Seasons 1–3 (2014–, US: FX).
Fargo (Pilot 1997–, Canada: Trio).
Hannibal (2013–2015, US: NBC).
Legion (2017–, US: FX).
Mildred Pierce (2011, US: HBO).
Nikita (2010–2013, US: The CW).
Shutter Island (In Production, US: HBO).
Taken (2017–, US: NBC).
Terminator: The Sarah Connor Chronicles (2008–2009, US: FOX).
The Departed (In Production, US: AMAZON).
This is a True Story (2003, UK: Channel 4).
True Detective (2014–, US: HBO).
Westworld (2016–, US: HBO).
Wolf Creek (2016–, Australia: STAN).

Film
Barton Fink. Dirs. Joel and Ethan Coen. 1991.
Blood Simple. Dirs. Joel and Ethan Coen. 1984.
Burn After Reading. Dirs. Joel and Ethan Coen. 2008.
Carrie. Dir. Brian d Palma. 1976.

Close Encounters of the Third Kind. Dir. Steven Spielberg. 1977.
Fargo. Dirs. Joel and Ethan Coen. 1996.
He Walked by Night. Dir. Alfred L. Werker. 1948.
Inside Llewyn Davies. Dirs. Joel and Ethan Coen. 2013.
Kumiko, The Treasure Hunter. Dir. David Zellner. 2014.
Millers Crossing. Dirs. Joel and Ethan Coen. 1990.
No Country for Old Men. Dirs. Joel and Ethan Coen. 2007.
O Brother Where Art Thou. Dirs. Joel and Ethan Coen. 2000.
Point Blank. Dir. John Boorman. 1967.
Psycho. Dir. Alfred Hitchcock. 1960.
Raising Arizona. Dirs. Joel and Ethan Coen. 1987.
Star Wars. Dir. George Lucas. 1977.
The Assassination of Jessie James by the Coward Robert Ford. Dir. Andrew Dominik. 2007.
The Big Lebowski. Dirs. Joel and Ethan Coen. 1998.
The Getaway. Dir. Sam Peckinpah. 1972.
The Man Who Wasn't There. Dirs. Joel and Ethan Coen. 2001.

CHAPTER 4

Orange Is the New Black as 'Living Text': From Memoir to TV Series

4.1 Introduction

Piper Kerman's prison memoir, *Orange is the New Black*, focuses on a specific period in time during which she was incarcerated in a federal penitentiary for a drug-related crime committed in her early twenties. Kerman's detailed observations, couched through the intimate filter of the memoir form, expose the inadequacies and injustices of a punitive prison system and its impact on the lived experience of women of varied race, creed, sexual preference and class. It is a text that lends itself to further in-depth exploration of that lived experience and herein lies its major appeal to the would-be adapter. First published in 2010, its transition to screen swiftly followed; with seasoned TV scriptwriter, Jenji Kohan (*Weeds*, 2005–2012), securing Kerman's permission to adapt her memoir for television, its release as a seven-season Netflix Original commenced in 2013. The series is by no means a 'faithful' adaptation of Kerman's life experience. Rather, it is an imaginative extension thereof: one that builds a fiction around character types and events noted in the memoir, engaging at the level of dramedy and comedy with the pressing social issues that inform Kerman's writing. At an intertextual level, the series is constantly in dialogue with screen texts that precede it, with the paratexts that continue to circulate it before, during and after each season release. As a prison narrative, it employs the tropes of the Women in Prison genre, and it shares the generic DNA of its cinematic and its televisual forerunners; as a populist female-centred narrative, often of a comedic bent and aimed at a mainstream female-centred TV audience, it becomes part of a body of televisual texts that dramatise contemporaneous female experience within a contemporaneous production context. But even as it speaks to other texts, through purposeful allusion and inference, *Orange is the New Black* subverts anticipated paradigms, taking the Women in Prison genre into new narrative territory, constructing a different and a more inclusive kind of female representation on screen.

4.2 'Every Sentence Is a Story': The TV Rewrite

Orange is the New Black is in part an adaptation of Kerman's experience of life within America's female prison system; however, while Kohan takes her narrative lead from the memoir, she asserts her intention, as series creator and primary adapter of *Orange is the New Black*, to move beyond its narrative boundaries, taking creative liberties with the text and using Kerman's observations as a springboard for a more detailed exploration of the lives of incarcerated women. In pursuit of conflict and character complexity, and as a means to creating engaging drama, Kohan shapes a narrative that revolves around the lives of women of varied race, ethnicity, sexuality and class, Kerman's memoir serving as 'a launching point' rather than a fixed narrative template. According to Kohan, Kerman remains 'the mother of all this', and she is afforded a writing credit on every episode, but as showrunner it was always Kohan's intention to 'veer left', taking the narrative 'in its own direction' (Kohan in Radish). From the outset, Kohan demonstrated 'this wasn't going to be …the story of Piper Chapman' (Kohan cited in McHugh 22) or Kerman, her real-life counterpart, but that of the incarcerated women Chapman interacts with during her time in prison. Chapman is but one of many complex female characters to emerge in a series that presents a kaleidoscopic range of female experience by foregrounding the narratives of the collective rather than the trials and tribulations of the white middle-class woman at the centre of the memoir that is being adapted. The prison environment represents, Kohan contends, one of the 'very few crossroads' left where 'you can slam really disparate people up against one another'; it is, she notes, a 'space' where the mythical cultural 'melting pot' becomes a rare reality of a kind that lends itself to further dramatisation (Kohan in Gross). By switching the narrative from the more reserved 'I' of memoir and its measured observations to focus instead on emotive universal relationship stories noted yet not developed in the memoir—stories centred on mothers and daughters, on innate desire for tribal/familial bonding and on supportive friendships and the elusive search for some kind of 'faith'—Kohan extends the scope of the narrative beyond its origins as memoir, foregrounding normative lesbian visibility and sexual relationships as well as addressing the issue of transgender experience as part of that transition process. As the Season One tag line so aptly notes, 'every sentence' is ripe for further narrative development at both a literal level and a metaphorical level and Kohan mines the prose of the memoir for points of potential fictional cultivation during its transition to the televisual platform. For the screen adapter, the interiority of the first person 'voice' is always problematic when narrative is transitioning from written text to the exteriority of the visual medium, but the shift from the 'I' of memoir is made less problematic by the fact that it is rooted in the context of place and external interaction as opposed to the highly individualised and internalised thought processes of autobiography.

Fictitious character, Piper Chapman, is loosely based on the Kerman of the memoir, but for Kerman and Kohan, she remains a distinct entity who has attained a fictional identity and narrative trajectory that goes beyond the parameters of Kerman's self-representation. Piper Chapman is initially introduced as series' protagonist and her story is presented as a prison 'coming of age' narrative that, over the course of the first four seasons, narrates her journey from naïve, self-absorbed 'yuppie' of limited standing within this all-female prison community to experienced prison inmate who eventually learns to accept her place within its self-styled hierarchy. Kohan builds a comprehensive picture of Piper through not only a series of backstories that relate intermittently her childhood and her experimental post-college years with her lesbian lover, Alex Vause, but through her more recent relationships with her family, partner Larry, her friend Polly and her brother while at the same time providing her audience with an ensemble cast of performers whose backstories represent very different experiences to those of this 'safe' and familiar white, middle-class WASP. Chapman provides 'a yuppie's eye view' of an alien prison environment for the series' predominantly white middle-class demographic and serves as the series' 'gateway drug' to open up access to the wide array of incarcerated women's stories that Kohan builds from the seeds of the memoir and beyond (Kohan in Radish). The pilot episode's opening montage involves numerous scenes depicting the life of Piper Chapman, accompanied by her guiding voiceover narration—a narration that functions as the cinematic equivalent of the memoir's personalised voice. It is, however, swiftly relinquished once the montage enters prison space and is not employed again throughout the series run. The use of voiceover in narratives such as *Sex and the City* (1998–2004) provides an ongoing framework that filters viewing experience through the personal lens of one individual, in that instance the show's protagonist, Carrie Bradshaw, but in *Orange is the New Black*, Kohan constructs a wider frame of reference for the stories about to unfold. Though Piper serves as 'Trojan horse' (Kohan in Gross) in its opening episodes, her experiences become part of the wider fabric of the narrative as Season One draws to a close, and at Kohan's insistence the show's signature credits sequence, in which the narrative was originally framed from Piper Chapman's point of view, was replaced with a montage of over seventy women's faces, all of whom have served time in a state penitentiary (McHugh 22).

Like Kerman, Kohan draws attention to women in prison and their particular predicament via the filter of shared experience; both writers explore the incarcerated female's desire to belong and to connect, ways to resist and yet, more often, ways to endure arbitrary authority and the injustices of the system. Kohan refers to the series as her own brand of non-didactic activism (Kohan in McClelland). True to its generic form, Kerman's prison memoir focuses on observation of life experience within prison confines and within a clearly delineated time frame—one that ends with her release from prison fifteen months later—and there are few references to life outside the prison environment or her relationship with her partner and family members. However, the story universe of *Orange is the New Black* extends beyond the confines of the prison environment depicted in Kerman's memoir, and the series' emotively charged backstories of incarcerated women and their families add other dimensions to its social critique of the prison system. Within the collaborative context of the writers room, led by Kohan as series showrunner, an ever-evolving fictional universe peopled by both constant and newly arriving inmates evolves; unlike the memoir, the TV series has no clear point of closure and can be added to ad infinitum across its projected seven-season story arc as the narrative shifts progressively away from the series' initial focus on WASP protagonist, Piper Chapman. Chapman remains a central part of the series' narrative momentum but by shifting the focus of the narrative from the 'I' of Kerman's memoir to the collective and individual experiences of the inmates Kerman interacts with, Kohan sustains our interest in her fictitious story world across years rather than the fifteen-month span of Kerman's memoir.

The series recurring credit sequence signals from the outset its ongoing nonlinear approach to storytelling; it employs what McHugh terms a 'horizontal' rather than a 'vertical axis' and a suitably 'reversible semantic flow' in which the various faces projected during the credit sequence are interchangeable (21). Shifting narrative momentum is presented as a given as the cycle of imprisonment is perpetuated indefinitely. In *Orange is the New Black*, the device of the recurring flashback is employed by Kohan as a means to creating complex characterisation across a wide-ranging community of imprisoned women from varying socio-economic and ethnic backgrounds. These backstories are tangential to the prison narrative's forward momentum, functioning instead as a means to spinning out the story universe but they help us to make sense of current actions, current preoccupations and relationships taking place within the story's mainframe and thus serve to create further layers of character complexity. Unlike the traditional Women in Prison genre in both its screen and memoir form the narrative shifts from the present-day fictional world of the prison correctional institution to a series of ongoing stories that move back in time, taking the viewer outside prison confines and presenting narratives that explore the circumstances leading up to the criminal act that results in the individual's incarceration. While the flashback may traditionally replace voiceover as a means to cueing and framing past events and inviting empathy (Grishakova and Ryan 88), its function in *Orange is the New Black* is much more complex. In this series, Kohan creates connections between current events taking place within the prison walls and those unfolding in the flashback scenarios relating to the lives of thirty female inmates over the course of the show's first five seasons; they both cue a past event and add further layers of complexity to the current moment. Some character backstories unravel over the duration of its five-season story arc, others are dealt with as one-off cameo scenarios that give us more limited background information. Season Three in particular rolls out the latter type of condensed pre-prison vignette recounting the disparate stories of Marisol 'Flaca' Gonzalez (5.3), Mei Chang (6.3), Norma Romano (7.3) and Leanne Taylor (9.3), while the one-off backstories of Maritza Ramos (5.4) and Lolly Whitehill (7.4) appear in Season Four, each detailing the crime that has led to their incarceration. But the series entails a far more complex take on the backstories of characters who, in addition to Piper Chapman, prove to be central to the narrative's momentum, or whose popularity warrants their further development as in the case of Poussey Washington, an initially minor character brought into the narrative's mainframe in response to favourable audience reception post-Season One.

One of the most detailed narratives developed by Kohan focuses on the life experiences of Season One villain Tiffany 'Pennsatucky' Doggett, written of in Kerman's memoir as one of the 'Eminemlettes' from 'the wrong side of the tracks' (156): an unstable crack addict serving two years for a minor drug-related offence, described as a 'lost girl' (247) who is 'perceptive and sensitive' despite her bravado (198). From such seeds, Kohan builds Doggett's fictitious life and prison experience, as presented through progressively revealing flashbacks that, in a purposefully nonlinear fashion, explore not only the crime for which she is now incarcerated but her impoverished upbringing. She is introduced in Season One as the evangelical anti-abortionist 'white-trash' villain of the series, imprisoned for the cold-blooded murder of a nurse at an anti-abortion clinic, but Kohan then adds to the paradoxical complexity of Doggett's crime through her opening backstory in which she is exposed as a serial abortionist, her criminal act the end product of rage and emotional indifference as opposed to moral outrage of the kind her anti-abortion league protectionists afford her (12.1). But her position as the prerequisite villain of Seasons One and Two is, however, gradually undermined via a series of sound-bite flashbacks that explore the social context of her 'white trash' upbringing. Her relationship with her exploitative mother is first introduced in the formative moments of Season Three (1.3) and her narrative goes on to dominate in episode ten through a sequence of backstories that intertwine her present prison experience with her past experience, building in particular a picture of her bewildering relationship with sex. Within the more tightly framed structure of one episode (10.3), compassion for Doggett is gradually layered into the narrative as the audience becomes increasingly aware that, in her past as well as in her present prison experience, she has been a victim of rape. The flashbacks in episode ten begin with her mother's advice to her ten-year-old daughter to view sex as 'a bee sting, something to get through', before cutting back to the present-day prison scenario, detailing what at first seem harmless, almost romantic moments shared with prison guard Charlie 'Donut' Coates. A further shift in flashback time to her teenage years details what we assume is the one romantic and sexually fulfilling relationship she has experience of, before the sequence concludes with the departure of her lover and the graphic depiction of her rape by a former sexual partner. In the closing moments of episode ten, we edit back to Doggett's current experience of rape at the hands of Donut, her disturbing backstory serving as a revelatory prelude to her present relationship with her rapist. This kind of storytelling strategy with its 'reversible semantic flow' and 'horizontal axis' (McHugh 21) has become synonymous with Kohan's complex approach to dramatisation of the lives of prominent characters in the series. Strategically positioned for maximum impact at various points throughout the narrative, the backstories play out alongside present-day prison narratives that connect with the former lives of these inmates on some level, Doggett's being withheld for dramatic purposes until Season Three at which point Kohan undermines viewer perception of Doggett as series' villain.

4.3 Dipping into the Gene Pool

Genre is one of several interpretive processes at work in the adaptation of text to screen; it sets up expectations, provides a viewing context and establishes connections with earlier iterations of narratives, ensuring a certain level of continuity between what has gone before and what comes after. More significantly, adaptations maintain a complex intertextual relationship with their generic forerunners: all are drawing from the same gene pool at some level, even though those genes are often mutated during the adaptive process. *Orange is the New Black* transcends generic boundaries, operating as an amalgamation of many yet it remains firmly within the purview of melodrama, despite its liberal use of comedy as a storytelling strategy.

TV adaptations like *Orange is the New Black* operate within what Mittell terms a 'discursive cluste[r]' (11) that in this instance mixes the Women in Prison genre with comedy and melodrama. It is what Guglielmo and Pescatore term 'a "hard core" version of the classic women's show' (5), though classified in industry terms as both 'dramedy' and 'comedy'. Despite the opening season's numerous EMMY awards and nominations in 2014 for its comedic rather than its dramatic properties, it was reclassified as an entry into the drama category in subsequent years and has been submitted as drama in other awards events like The Golden Globe Awards since its inception. Its comedic properties are, like melodrama, a facet of its modus operandi rather than its overriding generic identity. Each contributes to the series' unique style, and the tonal shifts between those two modes become part of its style signature throughout its five-season run thus far. Moreover, both are storytelling modes traditionally employed in the telling of female-centred narratives on screen—narratives that become part of the series' intertextual frame of reference. Its content, however, places it firmly within the parameters of the Women in Prison genre—a genre framed by its *own* unique set of traditional tropes and characterised by its hybridity. Its capacity to defy neat genre definition is, argues Netflix Chief Content Officer, Ted Sarandos, one of its strengths as 'a truly pioneering series' (Andreeva).

Kohan adapts not only Kerman's memoir but the tropes of the Women in Prison genre, reshaping and subverting said tropes in accordance with her own creative agenda for an audience more likely to be familiar with this genre than with the prison memoir that has inspired the series. Regarded as 'one of the most enduring genres in twentieth century American popular culture' (Ciasullo Containing 218), the Women in Prison genre is a formulaic, popular and populist classification that has traditionally been associated with sexploitation cinema and soft-core pornography (Millbank 160). From its earliest pre-Hays Code cinema iterations, it has been considered a low-budget and marginal genre, marked by risqué content that often constructs images of the 'fallen woman' as one of its central tenets. Its subject matter and the dramatic potential of its socio-situational context continue to attract mainstream audiences but it first thrived as a cinematic genre in the fifties when films like *Caged* (1950) addressed matters of female victimhood and repression within a system in need of reform (Bouclin 29). Yet even in this staple of the genre, produced within the moralistic context of fifties America, mainstream cinema's preoccupation with heterosexual romance is *subverted* by a subplot that focuses instead on female relationships and female-driven plotlines that generate other kinds of discourse around women. The 1970s marks a resurgence of the Women in Prison genre through the release of low-budget sexploitation films like Roger Corman's *Women in Cages* (1971), *The Big Bird Cage* (1972) and *Caged Heat* (1974), and the popularity of the genre as sexploitation cinema extends through to the late 1980s and early 1990s with the release of films like *Chained Heat* (1983) and *Chained Heat II* (1993). Several TV films also contribute to the genre and its risqué female-centred content. Swiftly adapted from a memoir of the same name 1973 prison memoir, *Born Innocent* (1974), starring Linda Blair one year after her iconic role as possessed child Regan in *The Exorcist*, explores the lives of girls in a reform school and presents a graphic and controversial scene detailing the gang rape of a fourteen-year-old inmate. Cheryl Dunye's TV movie *Stranger Inside* (2001) shifts the focus from the mainly white female protagonist of the genre to a black female protagonist; with its 'feminist agenda' and its narrative focus on a mother/daughter relationship, the film serves as one of many intertexts at play in Kohan's series (McHugh 28). Though traditionally more prominent in cinema than television, there have also been a number of populist yet groundbreaking TV series set in prisons since the mid-seventies. Within the microcosm of the patriarchally controlled prison setting, Kohan, her contemporaries and her predecessors are able to construct narratives that focus on female collectives of different class, colour, creed and age, placed in a shared position of inequality. From *Within These Walls* (1974–1978) and *Prisoner* (1979–1986, known on UK release as *Prisoner: Cell Block H*), to *Bad Girls* (1999–2006) which led the genre's revival at the turn of the millennium and set the scene for two current series—*Wentworth*, the remake of *Prisoner* released in 2013, and *Orange is the New Black*—the genre remains a part of mainstream culture, and it continues to engage with feminist issues within a decidedly populist frame of reference. The female prison remains a setting that presents 'fertile ground' for 'feminist authors' (Millbank 161) and as with all narratives associated with the Women in Prison genre, the majority of these screen texts, regardless of era and delivery platform, foreground the female collective over and above the individual.

Kohan employs the formulaic tropes of the Women in Prison genre during its transition from prison memoir to TV series but she destabilises and parodies many of its underlying attributes, creating a prison narrative that, even as it intertextualises its generic predecessors, operates outside the genre's anticipated conventions. Though she sees the series in general and its opening shower scene montage in particular as intentional 'homage' to the prison narratives that precede it, she also attests to her desire to 'subvert the paradigm' and to avoid some of its more tired clichés (Kohan in Willmore). Given the scope of a seven-season story arc, Kohan is also able to explore in greater depth and complexity the genre's varied yet somewhat limited stereotypes in ways that venture beyond the means of the traditional 90–120 minute Women in Prison film. The white middle-class woman at the centre of Kerman's memoir becomes the genre's seemingly prototypical 'young innocent' who, like *Caged*'s Marie Allen, has no idea of how to operate within an alien prison environment (Schwan 479). However, where the protagonist of the genre is traditionally framed by a generically preordained and passive downward narrative trajectory that sees her slowly consumed by the system, the narrative path of Kohan's Piper, who is neither 'innocent' of her crime nor inclined to passivity, is far more complex. Piper Chapman's crime, like that of memoir writer Kerman, is not actioned by the conventional call to support a male love interest but a female one, and she is not unwittingly involved in the drug-smuggling enterprise for which she is imprisoned, or simply caught in the wrong place at the wrong time. The heteronormative sexual positioning of the Women in Prison genre's lead is challenged and complicated here by Piper's already declared lesbian past, and the five-season on-off relationship between fictional Piper and Alex Vause bears little resemblance to that of Kerman and her lover, Nora, who in the memoir emerges as a 'figure of intrigue', a member of 'a clique of impossibly cool and stylish lesbians' with whom Kerman is only momentarily aligned (5), and whose appeal is in part attributed to Kerman's desire to rebel against her safe, middle-class upbringing. There is no return to the familial heteronormative fold of the fifties Women in Prison film for Piper Chapman as Kohan amplifies the lesbian relationship that is less overtly acknowledged in Kerman's memoir, creating an ongoing lesbian romance subplot that plays out across the seasons alongside her heterosexual relationship with Larry in seasons one and two only. Where Kerman's relationship with her male partner is recorded in the memoir as one that remains in place during and post-prison term, Kohan, as adapter, intervenes taking creative liberties with the source text in the service of dramatic conflict. Here, the 'love of a good man' is forsaken in favour of a rekindled attraction to a 'bad woman'.

Piper Chapman encounters the stereotypical characters of the Women in Prison genre: the 'older mother-figure', the 'mentally disturbed woman', the 'butch lesbian', the benevolent and/or malevolent warden/prison guard (Mayne 115). However, in *Orange is the New Black*, stock characters of the genre become more nuanced character studies, and contrary to the more sensationalistic and exploitative elements of the Women in Prison genre, most of the female prisoners who populate the narrative of the memoir and the TV series are incarcerated for minor offences, many as a consequence of their involvement in the drugs trade in a contemporary America preoccupied with its war on drugs. Similarly, the genre's representation of the singular butch dyke, traditionally present yet invariably marginalised, is replaced by a more normative and inclusive approach to lesbian visibility. The genre's preoccupation with the 'mother-figure', for example, becomes one of the series' ongoing story arcs, providing thematic links across seasons. Building on references found in Kerman's memoir and on the melodramatic tropes of the family melodrama, Kohan constructs a number of the Women in Prison genre's tribally based 'mother-figures', and in keeping with the tropes of the genre, all such 'mothers' are involved in organised 'crime' within the prison system to varying degrees. 'Good' mother Galina 'Red' Reznikov (based on Kerman's 'Pop', 73) is leader of the Caucasian tribe and the 'benevolent' provider of black market goods. As a means to validating Red's role as prison 'mother' and provider of black market goods (8.1), Kohan introduces a series of fictitious backstories that reveal Red's mafia affiliations. 'Bad' mother drug dealer Yvonne 'Vee' Parker, who represents the other 'motherly' extreme, is afforded a similar series of backstory moments that underscore her Machiavellian tendencies both in and out of a prison context. But Kohan complicates the trope of the prison mother in several ways. Piper's inception of the Felonious Spunk dirty panties enterprise in Season Three presents a comic subversion of the 'mother' trope. Piper's 'mothering' of her 'tribe' is of a different kind that works on a purely capitalist model of a type seldom seen in the genre; fealty to her criminal enterprise is dependent solely upon material reward and its failure demonstrates the system's reliance on family loyalty to the genre's 'mother figure' whose leadership of the tribe is predicated on more than personal gain. Unlike prison mothers Red, Vee and Maria Diaz, the newly affirmed 'mother' of the Dominican inmates who launches a successful takeover of Piper's dirty panties business, or Taystee, who emerges in Season Three as the good 'mother' of Vee's former 'tribe', Piper is unable to control her 'family' and her criminal empire crumbles. Kerman's more enlightened yet equally absent female warden, Kuma Deboo, is transformed in the TV series into Natalie (Fig) Figueroa, a successful neoliberal post-feminist career woman and parodic 'mother' figure who shows no 'maternal' interest in her charges' welfare and intervenes only in matters that may become a PR issue or that impact her capacity to syphon off funds for her husband's political campaigning.

Given its social agenda and the nature of its story content, melodramatic realism remains central to the narrative strategies employed in *Orange is the New Black*, but its melodramatic identity exists alongside its identity as comedy, and its frame of reference remains decidedly populist. For Kohan, comedy provides a much needed foil to the dramatic intensity of the memoir's dark content and its focus on the social injustices inherent in the current system. Humour, she argues, is a survival technique employed by individuals in 'even in the most horrific situations', and as a writer she harnesses humour as a means to highlighting 'the pathos and the struggle' that informs the series' disturbing narratives, intentionally 'slam[ming] it up against drama' to 'mak[e] both shine' (Kohan in Radish). Whether labelled comedy or dramedy, comedic moments form an intrinsic part of the series' style signature; in contrast, though Kerman employs the occasional humorous anecdote, comedy is not employed as a vehicle for communicating her response to either her own prison experiences or those of her fellow inmates in her memoir. The series frequently references other populist narratives in general[1] and those affiliated with the prison genre in particular, providing tongue-in-cheek intertextual references to screen texts that have gone before. Piper's sardonic referencing of sexploitation films *Chained Heat* and *Cellblock Sisters* undermines the popular perception that female prisoners' lives are dominated by 'lesbian sex and strip searches and naked cat fights in the shower' (7.3), while reference to films like *Cool Hand Luke* (1967, 7.4) and *The Shawshank Redemption* (1994, 3.4) pepper the script, and in a comedic nod to populist television series *Breaking Bad* Piper is reminded by her brother Cal that, despite her perception of herself as some kind of gangster leader of their illegal dirty panties enterprise, she's 'not Walter White yet' (13.3). There are few series that employ a comedic treatment of the Women in Prison genre; *Women in Prison* ran for one season (1987–1988), and contemporary web series *Kittens in a Cage!* (funded through Kickstart), is a comedic parody of the genre, but *Orange is the New Black* is the only long-running series of critical and populist acclaim that adapts the comedic tropes of female-centred narratives within the darker narrative template of the genre. Addressing matters as diverse as the systematic abuse of power in Season One, the commodification and exploitation of female labour in Season Three and Season Four, or the chaotic horrors of a prison riot in Season Five, Kohan and the series' writing team frequently explore disturbing issues through the lens of comedy.

---

[1] Litchfield's inmates remain engaged with popular culture, alluding in their conversations to pop cult icons like Beyonce and J. Lo (13.3) and to TV series like *Outlander* (2014, 13.2) and films from the *Harry Potter* franchise (2001–2011, 1.3).

4.3.1 The Women in Prison Genre as Comedy

As a mode, comedy is historically connected to the construction of a female subject position in mainstream television, and *Orange is the New Black* remains in dialogue with the many female-centred comedic television series that have preceded it. Since the advent of television back in the early fifties comedic series that foreground female protagonists—from *I Love Lucy* (1951–57) to *The Mary Tyler Moore Show* (1970–77), *Murphy Brown* (1988–98) to *Roseanne* (1988–97), *Ally McBeal* (1997–2002) to *Sex and the City*—have used comedy to challenge and disrupt established gender hierarchies (Rowe 1995; Dow 1996; Lotz 2001; Gray and Lotz 2012), and the sitcom has long been regarded as the genre 'from which tv's most resonant female representations have emerged' (Dow xviii). Though still confined in many ways, the women at the centre of such series provide a female subject position that has the capacity to confront gender-based limitations, even if the narrative's subversive material must be filtered and presented through the non-threatening vehicle of comedy. Kohan's use of comedy as a strategy for subversion is particularly apt given the double-edged confinement of the women at the centre of her narrative; their incarceration in an all-female environment amplifies their female subject position, their identity as women who have *already* challenged dominant hierarchies and systems a given since all are serving time for crimes against the state. Kohan takes the more subdued treatment of female representation found in Kerman's memoir to its unruly extremes, using comedy as a catalyst for her construction of women who choose not to conform to society's gendered expectations. Many of her female characters display an affinity with the figure of the 'unruly woman', defined in Kathleen Rowe's seminal study of women and television as one epitomised by womanly excess and whose 'female outrageousness and transgression' disrupts the dominant hierarchy; she is large, loud and outspoken, and she vocalises her discontent through humour (82–86). Comedian Roseanne Barr of the 1980s sitcom *Roseanne* presents as *one* such 'unruly woman' who challenges societal norms and expectations (82), but in *Orange is the New Black*, Kohan presents a host of 'unruly women' of various types who are intertextually connected to comedic counterparts who have gone before, their unruly status intrinsically shaped by earlier acts of outrageous resistance found in wide-ranging television series that identify as sitcoms.

Several women in *Orange is the New Black* (e.g. Boo, Cindy, Taystee or Red) qualify as 'unruly' under Rowe's terms, but Kohan builds on notions of female transgression and outrageousness by presenting women whose challenge to normative femininity comes through other means too. Boo, played by lesbian comedian Lea Del Ray, serves as the series' most overtly unruly woman: even within the confines of the series' prison context in which lesbianism is defined as a normative sexual position, her persona operates at the extremes of butch dyke representation, signalling 'transgression'. Fellow lesbian Nikki Nicholls emerges as a witty comedic agitator, a new kind of 'unruly woman', who, like Boo, confronts and challenges expectation through her openly sexual appetite. A parodic treatment of sexual game-playing is initiated and sustained throughout the second season by these two 'unruly' women who take up a position more readily associated with predatory male bravado as they embark on a 'Bing-off' competition to see who can seduce the most women. Couched here as comedic parody, Boo's claim that Nikki takes too long to bring her partners to a point of climax illustrates the distasteful nature of sexual bravado, Boo bragging that all it should take is 'two in the pink and one in the stink.' (3.2). The unruly woman's association with 'liminality, boundaries and taboos' that evoke disgust and fear, is again parodied in the series via Kohan's fictitious creation of lesbophobic prison counsellor Sam Healy who regards lesbians as the root of chaos and 'unruliness', their errant behaviour posing a challenge to the very existence of men. The series' depiction of female sexual desire and agency among older women is also both affirmation of a taboo female subject position and a parodic treatment of other female-centred shows such as *Sex and the City*. 'Desire' and 'transgression' (Rowe 83) are mined for comedic potential via moments of frank sexual discussion between older inmates Red and Sister Ingalls (13.2) that are far more shocking and thus challenging than those of Carrie Bradshaw and her well-heeled friends in the frequent moments of sexual frankness that characterise a text like *Sex and the City*. Having instigated a drug-fuelled threesome with prison guard Luschek and Yoga Jones, the series' imprisoned, celebrity chef Judy King breaks similar sexual taboos, defending her position as an older woman who enjoys sex and who out-rightly refuses to be 'desexualized' (11.4). She is, in Rowe's terms, the 'old crone' who 'refuses to become invisible' and who as a consequence is invariably considered 'grotesque' (31).

But it is Kohan's capacity to conflate the comedic and the tragic in her construction of the unruly woman that takes her series into a new and darkly subversive terrain. Post-op transgender figure Sophia Burset crosses the border between comedy and pathos via her positioning as an 'unruly woman'. Burset, an accepted member of the prison collective in the first two seasons, becomes the derided, unruly 'carnivalesque' woman (Rowe 83) of seasons three and four. Her biological origins ultimately set her up as a challenge to the perceived norm as empathy turns to antipathy, indifference to the fear and disgust Rowe deems the territory of the unruly woman. Transgender identity has often been included as a comic aside that explores female 'unruliness'—and Samantha Jones' altercation with the noisy transgender women who gather below her apartment window in *Sex and the City* ('Cock-a-Doodle-Do' 18.3) serves as a prime example of just such a treatment—but in Kohan's series, through the microcosm of prison experience, the comic aside is transformed into an in-depth exploration of society's complex response to transgender identity. The story of Sophia Burset's transition from male firefighter to transgender woman is addressed during the early stages of the series (3.1), but rather than dwelling on backstories related to Sophia's sexual transition, Kohan chooses to focus most of her narrative on Sophia's present predicament as a transwoman, exploring her current ongoing relationships with her supportive wife, her antagonistic son and her fellow inmates as her status within the prison system shifts from one of acceptance to rejection. From narrative threads embedded in Kerman's memoir, Vanessa Robinson, briefly noted as a 'full blown diva...male to female transsexual' and former contestant in the Gay Miss America pageant who, when denied her hormone treatment, regresses to the role of 'cheerful drag queen' (206–208), transitions within the series to Sophia Burset who serves as a conduit for media debate surrounding transgender identity. Through this storytelling strategy and the casting of transgender performer, Laverne Cox, whose media presence is sustained before, during and after each series' release, Kohan foregrounds the contemporaneous issue of transgender identity as part of the series' corrective social agenda, providing an added social dimension to the memoir's preoccupation with matters of much needed social reform of the prison system.

4.3.2 The Women in Prison Genre as 'Realist' Melodrama

The female-centred narratives at the heart of *Orange is the New Black* ensure the series may be coded as 'feminine subject matter' (Mittell 247), as do the romance narratives introduced during the course of its five-season run. However, unlike other American prison-based TV series that draw upon the soap opera and its melodramatic treatment of subject matter (Mayne 116), Kohan's series is not affiliated with the much derided TV soap opera genre nor with traditional definitions of melodrama as a genre or mode characterised by emotive excess signalled through loaded mise en scène and theatrically charged musical score. Rather, *Orange is the New Black* aligns itself with the kind of emotive and morally driven narratives employed in today's increasingly complex prime-time TV shows; through their focus on family drama and the centrality of women within their narratives, prestige TV crime series like *The Sopranos* and *Breaking Bad* employ a melodramatic modus operandi regardless of their other generic identities. Linda Williams sees melodrama as a mode of storytelling that has evolved from the 'lingua franca' of popular television's 'episodic melodramas' to contemporary 'multi-season serials' that operate beyond the realms of 'tried-and-true family-saga melodrama' (45) more readily associated with the 'woman's weepie' of cinema and the TV soap opera. Somewhat contentiously and despite the gritty realism of its content and its style aesthetic, Williams redefines groundbreaking TV series *The Wire* as melodrama. At its core it is, she argues, a 'melodramatic quest for moral legibility' at 'the personal and the institutional level' (119), in which realism rather than emotive excess is employed in order to evoke an impassioned response to the injustices of the flawed social institutions explored across its five-season story arc (114). Its exploration of institutional failure and its often Dickensian character constructs demonstrate the ways in which nineteenth-century melodrama connects with complex contemporary serial TV, its tales of the impact of corrupt and inadequate systems on the lives of individuals being equal to the more traditional melodramatic tropes of familial and romantic tragedy, with figures like Bubbles and Wallace presenting as 'Dickensian' modern-day victims of failed social systems (Williams 125). It is an ensemble drama of Dickensian scope that signals further synergies between contemporary realist drama and emotive nineteenth-century storytelling, and it is in this vein of melodrama that *Orange is the New Black* finds its dramatic modus operandi, Kerman's metaphor likening the current prison system to a ship, its 'wheel spinning while the sails fla[p]' (334), visualised on screen by Kohan as a series of systemic failures akin to those explored in David Simons' *The Wire*. Like *The Wire*, *Orange is the New Black* operates within the newly defined realms of 'melodramatic realism' outlined by Williams.

In Kerman's experience, it is America's War on Drugs and its government's 'ineffectual' drug laws, 'unevenly and unfairly enforced based on race and class,' that position America as a country which is 'intellectually and morally bankrupt' (Kerman 205). Her memoir details the experiences of incarcerated women who pass through what she terms the 'revolving door between our urban and our rural ghettos and the formal ghetto of our prison system'—a system that serves as a holding place for 'not only the dangerous but the inconvenient—people who are mentally ill, people who are addicts, people who are poor and uneducated and unskilled' (229). Kohan takes the narrative into darker territory, slowly filtering in details of the crimes of older women like Miss Claudette, Frieda Berlin and Red, all of whom we learn are former inmates of high security due to the murderous nature of their crimes, but the majority of her characters, like those who people Kerman's memoir, are incarcerated for minor infractions and drug-related misdemeanours. Through the creation of backstories, in which the actions of all of her female characters are explored, Kohan provides a rationale behind the crime as a means to ensuring audience empathy with their current predicament, but also as a vehicle for highlighting the inadequacies and failings of the system. The story of Taystee Jefferson's release and swift return to Litchfield Correctional Centre illustrates Kerman's observation that inmates, ill prepared for life outside, are presented with a 'revolving door' between the urban ghetto and the prison ghetto. Similar stories of system abuse prevail. Despite the onset of senile dementia and a broken arm, elderly patient Jimmy is granted early release as a means of alleviating the system's duty of care; deposited at the nearest bus station, she is left to fend for herself (7.2); and inmate Rosa Cisneros is denied an operation essential to her cancer treatment, while Sophia Burset is denied the ongoing hormone treatment she requires as a post-op transwoman. Stories of mentally ill patients lost in the system abound, from that of Suzanne 'Crazy Eyes' Warren and Maureen Kukudio to Lolly Whitehill, all of whom should be receiving psychiatric care outside the parameters of the prison system. The system is also revealed as inhumane in its treatment of mothers and children: pregnant inmates Daya and Maria are separated from their children at birth, while inmates like Maritza and Gloria are denied regular contact with their children due to their incarceration at a correctional facility far from their home state, in Massachusetts and Florida, respectively (5.2).

Like *The Wire*, *Orange is the New Black* presents as a Dickensian ensemble drama, rooted in a mode of melodramatic realism that is engaged in an emotionally charged social critique at the 'institutional level'; however, it remains historically coded as 'feminine subject matter' at the 'personal level', and through the populist medium of television, it facilitates mainstream debate about social injustice. Kohan's homage to Dickens is in part written into the series dialogue: at one point, female guard, Susan Fischer, compares listening into the prisoners' telephone conversations to 'reading Dickens' (6.2), and like Dickens, Kohan employs a similarly strategic comedic treatment of some of her character constructs and some of her storylines. But Kerman's factual recount of life in a women's prison lends itself more readily to a documentary treatment on screen and it is by combining the melodramatic facets of the narrative with a predominantly realist-style aesthetic that Kohan evokes entertaining and emotional engagement with the social injustices that underpin both source text and series. Just as *The Wire* focuses on the shortcomings of criminal justice systems and political systems, *Orange is the New Black* brings to the fore an equally flawed and corrupt correctional system that is presented as a by-product of each. The societal flaws that underpin the life experiences of Dickens' characters and characters like *The Wire's* Bubbles, Wallace and the 'corner kids' of the projects are foregrounded in *Orange is the New Black* through the fictitious creation of dysfunctional 'families' that operate both outside the system and as a consequence of the failures *of* the system. Season Two focuses on black matriarch Vee as the Fagin-like procurer of children the system has failed; taking on the role of 'Artful Dodger' to Vee's Fagin, Taystee, unable to find a foster family and later adequate employment, succumbs to Vee's attempts to recruit her as a member of her drug-running 'family' (2.2). The inadequacies of the system leave individuals like Taystee and fellow members of her dysfunctional 'family' in the hands of exploitative manipulative matriarch Vee. Vee's backstory further illustrates the extent of her flawed 'parenting' by detailing the revenge she exacts on a male 'foster child' who double-crosses her; playing the role of 'incestuous mother', she seduces him before actioning his pre-planned execution at the hands of a police officer on her payroll (12.2).

Orange is the New Black remains a 'family' melodrama of sorts since it employs the genre's 'tried-and-true family-saga' mode (Williams 45). The importance of its prison 'families' or 'tribes' becomes foundational to the narrative across its multi-season run. The breakdown of the prison friendship between Taystee and Poussey as a consequence of Vee's demand for Taystee's return to her familial drug-running fold, and Poussey's rejection of Vee's dysfunctional family, is central to Season Two's narrative momentum. The series' ongoing preoccupation with mother/daughter relationships is also explored in the wealth of emotionally charged backstories that recount mother/daughter relationships, most of which are central to the formation of character, contribute to the incarcerated woman's current predicament, and are in some way flawed. They provide empathetic points of connection between the characters in this drama and its predominantly female audience, all of whom are able to identify with the bonds of maternal ties, even if unable to identify with prison experience. Kerman's recount of Mother's Day becomes a central conceit that frames the Season Three narrative. Episode one is dedicated to this important date in the prison calendar: it serves to draw in narrative threads that have thus far explored the significance of the family/prison tribe in general and mother/daughter relationships in particular, many of which are, like that of Taystee and Vee, or Doggett and her mother, flawed and consequently destructive. More affluent characters like Suzanne, Nikki and Boo are also scarred by their relationships with their mothers. Nikki is constructed as a teen junkie whose addiction, at least in her estimation, is caused by parental over-indulgence which amounts to neglect, her society mother providing material rather than much needed emotional support (1.3). Similarly, Boo is denied the emotional support of a mother who refuses to accept her daughter's lesbian identity. In a comic parody of the makeover genre, as Boo prepares to con Doggett's fundamentalist church funders into believing she is a convert from the evils of lesbianism, she peers at her now feminised reflection and voices the universal timeworn concern: 'I look like my mother' (4.3). Though the big 'reveal' is presented as an exaggerated comedic moment, staged in Sophia's makeshift beauty parlour with the prison's guru of femininity, Lorna Morello, serving as advisor, the scene is nevertheless infused with melancholy since by this stage Boo's troubled post-puberty years and her refusal to make her peace with her dying mother have already been shared via her backstory. Mother/daughter relationship issues cross any perceived social or racial divide in Kohan's series. Suzanne Warren's mental instability is, in part, constructed as a consequence of her adoptive white mother's unrealistic demands of her (3.2), and Piper's mother is presented in the series as a class-conscious 'Southern Belle' who is afraid of what others may think, despite the fact that Kerman writes of her mother as a source of tireless love and support throughout her term of imprisonment and beyond (152).

The memoir's 'truths' become secondary to a narrative strategy that is designed to build on Kohan's preoccupation with problematic mother/daughter relationships and their emotively charged melodramatic potential. The exploration of mother/daughter relationships is at its most complex in the narrative of Aleida and Daya Dianarez constructed initially as one characterised by ongoing female rivalry. Both mother and daughter have slept with Aleida's partner, Cesare, and as a consequence of Aleida's motherly neglect, illustrated in the opening scenes of Mother's Day (1.3), Daya has become the much-loved surrogate mother to her siblings, while her unborn child becomes a contested possession, whose right to life Aleida defends yet is seemingly determined to exploit for monetary gain at a later point in the narrative. However, Aleida's insecurities and her maternal instincts are slowly unveiled in a decidedly melodramatic storyline that plays out across Season Three, beginning with her Mother's Day backstory in the opening episode and a further back story that recounts a growing resentment fuelled by love as child Daya learns to become less reliant upon her (12.3). Eventually, over the contested site of Daya's child, and in the lead up to Aleida's impending release, we sense that her harsh parenting is motivated by a desire to protect her daughter from a fate similar to her own—that of a young single mother with limited life choices, and in a final act of motherly protection she charges Gloria Mendoza with the care of her daughter (9.3), despite the fact that her jealousy has led her to obstruct Gloria's efforts to 'mother' Daya thus far. Negative constructs of mother/daughter relationships are nevertheless counter-poised by stories of positive bonds. With the love and support of her own mother before and during her incarceration, Gloria, like Red, emerges as the epitome of the 'good' mother to both her own children and to her prison family. The close bonds between mothers and daughters are also touched upon in the backstories of Alex and Poussey whose mothers are now deceased.

Poussey's overwhelmingly positive recollections of her loving and educated mother are presented as part of the series' traditional treatment of melodrama, and her story becomes one of several prerequisite melodramatic tragedies that unfold across the series' four-season run. Where Poussey's tragic death is mapped out across a long-form narrative arc that spans four seasons, the tragic life trajectory of Tricia Miller builds in flashback across the opening season. Tricia's backstory positions her as Season One's tragic victim; constructed as a Dickensian innocent, her decline is mapped out from her earliest days on the street as a naive teen runaway to her end of season demise as the genre's drug-addled mandatory suicide. First introduced as the gullible, naïve lover of soon to be released Mercy, her vulnerability is foregrounded in the backstory that follows on from this moment. The youngest inmate at Litchfield, her flashback details her time as a homeless street kid whose decision to leave the family home is again motivated by family dysfunction in general and her step father's abuse of her in particular, once again connecting her story to one of flawed parenting and to the inadequacies of the social services system. She is constructed as an honourable character, one who is keen to pay back what she 'borrows' to those she is forced to take from due to her poverty (4.1). Momentarily glimpsed in the guise of the genre's ' kind-hearted hooker', she becomes the series' only token prostitute but her imprisonment is not directly related to prostitution, and the reasons for her incarceration remain vague. Instead, her situation is one that Kohan highlights as all too familiar. Embedded in Tricia's backstory is the contrasting tale of a fellow homeless girl: unlike Tricia, who becomes an increasingly drug-dependent prostitute, this other girl finds a way to leave the streets (10.1). Tricia's victim status is similarly underscored in her prison narrative: despite her desire to remain drug free, she is coerced into selling drugs for prison guard villain Pornstache and is ultimately found dead of a drugs overdose later in this episode. Though her drug-related death is framed by Pornstache as a fake suicide in order to hide his own involvement, the audience is left without clear answers as to whether her demise is accidental or the last desperate, suicidal act of a teen prisoner, failed by a punitive prison system and ostracised from her prison family as a consequence of her perceived drug addiction.

While Poussey comes from a very different background, she and Tricia are both, in part, constructed as innocent, motherless victims on a quest for lesbian love, and the outcome of their respective narrative trajectories is equally melodramatic and emotionally loaded. Poussey's story is, however, a much more complex study of injustice, developed over a much longer period of time. Poussey is constructed as a virtuous character whose moral compass, unlike that of her white middle-class counterpart, Piper Chapman, remains in tact and whose search to find a replacement for her lost German lover (6.2) invests her with a romantic sensibility that singles her out from others seeking love within the confines of the prison system. Operating at both 'the personal and the institutional level', Poussey's narrative is constructed as the epitome of what Williams terms the 'melodramatic quest for moral legibility' (119). Her initial stand against Vee's drug trading in Season Two sees her ostracised from her prison family, leading her into an alcohol-fuelled depressive state; and though at a later point she joins the ranks of Vee's family, Poussey again rebels in a final act of defiance—or 'moral legibility'—when, on realising Vee's 'family' is dealing hard drugs, she purposely destroys their stash. Poussey's constant search for love provides a further melodramatic flourish to her characterisation and her narrative trajectory. In the vein of traditional melodrama, the loving relationship between SoSo and Poussey builds to a point where they are making plans to be together post-prison; having secured celebrity chef Judy King's promise of a job on the outside, the tentative promise of a happy ending for Poussey looms, but this is swiftly undermined (12.4). For despite Poussey's moments of moral triumph, her story leads to her tragic death in custody in the penultimate episode of Season Four and propels the season's narrative to its the dramatic climax as Litchfield's female inmates riot in protest at the handling of her death. Directed by *Mad Men* creator, Michael Weiner, this episode epitomises Kohan's approach to the politics of her story, a story Weiner was attracted to because of Kohan's capacity to frame its 'political context' within a highly emotive 'dramatic context' that connects first and foremost at the level of characterisation (Weiner in Strause).

Post the traumatic events of episode twelve, Poussey's backstory frames the opening and closing moments of the season's final episode, giving far greater intimacy to the moment, and far more prominence to Poussey's backstory than to any employed in the series thus far. In a decidedly melodramatic treatment of her last night of freedom, at a point in time where she is about to move on to a new life, she is caught up in America's 'war on drugs' and becomes the ultimate victim of a system that incarcerates individuals for what amounts to a minor offence in a country noted by Kerman as both 'intellectually and morally bankrupt' (205). The minor nature of her crime is revealed alongside the tragic consequences of her incarceration, adding to the pathos of her unnecessary death in custody. In the final moments, we edit from the riotous chaos inside the prison, as Daya holds a prison guard at gunpoint, to a wide-angled shot that pans down to a dramatic night-time New York cityscape, the scene overlaid with a soulful non-diegetic score, as the diminutive figure of Poussey, her back to camera, comes into frame against the expansive, brightly lit New York City backdrop and the litter-strewn river foreshore. The camera cuts to a medium close up shot of Poussey; as she stares at her native New York skyline, her serious demeanour is replaced by a tentative smile and finally a hopeful laugh as she gazes directly into the camera lens. By concluding with Poussey's direct gaze into the camera, a gaze that breaks the fourth wall that traditionally separates the world of the watcher and the watched, Kohan establishes an emotive intimacy between the audience and Poussey. At this moment of new beginnings, she is about to leave for Amsterdam, but by this stage the audience already knows her prison story has a tragic outcome. Even though the style aesthetic of the season finale is more in line with the kind of emotive excess associated with traditional women's melodrama, its treatment of Poussey's predicament also aligns it with the kind of socially driven, realist take on melodrama that Williams identifies as central to a series like *The Wire*.

Orange is the New Black does, however, employ the traditional romance trope as part of its melodramatic agenda. In addition to Poussey's tragic romance trajectory, a number of romantic storylines that play no part in Kerman's memoir are introduced to the narrative as a means to widening the scope of the drama. Valentines' Day (6.2), like Mothers' Day (1.3), becomes an essential part of the prison calendar and both become pivotal melodramatic moments in the series. The five-season on-off relationship between fictional Piper and Alex Vause bears little resemblance to that of Kerman and her lover, Nora. Similarly, Kerman's stable relationship with Larry becomes a source for dramatic conflict and uncertainty in the series as Piper Chapman's allegiances constantly shift from Larry to Alex over the course of Season One and Season Two, and a similar tale of romantic betrayal is added to the narrative in the form of a budding sexual relationship between Larry and Piper's best friend, Polly. But romance is rarely afforded the traditional melodramatic treatment. Series' serial romantic, Lorna Morello, is revealed as a disturbed fantasist, incarcerated for stalking Christopher, the man at the centre of her romantic obsessions (4.2). Her romantic desires are later realised when, in a ceremony that is comically far from her fantasy wedding dream, she marries prison visitor, Vinnie Muchio (13.3). But it is her relationship with Nikki that remains one of the series' most densely layered romances. Though initially presented as a mutually beneficial sexual arrangement that works for 'gay-for-the stay' Lorna and lesbian Nikki, the true nature of Nikki's unrequited love is slowly revealed across the current five-season story arc. A more conventional heterosexual romance is also sewn into the narrative from the outset with the inherently problematic pairing of prison guard John Bennett and inmate, Dayanara Diaz for whom 'true love' blossoms throughout Season One. Their romance provides an ongoing story thread that aligns the series with heteronormative mainstream melodrama, but here the complications that ensue also connect to the social implications indicative of social realist melodrama outlined by Williams. Finding herself pregnant as a consequence of her relationship with Bennett, Daya, like fellow inmate Maria, faces the prospect of motherhood in a system that separates mother and child at birth, and unlike Bennett, she remains trapped by the system.

At certain points in the narrative, there are moments that, in terms of both story content and style aesthetic, position the text as pure melodrama; the final scenes of season finales in particular align with its melodramatic identity. The closing sequence of Season Three depicts an unprecedented display of camaraderie as the inmates of Litchfield descend on the lake beyond the correctional facility's breached perimeter fence. This extended twelve-minute sequence employs a highly emotive orchestral score, and the saturated colours of the sunlit natural landscape are intensified to create a scene of visual harmony, depicting communal togetherness of the kind characteristic of the traditional melodrama's narrative closure and intimating that the season has a 'happy ending'. But this moment of intense melodramatic joy is ultimately undercut by a closing edit back to prison reality, focusing on the arrival of a bus containing more inmates, their walk into Litchfield accompanied not by the uplifting lakeside orchestral score but by the ironically portentous soundtrack to Foreigner's 'No More Lonely Life'. The series also employs the stylistic tropes of high drama at certain strategic points in the narrative: for example, the darker moments of Sophia's slow-motion entry into (12.3) and her zombie-like exit from the SHU (12.4) employ the kind of non-diegetic score, obtrusive editing and creative cinematography more reminiscent of the excesses of melodramatic storytelling. Sophia's removal to the SHU, couched by a PR conscious prison hierarchy as an act designed to protect her, provides a moment of emotionally charged high drama: flanked by three imposing guards, a mournful non-diegetic gospel soundtrack playing over the scene, the camera tracks her slow-motion walk in a continuous edit to the point where the jarring, exaggerated sound of the closing cell door breaks the melancholy mood; the camera then holds on a shot of a beaten Sophia, framed by the very small wired opening in the cell door, emphasising her isolation and her powerlessness within the system (12.3). However, though the style aesthetic of moments like these and its season finales are more in line with the kind of emotive excess associated with traditional women's melodrama, its treatment of the predicament of characters like Tricia and Poussey aligns it firmly with the kind of socially driven, realist take on melodrama that Williams identifies as central to a series like *The Wire*. The series' treatment of dramatic moments such as the death of Poussey (12.4) is devoid of artifice: there is no orchestral score and the chaos of the scene is captured in a series of obstructed shots, Suzanne's distress signalled only by her performance. In the episode's closing thirty seconds, the focus shifts to Taystee's grief as a non-diegetic score begins and the camera moves out to an aerial shot of Taystee and Poussey tightly framed by guards and prisoners, but it is Taystee's palpable grief that communicates the emotive energy of the scene rather than the accompanying soundtrack.

There are numerous scenes that employ a similarly loaded melodramatic style aesthetic, but such moments are a rarity in a series that, like the memoir it adapts, is grounded in the realities of prison experience. In *Orange is the New Black*, there are no surreal flights of fancy of the kind employed in *The Sopranos* or *Breaking Bad*: 'surreal' moments are realised instead via the powerful on-screen performance of psychological imbalance, characters like Lolly, Suzanne and Maureen acting out their particular psychoses within the mainframe of the narrative. The series' credit sequence is also rooted in documentary-style reality that reinforces the show's factual genesis. In her detailed critique of the show's opening credits, Kathleen McHugh addresses the ways in which it functions outside industry norms: while most credits serve as the point of transition from reality to the fictional world of the series, the credit sequence in this instance employs 'a documentary montage that marks the *limits* of the fiction that is about to unfold' (my italics) reminding the viewer instead that the stories are intrinsically connected to the real incarcerated women who remain a constant presence at the edge of the frame (22). Consisting of a series of fast-paced edits of a wide variety of faces, shot in extreme close up, the credit sequence presents the features of a vast array of convicted inmates past and present (including Kerman) of diverse ethnic backgrounds, forcing viewers to see people who are ordinarily invisible within mainstream society (21). But it also serves to create the illusion that there is a connection between these real women and the fictional constructs whose stories are about to be dramatised on screen; as curious and invested viewers, we seek out what one may assume are the eyes, nose and mouth of a particular character from the narrative, even when armed with the knowledge that these are not the faces of actors in role. The tight framing of the shots may limit our access to the 'individual woman' but as McHugh points out it does create an 'intimate anonymity' (20) that serves to pique audience interest and audience investment in the quest to know more about the life experiences of women like Kerman and her fellow inmates. The opening and closing moments of the Valentine's Day episode (6.2) similarly foreground the faces of female inmates in a series of roughly edited shots of various characters speaking directly into camera about their definition of 'love'. Initially, due to the breaking of the camera's objective fourth wall, these sequences jar with the realist-style aesthetic of the series thus far. However, they also resemble the kind of intimate 'talking heads' profiles employed in reality TV and documentary interviews, and at the end of the episode each is revealed as part of Piper's research for a story to be published in the prison newspaper. The melodramatic nature of the story content is thus juxtaposed with the tropes of realist storytelling, demonstrating its capacity to be a melodrama that, like *The Wire*, explores emotion through a more realistic and gritty lens. Despite the emotive, melodramatic nature of the narratives, some of which are developed from instances recalled in Kerman's memoir, while others are fictitious creations introduced for dramatic effect, Kohan's series retains its connection with reality, and an even more experimental mode of melodramatic realism prevails in Season Five at a structural level, with events unfolding over a three-day time frame across its established thirteen-episode run.

4.3.3 *Cellblock Sisters: The Sexual Politics of Orange Is the New Black*

Though Kerman's memoir is inherently engaged in women's issues, feminism per se is not a central tenet of her social agenda. In the TV series, Kohan, on the other hand, engages with feminist issues, contributing to the cultural conversations circulating contemporary feminism through the show's multilayered representation of both individual women and female collectives in a female-centric environment. Like other screen narratives belonging to the Women in Prison genre, it engages in prerequisite 'spectacles of female bonding, female rage and female communities with strong doses of camp and irony' (Mayne 115). The questionable sexual politics of sexploitation films like *Chained Heat* informs, at least at an intertextual level, the ongoing screen representation of Women in

Prison narratives, but the more exploitative elements of these low-budget films are tempered by a coded resistance to patriarchy. Although presented in part as exploitative sexual fantasy, they also represent a 'feminist backlash' (Mayne 132) through their 'problematiz[ation]' of issues related to the interconnectedness of gender, race and sexuality (142). Mayne argues that sexploitation films like *Caged Heat* (1974) and *Chained Heat II* (1993), for example, are seen to embody a 'sisterhood' that transgresses class and race through its construction of fantasy breakout endings that enact a populist 'feminist rebellion against patriarchy' (137), and unlike their fifties counterparts, such films affirm sisterhood over victimhood, female agency and acts of rebellion over the hollow spectre of prison reform, even if presented in the guise of camp sexploitation cinema. The Australian series, *Prisoner (Prisoner Cell Block H)*, shares a similar low-budget style aesthetic to that of sexploitation cinema and similar sexual tensions but it is informed by the feminist ideologies of writers Maureen Chadwick and Ann McManus (Curthoys and Docker 59; Herman 152): once again, female solidarity in the guise of the prison 'family' prevails (Herman 152), and the series' Larkhall HMP is constructed as a 'place of warmth, solidarity and community for women' (142–143), despite the harrowing storylines presented during the show's eight-year run. Neither Kerman nor Kohan speak of their position in relation to feminist politics in any overt manner in the memoir or the TV series: each writer is preoccupied instead with matters of social justice as they relate to women. But Kohan's introduction of a comedic edge to the relating of these tales of female experience builds on the comedy genre's propensity to provide ironic social commentary that can be employed in what Dow terms a 'negotiation for social change' (36–37), and any feminist critique becomes an intrinsic part of the series' narrative momentum and character development rather than a commentary that relates to particular feminist ideologies.

Orange is the New Black operates within an intertextually connected story universe that aligns it with not only the Women in Prison genre but with other TV shows that foreground the fictional representation of female experience. It remains in dialogue with the female-centred sitcoms that precede it but where these series are dependent upon presenting a microcosm of collective experience *Orange is the New Black* explores the complexities of the female collective along the more 'tribal' lines of the prison narrative. The sitcom is a genre which is traditionally championed as the site of most telling female resistance [Dow xviii], but it operates at the level of personal choice conditioned by personal circumstance appertaining to personal matters of class, race and sexual proclivity. Given its social and geographically contained context, the Women in Prison genre lends itself to a more diverse and complex representation of female collective experience of a kind that operates outside the parameters of personal politics characterised by the sitcom. Contemporary Dramedy of a comedic bent is likewise pre-conditioned along personal sociocultural lines. Dunham's *Girls* could never, the writer-performer contends, have been realised on screen without its forerunner *Sex and the City*: her young women are indelibly connected to this earlier representation of female experience (Dunham in Poniewozik). But for the diverse range of women represented in Kohan's series, a show like *Sex and the City* has limited currency. The latter's sexually liberated and financially independent women are synonymous with a consumer lifestyle that is, by circumstance, denied to Kohan's incarcerated women. The kind of neoliberal commodification that has become associated with post-feminism at large and with characters like Carrie Bradshaw, Samantha Jones, Miranda Hobbes and Charlotte York is at odds with the life experiences of Women in Prison, both within the confines of the prison system and for many in relation to their life experiences before and after serving time. If as many scholars contend, post-feminism is about white middle-class financially independent, 'straight' women (Lotz 2001, 2003; Whelehan 2005; Mc Robbie 2004, 2007; Gill 2007) then *Orange is the New Black* is not dealing in post-feminist politics in any direct way. Rather, it rejects the kind of neoliberal post-feminist frame of reference employed in mainstream female-centred TV narratives that focus on one protagonist, or at most a very small friendship group, in favour of a more inclusive exploration of female experience that crosses social, racial, sexual and gender divides. Piper serves as the series' emblematic white middle-class post-feminist but her rhetoric proves to be hollow and self-serving when measured against the solidarity of her cell block sisters and their allegiance to their own 'tribes', and her role as series' protagonist diminishes post-Season One.

Orange is the New Black offers a much wider, more complex critique of lived female experience than its Women in Prison forerunners, ensuring a female visibility that operates within yet transcends tired prison tropes. Friendships between women of differing age and background, outlook and sexual identity, are part of the narrative fabric of both Kerman's memoir and Kohan's TV series. The complexities of friendship between Taystee and Poussey are teased out across a four-season story arc that explores the boundaries between platonic and sexual love. Similarly, the growing friendship between black, transwoman Sophia and white nun Sister Ingalls illustrates one of the strengths of a genre in which women from different cultural and racial backgrounds interact; Sophia's initial overtures of friendship are predicated on her desire to secure some of Sister Ingalls' hormone treatment drugs, but the friendship is one that endures across the current five-season run. Kohan also develops a slow-burn relationship between seemingly disparate characters Boo and Doggett. Though first presented as a divisive and dogmatic white trash evangelist whose vitriolic hatred of anyone whose sexual identity sits outside of heterosexual norms, her growing relationship with the series' representative butch dyke, Big Boo—a figure whose size and sexual appetite are noted in Kerman's memoir (167)—serves as yet another illustration of Kohan's capacity to construct credible and diverse cameos of female bonding. In this instance, the two women bond over matters inherently aligned with ongoing feminist discourse of relevance to all women, regardless of sexual proclivity. Doggett's feminist 're-education' in Seasons Three and Four focuses on two major tenets of feminist concern—abortion and rape—but it is through the narrative richness of backstories and the growing trust between Doggett and Boo that the former's capacity to rethink her position as a woman in a patriarchal society is constructed on screen. As a grieving Doggett builds makeshift graves for all of her aborted children on Mother's Day (1.3), Boo discusses with her the ideological concerns behind the politically charged Row V. Wade abortion case, assuring her in a blackly humorous and ironic manner that her decision to abort her children was the right one (1.3), but the discussion is framed first and foremost by their relationship rather than as political diatribe. Boo points out that Doggett's role as serial abortionist has, ironically, helped to save society from the criminal activities of 'meth-head white trash pieces of shit' who are the unwanted offspring of 'meth-head white trash pieces of shit' like her, thus framing her decision as 'a blessing' rather than an unnecessary evil.

Kohan engages in central tenets of feminist ideology through a character-driven premise both here and in the later rape scenario. When Boo comprehends what has happened between Doggett and prison guard, Donut, it is Boo who helps her to both acknowledge that this constitutes rape, and that the victim status she so readily embraces and normalises should be rejected. Most tellingly, though, through the lens of personal relationships rather than as feminist polemic, Kohan explores their mutual incapacity to carry out their planned rape–revenge scenario. Boo advises it is time 'to do a "Girl with the Dragon Tattoo" on Do-nut', intertextualising the politics of rape and female empowerment already invested in this film—a foreign-language film that nevertheless bridges the mainstream/art house cultural divide—without forfeiting the series' dark yet comedic treatment of the issue. When neither Boo nor Doggett can ultimately action their planned revenge, the darker edge of the narrative is again tempered by the series' signature black humour, Boo claiming that contrary to society's belief that as a man-hating butch dyke she should be up to the task, 'foreign-object butt rape' is something that she has 'still not crossed off [her] list!'. But Doggett's understated response—'I don't feel rage, I feel sad'—undercuts the scene's darkly humorous treatment of the moment, leaving the audience to ponder the emotional as well as the physical consequences of female rape, especially when that rape takes place within what is initially constructed as a 'romantic' relationship. By devoting time to the slow-burn relationships between Doggett and Boo, and Doggett and Donut across a multi-season story arc, Kohan ensures the credibility of not only Doggett's complex response to rape but that of Boo and Donut, respectively. Doggett's disavowal here of the kind of 'eye for an eye' ethos that has characterised her actions in Season One and Season Two leads her to the realisation that rape takes many forms; she learns to identify some of her earlier teen experiences as acts of rape, and to see that the kind of power imbalance that informs her relationship with Donut can lead to a scenario in which he is unable to separate control and sexual lust from 'love'. Kohan's treatment of the issue of rape explores the emotional disconnect from both sides, and his bewildered response to her claim that he has raped her speaks to the complexity of the issue. When Donut says 'But I love you', Doggett is by now able to reply ' So that makes it different? It didn't feel any different' (4.3).

The lesbian on screen is historically aligned in mainstream media outlets with the threatening femme fatale or the abject 'other' of the horror genre, characterised by 'hegemonic imagery' of 'insanely aggressive lesbians' (Millbank 156) and 'pathologized as unbalanced and abusive' (168), but Kohan undermines such representation even as she situates the series in relation to what has gone before. Despite her own lesbian experience prior to entering the correctional system, Kerman does not dwell on this aspect of prison existence and notes that most inmates are only 'gay for the stay'; she likens the romantic relationships formed while women are incarcerated to a prison version of what she terms 'lesbian til graduation', as 'school-girl crushes' of the kind she experienced during her Smith's College dorm life (86). Her commentary infers that lesbian relationships are for the majority a temporary consequence of the prison environment. However, Kohan's focus on and treatment of lesbian relationships, and consequently lesbian sex, differs considerably from that of Kerman whose reference to lesbian prison experience in her memoir is minimal. In *Orange is the New Black*, as in *Bad Girls*, lesbian sexuality is not presented as anything other than the norm.

Lesbianism goes unremarked by all but counsellor Sam Healy, an increasingly parodic figure whose lesbophobic preoccupations form part of the series darkly humorous agenda without diluting its sexual politics. Where in most prison narratives, lesbian relationships are couched as temporary interludes seen only within prison walls, in Kohan's narrative lesbian characters are also given a lesbian presence in the world outside via the various backstories employed, and the fictitious Piper Chapman's story arc revolves around her conscious decision to reject her male partner in favour of her former female lover, Alex. Kerman, who remains loyal to her male partner throughout her prison stay and beyond, suggests that sexual desire is flexible according to circumstance but in the universe created by Kohan lesbian relationships range from those that are a temporary dalliance to those set up as ongoing partnerships for women whose lesbian identity is non-negotiable. Lorna Morello epitomises the 'gay for the stay' mentality that is afforded to lesbian relationships in Kerman's memoir, and many of the series' lesbian relationships are presented as interchangeable, as evidenced by the shifting allegiances of Mercy who, in Season One, plays off former lover Boo and current lover Tricia against each other. Boo and Nikki are Litchfield's hardcore lesbians, driven by sexual needs of a kind more readily identified with male desire in mainstream television, or with the comedic excesses of sexually driven characters like *Sex and the City*'s Samantha Jones. The Season Two 'bing-off' competition and their involvement with various women throughout the five-season run set them up as Litchfield's lesbian lotharios. However, though lesbian sex between numerous couples is represented on screen in graphic detail Kohan also ensures audience engagement with the life experiences that inform lesbian identity through the interventions of character backstories. Poussey, the series only black lesbian, is characterised by her quest for love and constancy in her relationships with women; ironically, she finds this 'love' in her relationship with the inconstant and shallow Brooke SoSo whose lesbian identity vacillates throughout the series. But whether lesbian, gay for the stay or decidedly straight, the women of the series are portrayed as complex individuals in search of more than sex, and Kohan's detailed and varied portrayal of women, some of whom happen to be lesbians, transcends the tired stereotypical images that have long prevailed.

However, what singles out the Women in Prison genre from all other female-centred narratives of collective solidarity is its treatment of the gaze—a gaze which, according to feminist film theory, is traditionally seen to be invested in female objectification (Mayne 117). Instead of performing female objectification for a male gaze, the genre engages with the premise that 'women observe other women' (117–118), inviting a non-threatening and potentially erotic female-centric gaze that works in opposition to mainstream television's dominant heterosexual norms. By contesting the 'heteronormativity of mainstream TV', it provokes instead a female viewing position that provides access to a wide range of female experience, including that of lesbian sexuality (Ciasullo Containing 30). Some shows like *The L Word* (2004–2009), with its array of consumable/consumer-driven 'lipstick lesbians' and couplings that aspire to a heterosexual norm, invite the would-be tourist lesbian to engage in a vicarious and decidedly glamorous version of homosexual desire; others, like *Sex and the City*, introduce lesbian desire as a comedic strategy, as simply yet another passing phase for the series' sexually curious Samantha Jones. In each, lesbian sex is presented as a potentially titillating experience for both straight and gay viewers but, ultimately, heteronormativity prevails. Though some depictions of women in *Orange is the New Black* may be deemed voyeuristic, employing as they do shots of image-conscious and carefully posed bodies (Pramagiorre 192), others provide candid depictions that convey the awkwardness of the sexual moment within the prison environment, presenting women of all shapes and sizes, both gay and straight, whose body image does not align with heteronormative ideals of feminine beauty of the kind constructed in shows like *Sex and the City* or *The L Word*. There are moments of vicarious engagement in *Orange is the New Black*; during the pilot episode, the camera lingers over the conventionally beautiful body of inmate Lorna Morello as she is brought to sexual climax by the show's lesbian lothario, Nikki, who through her forthright gaze, challenges Piper, and by inference the audience, not to look away during one of the series' many prerequisite prison shower scenes. There are numerous flashback moments of this nature too, such as nude sex scenes between nubile Poussey and her young German lover (6.2), but such moments are counter-balanced by the series overwhelmingly realistic treatment of sex and female nudity. For Kohan, sex works as a leveller that 'expresses everything. It's comfort, it's release, it's brutality, it's companionship' (Kohan in Radish). The sexual posturing of *Sex and the City* with its 'romanticised/sanitized portrayal of sexuality' (Nash and Grant 982), and the more overtly titillating portrayals of lesbian sex epitomised in *The L Word* have no place in a series like *Orange is the New Black* which incorporates candid sexual moments that serve to undercut voyeuristic titillation. As with *Girls*, sex in *Orange is the New Black* is often awkward and unsexy, the female body presented on camera without artifice. Scenes of graphic sex are realistically presented and often far from titillating. For example, the sexually titillating potential of shots that linger on the body of conventionally beautiful SoSo as she is brought to climax during an act of cunnilingus performed by Nikki (4.2) is undermined by what follows on from that moment, as Nikki stops Soso from talking incessantly during sex by hoisting down her unattractive prison issue underpants and unceremoniously thrusting her vagina into Soso's face. Similarly, during the Season Two 'bing-off' competition, the camera lingers on a decidedly unappealing moment of toilet sex between Nikki and another anonymous partner, the viewer positioned with Boo, able to see only their lower body parts as they engage in awkward, uncomfortable sex.

In keeping with the Women in Prison genre's affiliation with subversive 'sisterhood' and 'feminist rebellion against patriarchy' (Mayne 137), the series does engage in the critique of patriarchal systems. Kohan addresses female objectification and the commodification of female experience on numerous occasions through the vehicle of comedy and as part of the series' narrative momentum and character development. Larry's misappropriation of Piper's prison narrative, consciously crafted in his magazine as what she labels a 'cool story' to be told at 'a yuppie fucking cocktail party', serves as an instance of Piper's resistance to male acquisition of female narratives: she rejects his loaded white middle-class fantasy of prison experience as one that denies her reality and that of her fellow inmates. But in the eyes of these fellow inmates, it is Piper who is responsible for their betrayal and for the initial re-appropriation of their stories (8.1 and 11.1). In an act of female agency, couched as a call to arms in the name of sisterhood, her hyperbolic, rabble-rousing speech in defence of her dirty panties enterprise, Felonious Spunk, provides a similar tongue-in-cheek critique of female commodification and sexual objectification through a role reversal that commodifies male desire instead (8.3). But the moment also serves to reinscribe Piper's position as a middle-class neoliberal post-feminist—a position that few of her fellow inmates, including her lesbian lover Alex, subscribe to. Flaca's later stand against what she sees as Piper's capitalist exploitation of her and her fellow panties labourers is framed as an attempt to unionise the workforce; despite Piper's earlier satirical call to her 'sisters' to unite in an enterprise that exploits male desire, her response is that of the divisive capitalist entrepreneur—a response that escalates her ongoing alienation, even from Alex (11.3). Less dramatic yet similarly acerbic critiques of patriarchy and of capitalism pepper the dialogue throughout. When, with her planned wedding-day fantasies shattered, Lorna Morello asks her lesbian lover, Nikki, 'What kind of woman doesn't wanna pick her own wedding date?' Nikki replies in a wry one-liner: 'One who doesn't get excited by the wedding industrial complex and society's bullshit need to infantilize women' (3.2).

Despite the questionable sexual politics of Women in Prison, sexploitation films and their often camp and exploitative treatment of story content, low-budget films like *Caged Heat* and *Chained Heat II* offer what Mayne terms a 'celebration of female revolt': one that engages with feminist ideology and 'sisterhood' in a populist form (137). As part of a narrative that builds to a point of dramatic conflict by the close of Season Four, *Orange is the New Black* presents a similar 'celebration of female revolt' brought about as a consequence of the inhumane treatment of inmates. The complex 'tribal' tensions and divisions that play out across Seasons One, Two and Three culminate in a rebellion against a harsh, inept prison system, run by cruel, dictatorial prison guards. Blanca Flores emerges as a singular voice of enduring protest during Season Four, her stand against the guards' racial profiling and sexist maltreatment of female inmates serving as the catalyst for a revolt that ultimately unites women of all tribes, regardless of colour, creed and cultural prejudice (12.4). As with earlier ineffectual prison protests led by SoSo and Sister Ingalls in Season Three, Blanca's initial act of rebellion—her refusal to shower—is at first couched as a comedic story thread, but as conflict builds in Season Four Flores redefines this as a purposeful act of 'civil disobedience' used as protection against sexual harassment, and eventually her fellow inmates adopt a similar form of passive aggressive resistance. In the penultimate episode, Flores turns her earlier inhumane punishment into yet another form of silent protest that escalates into an act of collective resistance on a grand scale as fellow inmates stand with her on the canteen table tops, refusing this time to come down (12.4). The dramatic climax of the Season Four story arc culminates in a more active form of revolt, initiated this time by Taystee in response to the insensitive and unjust handling of Pousseys' death. As Daya Diaz points a gun to the head of sadistic prison guard, Thomas (Hump) Humphrey, the camp aesthetic more readily associated with such revolts in the Women in Prison genre (Mayne 115) is replaced by a collective female rage, engendered by the death of Poussey whose demise intertextualises contemporary moments related to the death of black Americans in custody, referencing and alluding to contemporaneous movements like Black Lives Matter, I Can't Breathe and Say Her Name. In an unprecedented move, Kohan takes the Women in Prison genre into new territory subverting the power paradigm in a Season Five dedicated to the prison riot and its aftermath. Litchfield's 'cellblock sisters' are now in charge and its once powerful guards take on the role of 'helpless victim', a role traditionally reserved for the genre's incarcerated women.

4.4 Beyond 'Story': *Orange Is the New Black* and the Paratextual Context

Adaptations are about more than the sum of their connections to one particular source text; screen adaptations, and in particular adaptations to serialised television, are also about the paratextual discourse that scaffolds them before, during and after release. Paratexts remain a highly influential part of the organic adaptive process. They shape our ongoing engagement with and our interpretation of story (Lotz and Gray 36); they become an intrinsic part of a larger brand identity that relates to both the TV series and its broadcaster or streaming platform. Most importantly, they serve to sustain and extend the narrative through the kind of 'intertextual dialogism' that Stam sees as an inherent feature of the adaptive process, in which 'every text forms an intersection of textual surfaces' (64). Within the context of TV production, *Orange is the New Black*, the memoir from which it evolves *and* the paratexts that circulate both, form what Gray identifies as an industry-based 'network of power' (Lotz and Gray 39): a network that in this instance sustains not only audience engagement with narrative but with matters of social injustice.

Kerman's memoir is driven by her agenda for social change within the women's prison system, and the series is similarly defined by its engagement with matters of social injustice. At a paratextual level, the series is constantly referenced through its identity as a show that addresses such matters, via reviewer discourse, the media presence of star performers like Laverne Cox (Sophia Burset), Lea Del Ray (Boo Black) and Danielle Brooks (Taystee Washington), and by the marketing strategies of Netflix. One of the most effective marketing strategies employed by Netflix involves Netflix sponsored native advertising placed in the prestigious *New York Times*. This *New York Times* snowfall project, couched in an editorial style yet commissioned by Netflix content strategists and penned by hired writer Michelle Delziel, addresses the inadequacies of the female prison system. Titled 'Women Inmates: Why the Male Model Doesn't Work', it subtly references *Orange is the New Black* through its use of the series' signature colour palette, and through the nature of its content, establishing an intertextual relationship between what appears to be a feature article with a strong editorial 'voice' and the prison system experience presented in both Kerman's memoir and Kohan's TV series. The piece generated a high level of social media discourse when it appeared in December 2015, and it was amongst the top 1000 *New York Times* articles accessed in that year (Wegert). In its capacity to highlight the plight of women in a failing prison system, the article highlights by inference the significance of narratives being explored in the TV series that sponsor Netflix is currently streaming.

The exploration of social injustices within the prison system is central to the series' overriding narrative momentum, but other contemporary issues such as transgender identity and the disturbing prevalence of stories about black deaths in custody are also incorporated into the storyline. For some reviewers, the death of Poussey is an 'earned tragedy', a credible narrative outcome that is built into the series' narrative momentum as it builds to its Season Four prison riot finale; its treatment of the issue of black deaths in custody is seen to be indicative of its willingness to engage with 'hard-hitting' and 'controversial issues of the moment' (Nussbaum). For others, it is an instance of 'exploitative voyeurism', a form of black 'trauma porn' designed for a 'white gaze' (Shackelford). Responses to this fictional on-screen 'appropriation' of such a topical issue demonstrate the series' capacity to generate sustained and heated debate around issues of social significance; current events become part of its intertextual frame of reference as does the discourse that surrounds them. In Season Five, Taystee Washington alludes to the many other black deaths in custody, once again widening out debate around this issue. Series cast members are also a part of the discourse that continues to circulate the show. Danielle Brooks (Taystee Washington) argues that the show's 'work doesn't end when you finally say "cut" and its out on Netflix'; rather, its cast is engaged in social activism that goes beyond the series' fictional boundaries (Brooks in Saraiya). Brooks went on to organise cast involvement in the Eric Garner protest.[2] Like Brooks, the series transgender actor Laverne Cox is involved in social activism.[3] As a vocal advocate of transgender rights, Cox adds a further dimension to the show's identity as a vehicle for social change, taking its issues-based agenda beyond the parameters of the prison memoir it adapts and out into the media arena. Cox is the first transwoman to appear on the cover of *Time* magazine, and her high-profile media presence ensures ongoing engagement with the issues faced not only by transpeople but, by inference, with her fictional on-screen persona, Sophia Burset. In print, TV and online interviews Cox openly debates the politics of transgender identity, highlighting society's transphobic attitudes and its unhelpful preoccupation with the physical rather than the emotional side of the transition process. In a now infamous interview with daytime TV host Katie Couric, Cox challenges Couric's invasive line of questioning, arguing that Couric's overriding 'preoccupation with transition and surgery objectifies trans people', negates their 'real lived experiences' and sidesteps the issue of transphobic violence which remains a prominent part of that lived experience (*Katie*, ABC, Jan 2014). Unlike Couric, Kohan chooses to focus on the reality of life as it is experienced by transpeople. Tellingly, from the outset of the series, Kohan avoids any invasive sexual objectification of Sophia as a transwoman. Such matters are not addressed, and during the five-season narrative thus far Sophia speaks of sexual organs only in her role as educator of her fellow inmates who, sadly, have little understanding of how their own bodies function (4.2). There is no backstory focus on medical transition procedures and throughout the first two seasons, Sophia's narrative focuses on her 'real lived experience' as a prison inmate and as a transwoman coping with

---

[2] Brooks went on to organise cast involvement in the Eric Garner protest, December 2014.

[3] Cox executive produced and appeared in the *Free CeCe* documentary (2016), speaking out against the unjust imprisonment of transwoman CeCe MacDonald.

emotional rather than physical transition both in and out of the prison environment. Her relationship with partner, Crystal, both before and after her transition, is handled with sensitivity, and the emotional transition of *both* women is explored as part of the 'lived experience' Cox notes as essential to a better understanding of transpeople. As the series progresses, her story also addresses the pressing issue of transphobia within the confines of the prison system and via MCC's inappropriate response to the violent transphobic treatment she experiences at the hands of fellow inmates.

Kohan's capacity to experiment with complex narrative strategies that go beyond the norms of serialised storytelling is enhanced by the fact that this is a Netflix Original, designed not for weekly release but for seasonal release on a streaming platform that makes available the back catalogue of seasons simultaneously. The need to sustain audience long-term memory is less pressing when a streaming library provides instant recap, just as seasonal release negates the need for the kind of repetitive episode recaps that are employed across mainstream and cable networks. Indeed, since Netflix originals operate outside the industry norms of 'gap-filled serial broadcast experience' in which the audience must anticipate and discuss the next narrative revelation, Mittell questions their very identity as 'serial' drama (41). The inference here is that such a release strategy in some way negates audience engagement beyond the parameters of the series itself, but in this age of media convergence and social media hype, a Netflix originals like *Orange is the New Black*, with its cult fan base as well as its populist following, maintains high levels of audience engagement and, between release of its seasons, a distinct paratextual presence of a kind that 'transcends the limits of a predetermined consumption' (Innocenti and Pescatore 8). Netflix is actively involved in cultivating and maintaining its social media presence through innovative social media strategies via Facebook, Twitter and Instagram. One such strategy involved cast interaction with fans via a 'Visiting Hours' Twitter account that hosted 'surgery' times in which fans could ask cast members questions; other Twitter initiatives invite fans to get personally involved by uploading images of themselves wearing orange to the 'On Wednesdays We Wear Orange #OTINB' Twitter feed, while downloadable apps provide fans with the capacity to upload images of themselves alongside characters from the series. A more inventive ploy created by Netflix involves curated character playlists accessible via the Pandora Radio streaming platform. All such strategies help to maintain a media presence before, during and after the release of each season; all extend the narrative's paratextual universe in a conscious effort to build the brand identity of both *Orange is the New Black* and Netflix.

Netflix has built on the series somewhat skewed identity as a product affiliated with the city of New York and, as a consequence, with other female-centred comedies and dramedies that identify with this locale. From *Sex and the City* to *Girls* and *Broad City*, New York is associated with the kind of 'hip' vibe that reflects the WASP persona of fictitious Piper Chapman rather than the life experience of fellow Litchfield New Yorkers, or indeed of Kerman as writer of the memoir. Marketing prior to the release of Seasons Two and Three focused on this locale, enacting a Times Square takeover, replete with cast appearances and photo booths ahead of Season Three, and the more elaborate ploy of a travelling food truck and food giveaways in targeted affluent locations like Lower Manhattan prior to the launch of Season Two. For some, the latter strategy was regarded as counter-productive: rather than foregrounding the series' exploration of social injustices, the stunt was seen to trivialise women's prison experience and mental illness, while promoting reductive racist stereotypes through its Crazy-Pyes logo and the accompanying 'pickaninny' images of black character Suzanne Warren (DeCarvalho and Cox 508–509). Reflected in this marketing ploy is one of the series ongoing dilemmas; the decision to employ comedy alongside high drama remains problematic, and response to the newly released Season Five attests to this. Episodes nine and ten in particular present the two extremes; the former serves as an homage to the horror genre and treats the prison riot as a source of slasher parody; the latter is a decidedly dark treatment of content, incorporating disturbing scenes of graphic torture that verge on torture porn. The series capacity to strike a balance between the comedic and the melodramatic across the first four seasons has ensured its continued popularity thus far; however, that balance has proved difficult to sustain in the prison riot context of the current Season Five. Reviewer discourse around Season Five focuses on its inability to find the right mix between the 'always-jarring tonal shifts' that have served the series so well up to this point (VanDerWerff); its established capacity to shift with ease between the extremes of 'ridiculous warm-hearted slapstick comedy' and 'serious drama' is challenged in a season that deals with the aftermath of a death in custody and the consequences of a prison riot, leaving it 'struggl[ing] to balance' these 'two very distinct tones' (Nicholson). Nevertheless, *Orange is the New Black* continues to move beyond the parameters of comedy into a cultural space that sits outside mainstream society—one defined *by* confinement and patriarchal control yet dominated by the female collective whose lived experience and the social injustices that abound within the system are effectively shared with its mainstream audience.

4.5 Memoir as 'Living Text'

Discourse surrounding *Orange is the New Black*, in both its prose and TV form, relates first and foremost to the sociocultural context of the narrative being presented over and above any projection of authorial self, even though its narrative framework is anchored in the lived experiences of Kerman as memoir writer. Memoir, a form of life writing historically regarded as a populist, informal mode of expression that lacks the high brow literary status of the autobiography, remains for some a 'less sophisticated' and 'passive form' of life writing, the domain of the less skilful writer observer (Mische 15), but for others it is a 'more tightly focused, more daring' and 'more penetrating' construction 'of self …of people or of a particular decade' (Fetherling vii). Both autobiography and memoir are concerned with personal life experiences yet the self-reflexive interiority that drives the autobiographical account is tempered in memoir by an equally important emphasis on place, social context and engagement with the lives of others: it is a mode of writing that vacillates between private and public discourse (Smith and Watson, Nancy K. Miller, Rak), reflective not just of the author's life experiences but of 'society, culture, and history' at a particular point in time (Mojab and Taber 33). Contemporary reassessment of the memoir is in part due to its engagement with 'the complexity of relations' between these 'public and the private spheres' (Rak 322), and it is the interplay between these spheres that becomes of central importance in the adaptation of Kerman's memoir to a complex, long-running TV series. For Kerman, her memoir serves as a vehicle for social change rather than as receptacle for personal reflection. It functions as a record of her life experience at a given point in time and in a specific locale but it also serves as a record of the life experiences of the women she shares that space and time with, and as a record of the inadequacies and injustices inherent in the American prison system. It is what Mojab and Taber would term a 'living text': one that presents the filtering of the 'social and historical through the voice of the individual' (933). She writes of and for incarcerated women whom she deems 'complicated and interesting and compelling and worthy of recognition' (Kerman in Figueroa), serving as the reader's guide into unfamiliar territory by taking her own experience as a starting point for social commentary that goes beyond the 'I' of autobiographical writing. Her 'story' has wide-ranging content, context and complexity ripe for adaptation to screen. Its far from stable meanings open up a wealth of possibilities for the would-be adapter of her memoir, and like autobiography it is a writing mode that is inherently involved in process: selecting, editing, pausing and rewinding, the life writer adapts her life story according to her own creative agenda, no matter how much the events are anchored in a lived reality. When adapting Kerman's memoir for a TV audience, Kohan engages in further acts of selection, omission and addition in order to create a series that builds on the lived experience of not only Kerman but of those many women who form part of her lived experience during the period of her incarceration.

Historically, memoirs are a rarely adapted commodity in the film industry; adaptations of memoirs in the TV industry remain an even greater rarity. Nevertheless, there has been a post-millennial upturn in the cinematic adaptation of memoir directed by notable film auteurs. Alan Parker's successful screen adaptation of Frank McCourt's *Angela's Ashes: A Memoir*, produced at the very end of the twentieth century, was at the vanguard of a stream of auteur-driven memoir adaptations released in its wake, from *The Pianist* (Roman Polanski 2002); *The Motorcycle Diaries* (Walter Salles 2004); *A Mighty Heart* (Michael Winterbottom 2007); *The Diving Bell and the Butterfly* (Julian Schnabel 2007); *My Week with Marilyn* (Simon Curtis 2011); to the recently released *127 Hours* (Danny Boyle 2017). Though fewer in number, the memoir is becoming an increasingly popular template for adaptation to the serialised TV form. Popular BBC TV series, *Call the Midwife* (2012–), based on Jennifer Worth's best-selling memoir, precedes the success of Kohan's TV serial adaptation of Kerman's *Orange is the New Black*, and in their wake and that of a number of recently released memoir adaptations[4] several high-profile TV auteurs are currently working on projects that involve memoir adaptation. Shawn Ryan (*The Shield*, 2002–2008) is series creator for an upcoming AMC serial adaptation of journalist David Carr's memoir, *The Night of the Gun*, while John Logan

---

[4] *Fresh Off the Boat* (2015–); *The Family Law* (2016–).

(*Penny Dreadful*, 2014–2016) is working as series showrunner on a forthcoming Showtime adaptation of Patti Smith's memoir, *Just Kids*. Post-millennium, the memoir has become the publishers' preferred marketing term for life writing (Smith and Watson 3): the very popularity once seen as its limitation is now seen as its strength, and its commodity-driven identity an asset that lends itself to further commodification in the guise of adaptation, particularly within the realms of commercially driven mainstream film and television, as its increasing popularity as a form that translates to screen in recent years indicates. Just as television series have entered a 'golden age' of prestige TV, the memoir has emerged as the chosen subgenre of life writing post-millennium, life becoming 'art' within a decidedly populist cultural milieu.

Works Cited

Andreeva, Nellie. "Emmies: *Orange Is the New Black* to Run as Drama, Ruled Ineligible for Comedy Race." *Deadline Hollywood*, 20 Mar. 2015. Web. 10 April 2015.

Barker, Cory. "Who Is Ruining *Orange Is the New Black*: Jenji Kohan or Netflix?" *Complex.com*, 17 June 2016. Web. 3 Aug. 2016.

Bouclin, Suzanne. "Women in Prison Movies as Feminist Jurisprudence." *Canadian Journal of Women and the Law* 21 (2009): 19–34. Print.

Ciasullo, Ann. "Making Her (In)visible: Cultural Representations of Lesbianism and the Lesbian Body in the 1990s." *Feminist Studies* 27.3 (2001): 577–760. Print.

———. "Containing 'Deviant' Desire: Lesbians, Heterosexuality, and the Women-in-Prison Narrative." *Journal of Popular Culture* 41.2 (2008): 195–223. Print.

Curthoys, Ann, and John Docker. "In Praise of Prisoner." *Australian Television: Programs, Pleasures and Politics*. Eds. John Tulloch and Graeme Turner. Sydney: Allen & Unwin, 1989: 57–63. Print.

DeCarvalho, Lauren J., and Nicole B. Cox. "Extended 'Visiting Hours': Deconstructing Identity in Netflix's Promotional Campaigns for *Orange Is the New Black*." *TV and New Media* 17.6 (2016): 504–19. Print.

Dow, Bonnie J. *Primetime Feminism: Television, Media and the Women's Movement Since the 1970s*. Philadelphia: University of Pennsylvania Press, 1996. Print.

Fetherling, George, Ed. Preface to "The Vintage Book of Canadian Memoirs." Toronto: Vintage Canada (Random House Canada), 2001: vii–x. Print.

Figueroa, Alyssa. "*Orange Is the New Black*'s Piper: 'The biggest Thing I Took from Jail Was Complete Awareness of Inequality'." *Alternet* (Culture), 4 Apr. 2014. Web. 20 Aug. 2015.

Gerhard, Jane. "*Sex and the City*: Carrie Bradshaw's Queer Postfeminist." *Feminist Media Studies* 5.1 (2005): 37–49. Print.
Gill, Rosalind. "Postfeminst Media Culture: Elements of a Sensibility." *Cultural Studies* 10.2 (2007): 147–66. Print.
Gray, Jonathan, and Amanda D. Lotz. *Television Studies*. Cambridge: Polity Press, 2012. Print.
Gross, Terry. "Interview with *Orange* Creator Jenji Kohan: Piper Was My Trojan Horse." *NPR* (Fresh Air), 13 Aug. 2013. Web. 20 Aug. 2015.
Harvey, Chris. "*Orange Is the New Black* Author Piper Kerman: 'People Are Sexual Beings, Even if You Lock Them in a Cage.'" *The Telegraph* (Film & TV), 5 June 2014. Print.
Herman, Didi. "Bad Girls Changed My Life: Homonormativity in Women's Prison Drama." *Critical Studies in Media Communications* 20.2 (2003): 141–59. Print.
Innocenti, Veronica, and Pascatore, Guglielmo. "Changing Series: Narrative Models and the Role of the Viewer in Contemporary Television Seriality." *Between* 4.8 (2014): 1–15. Print.
Kerman, Piper. *Orange Is the New Black: My Time in a Women's Prison*. London: Little, Brown Book Group, 2013. Print.
Lotz, Amanda D. "Postfeminist TV Criticism: Rehabilitating Critical Terms and Identifying Post attributes." *Feminist Media Studies* 1.1 (2001): 105–21. Print.
———. "Communicating 3rd Wave Feminism and New Social Movements: Challenges for the Next Century of Feminist Endeavour." *Women and Language* 26.1 (2003): 2–10. Print.
Mayne, Judith. *Framed: Lesbians, Feminists and Media Culture*. Minneapolis: University of Minnesota Press, 2000. Print.
McClelland, Mac. "*Orange Is the New Black*: Caged Heat—How Did the Unlikely Stars of *Orange Is the New Black* Revolutionize TV?" *Rolling Stone*, 12 June 2015. Web. 20 Aug. 2015.
McCourt, Frank. *Angela's Ashes: A Memoir*. Leamington Spa: Scholastic, 1996. Print.
McHugh, Kathleen A. "Giving Credit to Paratexts and Parafeminism in *Top of the Lake* and *Orange Is the New Black*." *Film Quarterly* 68.3 (2015): 17–25. Print.
Mc Robbie, Angela. "Postfeminism and Pop Culture." *Feminist Media Studies* 4.3 (2004): 255–64. Print.
Millbank, Jenni. "It's About This: Lesbians, Prison, Desire." *Social & Legal Studies* 13.2 (2004): 155–90. Print.
Miller, Nancy K. *Bequest and Betrayal: Memoirs of a Parent's Death*. New York and Oxford: Oxford University Press. 1996. Print.
Misch, Georg. *A History of Autobiography in Antiquity*. 2 vols. London, UK: Routledge & Kegan Paul, [1907] 1950. Print.

Mittell, Jason. *Complex TV: The Poetics of Contemporary Television Storytelling*, New York and London: New York University Press, 2015. Print.

Mojab, Shahrzab, and Nancy Taber. "Memoir Pedagogy: Gender Narratives of Violence and Survival." *Canadian Journal for Study of Adult Education* 27.2 (2015): 31–45. Print.

Nicholson, Rebecca. "*Orange Is the New Black* Season 5: So Jolty It Will Give You Whiplash." *The Guardian* (Culture), 10 June 2017. Print.

Nussbaum, Emily. "Empathy and *Orange Is the New Black*." *The New Yorker*, 11 and 18 July 2016. Web. 30 July 2016.

Nash, Meredith, and Ruby Grant. "Twenty-Something Girls V Thirty-Something *Sex and the City* Women." *Feminist Media Studies* 15.6 (2015): 976–91. Print.

Patterson, Eleanor. "Fracturing Tina Fey: A Critical Analysis of Postfeminist Television Comedy Stardom." *The Communication Review* 15:3 (2012): 232–51. Print.

Poniewozik, James. "Lena Dunham Interview Part One: What *Girls* is Made of." *Time* (Tuned In), 12 Apr. 2012. Web. 20 Aug. 2015.

Pramaggiore, Maria. "Privatization Is the New Black: Quality TV and the Re-fashioning of the US Prison Industrial Complex." *The Routledge Companion to Global Popular Culture*. Ed. Toby Miller. New York: Routledge 2017: 187–96. Print.

Radish, Christina. "Creator Jenji Kohan Talks *Orange Is the New Black*, Her Research into Prison Life, and Graphic Sex Scene." *Collider*, 7 July 2013. Web. 20 Aug. 2015.

Rak, Julie. "Are Memoirs Autobiography? A Consideration of Genre and Public Identity." *Genre* 36.3–4 (2004): 305–26. Print.

Rowe, Kathleen K. *The Unruly Woman: Gender and the Genres of Laughter*. Austin: University of Texas Press, 1995. Print.

Sairaiya, Sonia. "*Orange Is the New Black* Season 4: Danielle Brooks on Big Death, Giving Voice to the Left Behind." *Variety*, 24 June 2016. Web. 15 July 2016.

Schwan, Anne. "Postfeminism Meets the Women in Prison Genre: Privilege and Spectatorship in *Orange Is the New Black*." *Television and New Media* 17.6 (2016): 473–90. Print.

Shackelford, Ashleigh. "*Orange Is the New Black* is Trauma Porn Written for White People." *Wear Your Voice: Intersectional Feminist Media*, 20 June 2016. Web. 15 July 2016.

Smith, Sidonie, and Julia Watson. *Reading Autobiography: A Guide for Interpreting Life Narratives*. 2nd ed. London and Minnesota: University of Minnesota Press, 2010. Print.

Stam, Robert. "Beyond Fidelity: The Dialogics of Adaptation." *Film Adaptation*. Ed. James Naremore. New Brunswick: Rutgers UP, 2000. 54–78. Print.

Strause, Jackie. "*Orange Is the New Black*: Director Michael Weiner on 'Choreographing the Chaos' of the Tragic End." *Hollywood Reporter*, 27 June 2016. Web. 15 July 2016.
VanDerWerff, Todd. "*Orange Is the New Black* Season 5 Review: A Staggeringly Ambitious Mess." *Vox.com*, 11 June 2017. Web. 20 June 2017.
Walgrove, Amanda. "The *New York Times* Just Created an Incredible 'Snow Fall' for *Orange Is the New Black*." *Contently.com*, 7 June 2015. Web. 30 July 2015.
Whelehan, Imelda. *The Feminist Best Seller: From Sex and the Single Girl to Sex and the City*. Houndsmill: Palgrave Macmillan, 2005. Print.
Wegert, Tessa. "Why the *New York Times* Sponsored Content Is Going Toe-to-Toe with Its Editorial." *Contently.com*, 27 Mar. 2015. Web. 30 July 2015
Williams, Linda. *On the Wire*. Durham and London: Duke University Press, 2014. Print.
Willmore, Alison. "*Weeds* Creator Jenji Kohan on Her New Netflix Series Orange Is the New Black and Why 'Likeability Is Bullshit.'" *Indiewire*, 8 July 2013. Web. 20 Aug. 2015.

Screenography

Television

Ally McBeal (1997–2002, US: FOX).
Bad Girls (1999–2006, UK: ITV).
Breaking Bad (2008–2013, US: AMC).
Born Innocent (1974, US: NBC).
Fresh Off the Boat (2015–, US: ABC).
I Love Lucy (1951–1957, US: CBS).
Just Kids (in production, US: SHOWTIME).
Murphy Brown (1988–1998, US: CBS).
Outlander (2014–, US: STARZ).
Prisoner (1979–1986, Australia: Network Ten).
Roseanne (1988–1997, US: ABC).
Sex and the City (1998–2004, US: HBO).
Stranger Inside (2001, US: HBO).
The Family Law (2016–, Australia: SBS).
The L Word (2004–2009, US: SHOWTIME).
The Mary Tyler Moore Show (1970–1977, US: CBS).
The Night of the Gun (in production, US: AMC).
The Shield (2002–2008, US: FX).
The Sopranos (1999–2007, US: HBO).
Within These Walls (1974–1978, UK: LWT).
Wentworth (2013–, Australia: SoHo).
Weeds (2005–2012, US: SHOWTIME).

Film

Hours. Dir. Danny Boyle. 2017.
A Mighty Heart. Dir. Michael Winterbottom. 2007.
Caged Heat. Dir. Jonathan Demme. 1974.
Cellblock Sisters: Banished Behind Bars. Dir. Henry Charr. 1995.
Chained Heat. Dir. Paul Nicholas. 1983.
Chained Heat II. Dir. Lloyd A Simandl. 1993.
Cool Hand Luke. Dir. Stuart Rosenberg. 1967.
My Week with Marilyn. Dir. Simon Curtis. 2011
The Big Bird Cage. Dir. Jack Hill. 1972.
The Diving Bell and the Butterfly. Dir. Julian Schnabel. 2007.
The Exorcist. Dir. William Friedkin. 1973.
The Motorcycle Diaries. Dir. Walter Salles. 2004.
The Pianist. Dir. Roman Polanski. 2002.
The Shawshank Redemption. Dir. Frank Darabont. 1994.
Women in Cages. Dir. Gerardo de Lyon. 1971.

Web Series

Kittens in a Cage! Stoic Entertainment. June 2013–. Web. 1 Feb. 2015.

CHAPTER 5

The Night Of: A Remake 'Original'

5.1 Introduction

The Night Of (2016) is a conspicuously authored and more expansive HBO remake of the first narrative in the BBC series *Criminal Justice* (2008–2009). This remake, like its precursor text, follows in close up the harrowing journey of a young suspect through the complex labyrinth of custodial systems and is characterised by its generic hybridity. Affiliated with the generic markers of the crime drama, the courtroom drama and the prison drama, each series builds upon a set of preordained and culturally embedded codes that intertextualise both former and contemporary screen iterations of all three types of drama, creating a complex web of cross-cultural connectivity. Yet, despite their shared generic DNA and their shared narrative template, these series differ in terms of their stylistic treatment of generic tropes and, as a consequence, not only the visualisation of the narrative but also the construction of figures involved in that narrative are recalibrated in the narrative's transition to an American televisual context. Though contested notions of 'originality' have less sway within the TV industry, where shared authorship is fundamental to TV production and the migration of narrative templates to a different national/cultural platform is an established practice, claims of 'originality' remain synonymous with quality. The scripted drama remake is emerging as an increasingly legitimate mode of production in this latest 'golden age' of television (Chalaby 4), with prestigious cable channels like HBO entering into programme exchange in order to maintain a competitive market edge, but maintenance of its quality brand identity remains of paramount importance. By definition *The Night Of* is a remake and thus a 'derivation' of a precursor text; however, as a prestigious product affiliated with the HBO brand, it cannot be seen to be 'derivative' (Hutcheon 7), and its identity as a remake is afforded little traction in its marketing and reception. This 'limited' series emerges instead as a prestige HBO product representative of the HBO brand. It is 'its own palimpsestic thing' (8) capable of imbibing yet also eclipsing the prior text, and thus of overriding its own status as a remake.

The remake is the most recognisable form of adaptation in populist terms: instantly, it identifies itself as something that remakes or reproduces a prior text, and it is a common mode of production in a televisual context. It is, nonetheless, a particularly problematic mode of adaptation that crystallises the combative nature of discourse surrounding notions of adaptation as legitimate creative endeavour. For some, it epitomises 'copycat' mimicry that, as the label 'remake' infers, lacks all semblance of originality and authorial authenticity. Yet, like all adaptations, it involves the kind of '"reformatting"' that inevitably entails 'both gains and losses' (Hutcheon 16); it can be 'highly derivative or highly innovative' (Gil 23). Its status is also in part defined *by* its production context, and its perceived value as a cultural artefact differs according to not only the quality of its 'reformatting' but also its acceptance as a legitimate mode of storytelling. The often negative *perception* of the cinematic remake as inherently imitative and inferior (Braudy 1998: 327) has, however, limited currency within the production context of the television industry. Despite (or perhaps because of) its mass media identity and its populist appeal, the TV remake, unlike the film remake, is able according to Grindstaff to 'realize most fully [André] Bazin's vision of the adaptation as capturing, not the *letter* of the original, which can be emulated in mechanical fashion....but the *spirit* of the original—its tone, values, and rhythms' (2001: 157). Even in this 'golden age' of TV drama, authorial authenticity remains something of a misnomer within the collaborative, commercially driven environs of the TV industry where the practice of reworking existing narratives is not mired in the kind of tired fidelity-driven debates that traditionally circulate the field of adaptation studies.

Like all adaptations, the remake evolves by a quasi-biological process of 'cultural selection' (Hutcheon 177): it builds on the status of a prior text while also 'challenging the fixity' of that text's 'meaning'

(Grindstaff 138) during its transition to different cultural, geographical and often temporal storytelling spaces, performing what Horton describes as an 'intensified' and 'self-conscience balancing act between the familiar and the new' (173). The nature and quality of the remake is in part dependent upon the selected source text's capacity for 'continued cultural production': more pressing than the issue of fidelity to source is the issue of the prior text's capacity to 'inspire or stimulate' further iterations of that narrative (156). Selection of a prior text involves an intuitive act on the part of the adapter who must recognise a story's mythic potential and its aptitude for further exploration of the compelling fable at the heart of its narrative if it is to succeed in the guise of the remake (Braudy 328). Given a makeover that aligns the adapted story with its new audience within its new cultural, geographical and temporal space, TV series in particular argues Moran are ripe for remake (Makeover 462) but the careful grafting of a prior text onto that new landscape is of paramount importance, especially when working with texts that require no linguistic translation. The 'tone, values, and rhythms' (Grindstaff 157) of the prior text must be recalibrated if in its remade form it is to evolve as a product that functions effectively in a different cultural environment.

5.2 The Remake and Its Production Context

TV production works on the 'premise that a good creative idea in one place can be successfully established elsewhere' (Moran Makeover 462) but the act of remaking an existing cultural artefact is nonetheless an act characterised at the fundamental level of semantics as a lesser art, the terms 'remake' and 'original' being culturally loaded in favour of the latter and signifying a prior claim to 'creative agency' (Gil 21). It is still frequently couched as an act of stealth in critical and scholarly discourse—a sanctioned act of 'creative stealing' (Klein and Palmer 9) that may result in the creation of excellent TV, but one aligned with the negative language of thievery nonetheless. Stam's concerns about the negative language employed in the discourse surrounding adaptations in general (54) remains a pressing issue. However, the remaking of narratives for ever-expanding audiences is embraced by the financially driven TV industry where the sharing of successful formats is a recognised part of good work practice, and the recycling of narrative forms an established mode of production (Moran Global 1–5). Programme transfer has been an accepted mode of TV production since the 1950s;

while initially related to easily relocatable formats like the game show (6), the nineties saw the unprecedented rise of the reality TV show format (Madger 145)—a format which continues to provide readily accessible product for an ever-burgeoning global TV market. For both financial and cultural reasons, in a contemporary TV landscape characterised by trans-media storytelling, producers are turning increasingly to the stability of pre-loved narrative formats too. Quality TV of the millennial era is, argues Perkins, increasingly 'rel[iant] upon the concept of transformation' (784). Yet, while formats like the game show or reality TV migrate to other national TV audiences with malleable ease (Moran Makeover 467), the scripted TV drama is a more culturally sensitive format that has emerged as a favoured mode of remake only in recent years (Chalaby 4). Since TV scripted drama is a notoriously expensive commercial enterprise, the opportunity to build on the proven success of an existing scripted format presents a means to managing financial risk, the possibility of repeating favourable audience reception in a new market adding incentive for producers and broadcasters to turn to the remake as a relatively risk-free creative endeavour—one that 'heral[ds] a new era in the development of adaptation and imitation' (Moran in Lavigne, 38). This current 'golden age' of prestige TV drama and the rise of the scripted format drama remake is in part fuelled by the recent deluge of viewing outlets, with streaming services like Netflix, Hulu and Amazon Prime no longer defined solely by their function as platform providers for existing films and television programmes but as makers of original material in their own right. In the wake of HBO's phenomenal success, cable channels like FX, Showtime and AMC have also entered the scripted drama fray, quality drama being seen as a way to distinguish brand identity in a highly competitive market (Chalaby 6). The notion of 'original' is also redefined for similar purposes, with a remake like *House of Cards*, for example, being marketed as a highly successful Netflix original, despite its origins as a drama adapted for the BBC by Andrew Davies.

In general, the days of recycling TV product under the radar are long gone as affiliation with a prior text is more readily employed as part of a remake's marketing strategy. Remakes of Nordic Noir crime drama series illustrate the contemporary preoccupation with this transparent mode of transcultural adaptation. These series offer a fertile site for further mediation of populist stories within a complex transmedial narrative network that transcends geographical and cultural borders. They are 'travelling stories' able to 'adapt to local cultures' and 'local environments' with 'relative ease' (Hutcheon 177) and have evolved in recent times into a transglobal brand characterised by a distinctive yet highly adaptable style signature. Their crime-based narrative templates can be grafted onto other cultural and geographical locales, resulting in the production of remakes that find their place within different national contexts. American remakes like *The Killing* (a remake of the Danish series, *Forbrydelsen*) and *The Bridge* (a remake of Danish/Swedish production, *Bron*), or *The Tunnel* (the British remake of *Bron*), retain the style signature of the Nordic Noir brand and are characterised by their capacity to stay close to each source text's narrative template and generic identity; yet adapters are also able to translate these narratives into new cultural and geographical locales. Similarly successful translation of Israeli TV series like *Be Tipul* (2005–) and *Hatufim* (2009–2012) as American remakes *In Treatment* (2008–2010) and *Homeland* (2011–) respectively demonstrate the capacity for stories to 'travel' and evolve within a different cultural production environment. Both of these remake series have garnered commercial and critical acclaim, extending the premise of the prior text into new multi-season narratives and establishing each remake as a creative endeavour in its own right. Like *The Night Of*, both have in many respects eclipsed their precursor texts. Within an American context, the likelihood is that the original Israeli series and the Scandinavian Nordic Noir series would not present as familiar to an American audience traditionally averse to subtitled fare and as such the adapter is more likely, in this instance, to be presenting narrative in which outcomes are not already known. But while there is a clear rationale behind the impetus to translate and relocate these successful narratives, there is a less straightforward rationale behind the remake of a product that requires no linguistic translation.

Nevertheless, there is an established tradition of scripted remake transfer between the USA and the UK—one that precedes current trends for cross-cultural sharing of scripted drama. The USA forms the UK's largest export market, the latter being historically lauded as a 'niche purveyor of high culture' (Steemers 2–3), and its 'reputational capacity' for producing quality crime and period drama ensures a steady flow of product into the American TV market (O'Regan 33–34). Lavigne and Markovitch note that the discourse surrounding the remake is historically dominated by the transformation of American product for British consumption, suggesting matters of 'cultural imperialism' are seen as central to this established relationship of programme exchange (x), but the remaking of British product for the American market is also 'part of the

American cultural fabric' (xv). Product exchange between the UK and the USA is an established tradition; early comedy series like the UK's *Steptoe and Son* (1962–1967), re-emerging as the American *Sanford and Son* (1972–1977), and more contemporary series like *The Office* (2001–2003) remade as the long-running American iteration thereof (2005–2013) serve as prime examples of successfully translated series. Content that is steeped in British culture and of a decidedly British locale does, nonetheless, require a carefully executed cultural makeover if it is to thrive in an American market, and even then there is no guarantee of success. The poor reception of the recent remake of *Broadchurch* (2013–2017) as *Gracepoint* (2014–) demonstrates the remake's capacity to fail despite its relatively 'risk free' format and the success of the prior text. Indeed, Turnbull argues that in today's 'transnational' TV climate the 'impulse' to remake and relocate a series is 'more questionable than ever', with remakes of crime drama series like *Cracker*, *Prime Suspect* and *Life on Mars* all experiencing limited success as American adaptations of the UK source text (708). The notion that 'British-made entertainment' remains 'inherently superior' (Lavigne and Markovitch, ix) is also open to debate given the wealth of quality TV series currently being produced by American streaming providers like Netflix, and cable channels like Showtime and its well-established rival, HBO. De Fino sees HBO as 'the well-spring' of the current 'Golden Age' of American TV(2); its scripted drama has a global reach (15), and along with what De Fino terms its 'imitators' (Netflix, Showtime, FX and AMC) has 'superseded cinema as the pre-eminent narrative medium of our time' (7). HBO dramas are innovative and though they are more often than not 'originals', some of HBO's innovative dramas have their genesis in prior texts, ranging from those that, like *Boardwalk Empire*, 'adapt' historical and biographical material, to series that adapt established literature (*Olive Kitteridge*) or literature as it evolves (*Game of Thrones*), and remakes of films like *Mildred Pierce* or *Westworld*. However, the TV series remake is a rare HBO product.

5.3 Televisual Quests for 'Authorial Authenticity'

Claims of 'originality' inevitably become synonymous with quality, and both HBO and the BBC are aligned with the production of quality TV. Through the marketing catchphrase 'It's not TV, it's HBO', HBO has built a brand identity that distances this cable channel from low-brow, mainstream TV, while the BBC remains a 'purveyor of high culture' (Steemers 2–3) and of original drama. And yet, as Hutcheon notes, adaptations 'by their very existence...remind us there is no such thing as an autonomous text' penned by an 'original genius' (111). This is particularly pertinent to the study of the TV remake which through its very classification problematises notions of 'original' authorship within an industry where text is invariably conceived, written and produced in a context of collaboration. In the field of adaptation studies as in screen studies, the quest for authorial authenticity as a means to validation still prevails and authorial authority has historically been ascribed as the domain of the director-auteur (Murray 133). But romantic perceptions of authorship and of a fixed text are relatively recent (Bazin in Naremore, 23). While cinema ascribes authorship 'responsibility' to the director-auteur, TV has long been regarded as the producer's medium, where 'authorship by management' is the norm—a norm that signals a directional shift in emphasis and perception of creative process away from notions of singular authorship to a much more product-driven mode of shared textual production. Mittell dismisses any idealised perception of '"pure" authorship' in the realms of the TV industry, arguing instead that its creative processes are collaborative from the outset, its creative strategies continuously shaped by commonly shared 'commercial concerns' (92). Nevertheless, despite the fact that authorship is seen as attributable not to an individual but to TV's large-scale production industry and its broadcast institutions, a series' creative direction and its distinctive style is shaped by its showrunner who retains overall managerial and authorial control of the project. In general, series directors change from episode to episode as well as season to season but the TV showrunner, ascribed the role of series creator, *oversees* its ever-evolving creative vision. Within an American TV industry context in particular, the showrunner leads a writing team, shepherding ongoing narratives across complex multi-seasonal story arcs: neither literature's romantic vision of the solitary writer or cinema's vision of the omnipotent director-auteur has currency in the context of contemporary TV production. The *sharing* of creative authenticity and authorship is fundamental to both TV production *and* adaptation as a mode of legitimate creative endeavour.

Somewhat ironically, though, the writerly process is given far greater credence and kudos in the environs of TV drama production than it has ever been given in cinema. In direct contrast to the lowly position of the screenplay writer in the film industry (Boozer 2), the TV scriptwriter plays a significant role in a TV industry that has traditionally valued 'writing, and words, above other aesthetic aspects' (Cardwell 172). Furthermore, as head writer and series creator the showrunner, working on certain prestige scripted dramas produced by certain networks, has emerged of late as what is now liberally termed the 'TV auteur' (Newman and Levine 2012; Mittell; Chalaby 2015). Though film auteur David Lynch's enigmatic TV series *Twin Peaks* was first screened in 1990, the concept of the 'author-driven series' with a 'distinctive voice' did not gain momentum until the late nineties and early 2000s (Poniewozik, Time). Series writers like David Chase (*The Sopranos*, 1999–2007), Alan Ball (*Six Feet Under*, 2001–2005) and David Simon (*The Wire*, 2002–2008) have emerged as showrunners with the kind of 'distinctive voice' that attracts what McCabe terms a 'consecrating consensus' of critics that promotes amongst its readership notions of auteur-driven television (188). Despite the fact that television is a medium that is '*produced* rather than *authored*' (Mittell 95), authorship discourse employed by critics and network marketing strategists alike set apart particular series deemed worthy of the mantle of auteurship, adding respectability to a medium that has long been regarded as a purveyor of low-brow culture. The presence of a 'showrunner-auteur' associated with an 'authored series' lends a show a mark of distinctive quality that forms a sought after facet of brand identity for broadcasters, cable channels and streaming providers alike, but it is no coincidence that industry writer-showrunners first emerged from the HBO stable. HBO plays the 'auteur TV' card at every opportunity, whether in relation to its auteur showrunners or its ('not TV') auteur products, actively 'mobilizing tropes of authorship' and establishing an 'aesthetic' perception of series and by inference the brand (Newman and Levine 44–5). The rise to prominence of the 'author-driven' series was first championed by HBO as part of a 'rebranding strategy' designed to reconstruct its image as something much more than the run-of-the-mill cable channel; by seeking to emulate established auteur art forms like literature, theatre and most tellingly art house cinema, HBO worked to establish itself as a 'purveyor of contemporary TV art' (McCabe 186). With the aid of writers like Chase, Ball and Simon HBO established itself as a 'beacon of originality' within the confines of the commercially driven TV industry (187). The practice of attaching auteurs from the film industry to television series is fast becoming an industry norm with rival cable channels like Showtime and Netflix also attracting screenwriters, directors and celebrity performers to engage in creative endeavours on the small screen.[1] HBO, nevertheless, remains the channel with the highest proportion of creatives who can boast auteur credentials either prior to working on HBO products (Martin Scorsese, *Boardwalk Empire*, 2010–2014; Todd Haynes, *Mildred Pierce*, 2011; and Stephen Soderbergh, *The Knick*, 2014–2015; Cary Fukunaga, *True Detective*, 2013) or as a consequence of doing so (Chase, Ball, Simon, Lena Dunham). With an increase in the number of film creatives, including screenplay writers, moving into the TV industry and the contemporary preoccupation with TV auteurship, notions of authorial 'voice' have become a powerful source of branding differentiation that affords a TV series certain cultural kudos.

However, in the TV industry as in the film industry, those heralded as the medium's auteurs do not always take up that mantle, some writer/showrunners of renown like Vince Gilligan, series showrunner of *Breaking Bad*, preferring instead to embrace the collaborative nature of TV and its production modes:

> The worst thing the French ever gave us is the auteur theory.
> It's a load of horseshit. You don't make a movie by yourself,
> you certainly don't make a TV show by yourself (Gilligan in Martin).

Attribution of the mantel of auteurship is inherently problematic in a TV production context, especially on those less frequent occasions where a series retains one director for an entire season. HBO's *True Detective* illustrates this dilemma: the success of Season One was readily attributed to showrunner/creator Nic Pizzolatto, with passing mention of the directorial finesse afforded by film auteur Cary Fukunaga who worked on every episode; but with the failure of Season Two, marked by the absence of Fukunaga's directorial presence, critics began to question the auteurial credentials initially afforded to Pizzolatto, positing the idea that it was Fukunaga's creative endeavours that made Season One such

---

[1] See, for example, Jane Campion, *Top of the Lake*, BBC, 2013–; John Logan, *Penny Dreadful*, Showtime, and *Just Kids*, in production, Showtime; Guillermo del Toro, *The Strain*, FX 2014–; David Fincher, *House of Cards*, Netflix, 2013; Spike Lee, *She's Gotta Have it*, Netflix, 2017; Cary Fukunaga, *Maniac*, Netflix, 2017.

a resounding success. Moreover, the 'promo[tion] and consump[tion]' of TV dramas as *authored* television texts' (Newman and Levine 39) is not a practice embraced by all who write for or about television. Nichols-Pethick argues that critical discourse surrounding television writing works on a commonly held (and misplaced) assumption that it is an inferior form (Nobody 153). For some writers too, writing for television will always be deemed a secondary art, even when it has resulted in a writer's overwhelming success; Chase is known for his disdain of the medium despite the critical acclaim garnered for his work on *The Sopranos* (Chase in Biskind) while Richard Price, series co-writer on *The Night Of* and a writer of episodes for *The Wire*, rejects any suggestion that writing for television could ever be the cultural equivalent of writing a novel, referring to it as merely 'a job' (Hughes). Despite the increased prominence of the 'author function' and its capacity to 'anchor the [TV] medium's cultural worth', this 'attribution' of authorship remains not only a 'comparatively new phenomenon' (Mittell 97), but one that has to be constantly qualified on many levels. Claiming a series has 'novelistic' attributes serves as one such means of validating its authorial credentials, but Nichols-Pethick refutes the assumption that TV writing is 'inferior to other forms', and challenges the assertion that it is only able to attain cultural kudos by emulating the writing formats and processes of more 'prestigious' genres like the novel (153–154); series like *The Wire*, for instance, are frequently lauded as TV calibrated as 'novelistic' (Nichols-Pethick, De Fino, Mittell, Bigsby).

In a time-conscious TV industry driven by tight production schedules, the concept of the time-rich solitary writer lacks credibility: as Noah Hawley, much-lauded showrunner/creator on FX series *Fargo* pointedly notes, 'if you're writing for television, you can't wait for the muse to strike' (Hawley in Tate). Writing for TV is a 'negotiated activity' (154); in an American production context, it invariably involves a writing team and a showrunner who, like Gilligan strives to 'invest people in their work', to 'make people feel comfortable in their jobs', to 'keep people talking'; clearly, auteurist posturing has no place in Gilligan's writers' room (Gilligan in Martin). Wells-Lassagne argues, however, that while showrunners are not necessarily seeing themselves as auteurs, they are 'engaged in making their series "auteur TV" in order to posit TV as art' (123), and to project a certain kind of brand image associated with not just the TV series but with the cable channel, broadcaster or streaming provider it is produced for. This quest for auteur status comes not from showrunners but from those who finance and market the end product, with showrunners becoming yet another celebrity property promoted alongside star performers and star directors through their increased media presence (Chalaby 101). Debates about authorship and authorial authenticity continue to permeate the practice of adaptation, especially when a prior text is being revisioned for the screen. But how does the TV industry's contemporary preoccupation with auteurism and authorial authenticity inform the processes involved in the adaptation of prior texts to this specific production landscape? It certainly complicates the relationship that ensues by adding another layer to the discourse surrounding authorship and its sacrosanct status, bringing considerations of authorial authenticity back into the frame—and this, despite TV's traditional mode of collaborative, co-operative creative endeavour, and the prevalence of contemporary scholarly discourse that steers the study of adaptations away from the tired fidelity debate.

As a well established and accepted mode of product sharing within the TV industry, the TV remake is inherently less fraught with difficulties when it comes to matters of 'authorial' ownership since some element of shared ownership—between the writer of the adapted text and its remake—is a given. It is now common practice to involve members of the originating country's production team in the translation of a drama series to its new geographical and cultural locale. Series creator and sole writer of the BBC's *Criminal Justice*, Peter Moffat, shares executive producer credits with *The Night Of*'s adapters, Stephen Zaillian and Richard Price, and with the BBC's former head of commissioning, Jane Tranter, who first brought the BBC series to the attention of HBO as a potential American remake ripe for further expansion (Ellis-Petersen). Nevertheless, traditional modes of writing and production differ considerably between the UK and the USA. According to TV producer Gareth Neame (*Downton Abbey*), the British model is 'much more like the film model' in which the writer has specific responsibility for creating a screenplay: there is no established tradition of a writers' room ethos within a UK production context (Neame in Birnbaum). However, Neame also insists the two writing models—'the American writers' room' and 'the British single author'—are increasingly likely to find traction in each production context, providing American and British programme-makers with the opportunity to 'steal from each other and find the best of both worlds' (Neame in Birnbaum). Peter Moffat is a writer whose work is firmly anchored in the world of British television, and in most of the series Moffat works on he takes sole responsibility for generating the series' script. He has been writing and executive producing in TV since the late nineties, and with the exception of his adaptation of *Macbeth* as part of the BBC's *ShakespeaREtold* series is involved in the writing of 'original' drama (*Cambridge Spies*, 2003; *North Square*, 2001; *Criminal Justice*, 2009; *Silk*, 2011; *The Village*, 2013; *Undercover*, 2016). His is the kind of 'individual writer's voice' that is 'central' to the traditional British TV series (Stephen Moffat in Birnbaum).

HBO's *The Night Of* adopts a mode of writing that is more in line with the author-centred British model; it serves as a clear example of the ways in which the *British* model is influencing its *American* counterpart. The 'singularity of authorship' that characterises *The Night Of* affords the series a 'singular vision' with a 'distinct and present voice' (Idato) of a kind that distinguishes it from the kind of American production norms that overwhelmingly favour the writers' room model of script production. Price and Zaillian come from a very different writing background to that of Moffat; yet their approach to the revisioning of Moffat's series emulates the British model which, regardless of the collaborative nature of the TV industry in general, still tends to afford writerly accountability to a very specific authorship. Both Price and Zaillian are screenwriters with an established pedigree, and are experienced in the art of adaptation. Many of their projects have involved the transformation of novels to film. Zaillian has penned seven screen adaptations since 1990, and won an Oscar for Best Adapted Screenplay for *Schindler's List* (1993). Price has written six screen adaptations since 1986, and some of his screenplays are adaptations of his own novels. Both have also worked with respected film auteurs: Zaillian has written for Martin Scorsese (*Gangs of New York*, 2002), David Fincher (*The Girl with the Dragon Tattoo*, 2011) and Ridley Scott (*American Gangster*, 2007), while Price has written for Scorsese (*The Color of Money*, 1986) and Spike Lee (*Clockers*, 1995). The initial outline for the remake of *Criminal Justice*, retitled *The Night Of*, was shaped by Zaillian but the series was then written collaboratively, with Price taking the scripting lead on the first four episodes and Zaillian the final four (Zeitchik). For Zaillian and Price, the series had to have 'the cohesion and feeling of a film—in this case a nine hour film' (Zaillian in Gill), for which the 500-page script was written in its entirety before being 'parsed' into discrete episodes (Zaillian in Ellis-Petersen). Tellingly, Zaillian also directs all but one episode of the series, amplifying its status as a text that has a certain 'singularity of authorship' (Idato) at the level of script and on-screen visualisation. In a TV landscape characterised by the rise of rival cable channels and streaming providers, HBO's edge is dwindling as strong competitors emerge in the market for quality prestige drama series, but the authorial pedigree of *The Night Of* serves to strengthen the cable channel's currently at risk identity as the main provider of quality high-end TV product. In contrast to other recent HBO series like Season Two of *True Detective* (2015) and the Scorsese/Mick Jagger helmed *Vinyl* (2016), both of which failed to attract substantial audiences, *The Night Of* has attained critical acclaim and commercial success.

Jane Tranter, executive producer on *The Night Of* and BBC drama commissioner responsible for the commissioning of *Criminal Justice*, sees *The Night Of* as a 'very unique series' that is 'different from other television pieces' due its 'meticulous attention to detail' (Tranter in Ellis-Petersen). *Criminal Justice* is, she argues, an 'unfinished conversation', ripe for further adaptation and expansion; its compressed five hour narrative results in the 'cramming of a huge and complex story into a too small space' (Idato), whereas the eight-episode structure of *The Night Of* leaves room for the narrative to develop fully, taking both its plot and its characterisation into different territory and resulting in television 'of a kind that has yet to happen in the UK' (Tranter in Ellis-Petersen). Clearly, the nature of the viewing experience differs too: *Criminal Justice* was aired in a manner that works against BBC norms with all five episodes broadcast within one week while HBO maintained its weekly episodic release schedule. The former builds viewer engagement around the momentum of the narrative, its harrowing prison scenes lending a sense of urgency to the piece; the latter leads viewers on the more traditional kind of slow-burn 'who-dunnit' trail, placing its audience in the role of what Mittell terms 'sleuths at work' engaged in a kind of online 'forensic fandom' in pursuit of answers to the conundrum posed by such narratives (52). It is, argues Price, 'the antithesis of *Law and Order*', a programme he sums up as a formulaic 'put it in the microwave, hit 60 seconds and serve' mode of storytelling (Price in Stanhope). With its ensemble cast and its novelistic depth, *The Night Of* has been favourably compared to both *True Detective* and *The Wire*. The latter, a series for which Price wrote several episodes and which, like *The Night Of*, addresses institutional flaws, also draws comparisons with other character-driven narratives as 'a television drama of the rarest kind, the once-in-a decade sort which stands shoulder to shoulder with *The Sopranos* and *Breaking Bad*' (Idato). *The Night Of*'s status as a remake has not impinged on its capacity to be seen as 'quality TV' on a par with some of the most revered and original series produced during this 'golden age' of television.

5.4 Recalibrating the Text

Despite its identity as a remake, *The Night Of* is a conspicuously authored piece of HBO TV drama. As an adapter, Zaillian cites the thematic appeal of a narrative as the main driving force behind his desire to become involved in its transformation; his numerous adaptations from novel to film demonstrate his commitment to maintaining the dominant themes explored in the source texts he chooses to work with, and his approach to the remake of *Criminal Justice* in which it is exploration of 'the system itself' that he is drawn to is no exception (Zaillian in Hughes). Moffat, as creator of *Criminal Justice*, cites the UK's 'adversarial system' as the driving force behind *his* narrative. It is a system 'which isn't interested in arriving at the truth'; it is, states Moffat, 'the narratives that matter in a trial' where 'the best story, the most compelling story, wins' (Moffat in Galloway). Versions of 'truth' provide the structural framework and plot momentum of both Moffat's series and the HBO remake. The quest for truth is subsumed by vested interests within the justice system, with versions of truth presented as fact by the various parties involved—from prosecution and defence lawyers to law enforcers and expert witnesses procured by both sides, all of whom are 'just telling different stories' (Moffat in Galloway). Moffat's script, as part of its exploration of the justice system and those whose lives are affected by it, focuses much of the narrative on the prison scenes that punctuate the trial, and this is something that Price and Zaillian also choose to focus on when recreating the narrative within a contemporary American context. However, *The Night Of* also emulates the generic hybridity of its precursor text by drawing on the tropes of the crime drama, the courtroom drama and the prison drama. Building upon the preordained and culturally embedded codes of former screen iterations of all three types of drama, the generic tropes of each are re-contextualised within the specific framework of American TV production: American police dramas, American courtroom dramas and American prison dramas that both precede and are contemporaneous to *The Night Of* provide further cultural referents, its narrative transitioning to a decidedly American context that situates the story within the minutiae of the American justice system and its institutions. The series examines America's flawed prison system and reflects the country's currently problematic social and political landscape. Yet Price insists this was not a conscious choice, even if such matters inevitably seep into the series' subtext:

> We didn't come at this with the idea of, 'Oh, we're going to expose social justice or the hellhole that is Rikers'. Everybody knows it's a hellhole. Prisons always are. We weren't to know what would happen with Donald Trump—when we were first writing, who the hell was Trump?—or Eric Garner or Isis. It's more that if you write stuff that reflects the vibrations in the air, some of it will make headlines (Price in Hughes).

Moreover, despite the series' shift from the source text's white suspect/black victim to black Muslim suspect/white victim, Zaillian is adamant that such changes are not actioned in order to turn this into a politically motivated post 9/11 'immigrant story' (Zaillian in Travers). The functional rationale for the change comes from the chosen geography of place—New York cabbies are, argues Price, from ethnic backgrounds in general and are of Pakistani nationality in particular, and that in itself 'adds a whole new dimension' (Price in Zeitchik). Murder suspect Nasir Kahn is not, according to actor Riz Ahmed, defined by his heritage and immigrant background but neither is his cultural identity erased (Ahmed in Okeowo). Rather than 'chasing headlines' with a topical immigrant story, the writers of *The Night Of* focus on the system and what it does to individuals who enter into that system, regardless of colour or creed, and by centring the narrative on an everyman suspect whose guilt or innocence has yet to be clearly defined, this series and its precursor text invite vicarious viewer engagement with the disturbing realities of prison experience. Zaillian wants his audience to share the fear of being caught up in an arbitrary system that detains '10,000 male and female detainees each day', hoping that we come away from the series 'with this feeling of "Please God, I don't ever want to get arrested and not make bail and have to go there"' (Zaillian in Ellis-Petersen). Ahmed recounts stories that both inform his character's situation and reflect the series' exploration of a flawed system in which people are unfairly exposed to the dangers of a place like Rikers Correctional Centre from which they emerge as markedly changed and damaged individuals; he recalls the story of sixteen-year-old Kalief Browder which came to attention during the filming of *The Night Of*:

> He was a young man accused of stealing someone's backpack. He was detained awaiting trial, for three years just because of the backlog of cases. He came with no previous, came out and killed himself from the PTSD of that….it's crazy (Ahmed in Ellis-Petersen).

Browder's story of judicial injustice within the American system becomes one of many that are in intertextual dialogue with a series like *The Night Of*—a series that, like *Orange is the New Black*, 'reflects the vibrations in the air' of contemporary American society (Price in Hughes).

However, both the source series and the remake maintain a political dimension through the very nature of their content. Class and race politics play a part in each, whether at a consciously crafted level or an inferred level. In *Criminal Justice*, white working-class suspect Ben Coulter is accused of the murder of a black working-class girl from the Stockhill Estate area of south London where racial tensions abound, and failure to convict this white suspect would, as the Chief of Police notes, result in 'bad PR' for the police force and a potential race riot on the estate: here, a plea bargain is sanctioned as a form of 'damage control' (episode 3). Though racial politics play their part in *The Night Of*, with tensions and racial backlash in the Pakistani community built into the narrative, it is the financial constraints and system overload that are foregrounded as the rationale behind the plea bargaining that takes place within this American context, bringing the thematic focus back to moral questions related to the arbitrary nature of 'justice' and the similarly financial strain placed on working-class families of suspects caught up in the system. The *success* of any remake is invariably dependent upon an adapter's capacity to resituate the story and its characters within the sociocultural framework of its host nation, adding cultural referents that speak to the viewer's experience, and that present familiar cultural territory, whilst retaining key narrative elements. The nuances of the systems that underpin this HBO narrative—from the police and courtroom procedures to the ways in which correctional facilities operate—are successfully translated in *The Night Of* to a new cultural and political scene as well as a transformed geography of place.

Remakes are, in general, further characterised by their inherently intertextual potential, and *The Night Of* in particular incorporates further layers of intertextual complexity to what is an already rich crime drama hybrid via its intertextual affiliation with a number of non-fiction series.

As a consequence of its narrative content, *The Night Of* is in dialogue with other contemporary American series that employ plot momentum which builds around the guilt or innocence of a given protagonist within the American justice system; though both *Criminal Justice* and *The Night Of* are fictional dramas, they share an affiliation with populist true-crime drama series like *Serial* (2014–2016), *Making a Murderer* (2015–) and *The Jinx: the Life and Death of Robert Durst* (2015–), all of which take a semi-procedural approach to the investigation of contested convictions that entail a possible miscarriage of justice. *Making a Murderer* and *The Jinx* present as legal procedural non-fiction series that document the flaws in the American justice system by following particular cases of potentially wrongful conviction while *Serial* is a non-fiction podcast that has attained populist acclaim, despite the podcast form's more niche appeal up to this point. Zaillian acknowledges the influence of a much earlier French TV docu-series (*Soupçon*, 2004) that similarly details another problematic murder trial (Zeitchik). In all, punishment is meted out according to whatever version a jury (and by extension a viewing audience) chooses to believe. Since *Serial* follows the flawed case of Pakistani Muslim Adnan Masud Syed who is accused of murdering his ex-girlfriend, there are further intertextual points of reference between the podcast and the HBO series, each following the narrative trajectory of a Muslim suspect within a post-9/11 context. Moral quandaries also play out in dramatised forms in contemporary series like *The People v O. J. Simpson* (2016). The BBC series predates all of these populist series, and the HBO remake is a project that was in pre-production well in advance of the aforementioned fictional and non-fictional programmes, but all of these texts remain in dialogue with each other through shared narratives that centre on the moral ambiguities surrounding justice systems and the impact those systems have on the lives of those who find themselves caught up in their often arbitrary procedures.

In *The Night Of*, changes to the source text are engendered not only by changes prescribed by the different judicial systems each narrative plays out in but by conscious choices related to characterisation, generic treatment and style aesthetic. While Price and Zaillian take *The Night Of*'s basic premise from the first five episode series of *Criminal Justice*, their eight-episode adaptation of that premise differs at both the level of plot and treatment. Their story still focuses on one individual's journey through the judicial system and its correctional facilities; similarly, the guilt or innocence of that individual remains an ongoing moral conundrum for much of the narrative, and the characters from the source text are, on one level, translated into their American counterparts within an American system and an American sociocultural context. Certain cause and effect plot points are retained; the narrative revolves around the same incidents—it begins by following events on a particular night in which a young man takes his father's taxi without consent, and ends up being arrested for the murder of a girl he has picked up and spent the night with; it then proceeds to detail the suspect's experience of the judicial system and his prison experience while on trial for her murder. However, the plot trajectory, the on-screen treatment of the genres with which the series engages, and the character constructs employed differ in this remake of the source text. The writers adopt a similarly 'classic three act structure' to the narrative but the 'overall architecture' of the piece is informed by its attention to the details entailed in the judicial process, from arrest, to charge, to arraignment (Zaillian in Radish). Price is interested in communicating the minutiae of the experience, aiming for a 'heightened reality' that explores the 'dead time' between the moments that take the plot forward—dramatised moments that 'capture the interminableness' of the system 'without being interminable' (Price in Radish). For Zaillian, it is 'the scenes on either side of the plot' that are sometimes 'the most interesting thing': the waiting around in the police station, the build-up to the inevitable interrogation and so on become, in *The Night Of*, detailed moments redolent with tension:

> When you go to a police station, you wait. When you're going to get interrogated, the scene doesn't start with the interrogation. It starts with him dreading the interrogation. We're here for a minute or two, just with [Naz] (Zaillian in Radish).

Though seeking to write a narrative that deals in the experiential minutiae of the system, Price acknowledges the challenges presented by a source text that in his estimation was already 'too dense' and contained 'too much that was good' (Price in Zeitchik). Faced with this dilemma, Price and Zaillian, as adapters of the story chose to expand the series to eight episodes, reworking certain plot points, through omission and revision, in pursuit of narrative clarity and in response to their own reconfiguration of the various characters that people *their* story as opposed to that of Moffat. Zaillian maintains *The Night Of* is, in its adapted form, first and foremost 'a character study—a study of many characters, really' rather than a 'procedural' (Zaillian in Zeitchik), suggesting that complex characterisation is the crux of the drama. Its plot revisions are actioned in response to the reconfiguration of characters involved in the narrative as well as matters related to genre and plot momentum. Zaillian and Price engage in a more layered, drawn-out exploration of characters involved—not only in relation to the suspect but to his family members, his lawyer John Stone, and prison 'king-pin' Freddy Knight. Here, characters like Detective Box and Chandra Kapoor, who function primarily as plot drivers in *Criminal Justice*, also become more complex character studies with their own backstories.

However, despite Zaillian's assertion that this is a 'character study' rather than a 'procedural', it is the procedural nature of the narrative that is foregrounded in both *The Night Of*'s trailer and its credit sequence, each of which differs in tone and content to that of the precursor text. The credit sequence employed on *Criminal Justice* places the narrative focus directly on Ben Coulter as protagonist. A tense, hollow-sounding single note score plays throughout a 46 second credit sequence that opens on a black screen, invaded by fine, ever-shifting electric blue and metallic grey vertical lines entering from the edges of the frame, and creating feelings of disorientation and enclosure. A face forms right of frame, the startling clarity of the image exposing every nervous mannerism and eye movement as the looker is held in the camera's scrutinising lens. The very human aspect of the narrative, and this figure's part in that narrative, is foregrounded from the outset, suggesting that some kind of personal drama is about to ensue though little is provided in terms of narrative detail and direction. The longer and more hypnotic 1990s credit sequence employed in *The Night Of* provides a much clearer sense of the fictional world of the series and its narrative direction; its focus is not on individuals, who are markedly *absent* from the sequence, but on inanimate objects and locale, establishing instead a sense of place and of the disturbing events that unfold there. This credit sequence, with its chiaroscuro lighting, its predominantly monochromatic palette and its decidedly urban locale, is a stylised homage to the noir detective narrative, and the procedural nature of its itemisation of objects infers that the series is identifiable first and foremost as a crime drama. Created by Method Studio's John Likens and Jon Noorlander to Zaillian's brief (Decider), the New York constructed in the opening credit sequence is purposely devoid of the city's iconic buildings and landmarks, its black and white images focusing instead on the cityscape of New Yorkers, representing New York in the 'abstract' yet establishing it as a major part of the narrative that is about to unfold (Noorlander in Decider). From the outset, the dimly lit monochromatic images are accompanied by the tension building staccato of an orchestral score that adds a rhythmic quality to a series of edits between claustrophobic shots of anonymous city streets, stairwells, the undercarriage of bridges, the subway and so on, each lensed by a constantly mobile prowling camera, before moving to a series of aerial shots of the city's roads and buildings that present night-time New York in an almost painterly abstract form. Locale shots give way to a series of seemingly random images of inanimate objects, from an abandoned New York taxicab and a cat shot in slow motion crossing a deserted street, to close ups of ecstasy pills, a broken necklace chain, rings falling into smoky black frames; as the intensity of the orchestral score builds, the sequence shifts to further shots of objects and locales that will become central to the unravelling of the plot. An almost procedural documentation of clues singled out by hints of colour ensues: shots of police tape tinged with red, blue and yellow hues on the petrol pumps of a deserted gas station, a close up of a stained, ring-clad hand, a rain-soaked screen infused with red, a blood-soaked floor, and a close up shot of a yellow-tinged taxi cab's ID light. Moving out again to various shots of the cityscape, the sequence finally rests on a static wide-angle shot of the city at dawn, the closing frame implying that at daybreak all will be revealed. Already, this American series is adapting to a different geographical context and to a style aesthetic that aligns its narrative with the long-standing traditions of American cinema's film noir and the televisual tropes of TV noir, the 'tones, values, and rhythms' (Grindstaff 157) of the precursor text recalibrated here to produce a remake which attains its own distinctive identity.

The trailers for each series are similarly disparate in their approach to genre and narrative. Performance takes centre stage in what is set up as a very British social realist drama in the trailer for *Criminal Justice*. It maps out the series' narrative trajectory via a sequence of swift edits between dramatic scenes taken from its five-episode run, and much of the emphasis is placed on the accused's daunting experiences within judicial and custodial systems. In contrast, the trailer for *The Night Of* is a meticulously crafted sequence that again constructs its identity as that of crime drama, the accused appearing only briefly. It is less revealing of story content than the trailer that accompanies its British counterpart, and it invites the audience to *engage* in the unravelling of a crime rather than in any kind of emotive identification with its protagonist in the aftermath of a crime: the narrative focus here is on the intensity of events on the night of the arrest and on the crime committed on that night rather than on the experiential story of its suspect. The locale created in the marketing trailer for *The Night Of* is much more specific than that of the night-time New York landscape of its credit sequence; several characters are also introduced in the trailer, providing the potential audience with not only a crime narrative but players involved in the perpetration and the solving of that crime. A series of syncopated shots slowly tracks the interior spaces where the crime took place, and as in the credit sequence, significant objects are framed in close up: an old-school push-button telephone, a bloodied eye on a stag head, a grimy push-button service bell on an equally grimy counter, pills in a clear plastic bag, an open refrigerator. These images and the subsequent images of a young man in a holding cell are accompanied by voices out of frame that discuss the crime, constructing a narrative that focuses on assumptions of guilt:

> *Box*: 'What am I not seeing? Explain to me what I'm not understanding'.
> *Naz*: 'It looks like I killed her, I know that'.
> *Box*: 'That's how it looks. But it's not that simple is it'.

Voices and sounds out of frame—the piercing ring of the counter bell, the incessant ring of a telephone that is later revealed as the one seen in the opening frame, and the diegetic sounds of prison doors opening and closing—play out over a series of fast edits that revisit earlier shots of evidence from the crime scene. The penultimate frame returns to the opening shot of the old-school telephone as hands dart into the static screen space to pick up the call. The cacophony of sound that has built to this moment ends abruptly as we edit swiftly between a momentarily black screen and a static medium close up shot of the suspect, now placed firmly at the centre of the series' narrative trajectory. Similarly, its pilot episode foregrounds the generic markers of the crime genre, highlighting en route moments that will later implicate Nasir Kahn in the murder of Andrea Cornish, from added scenes of officers intervening to eject unwanted male passengers from his cab to CCTV footage of his purchase of alcohol at the gas station and toll booth cameras placing him in a specific place at a specific time. The audience is also introduced to characters who are part of that evening and who become potential suspects during the course of Stone's investigative work as the series unfolds—from the driver of the funeral car, to the males who taunt him outside Andrea's house—adding another sleuth-like layer to the narrative. In comparison with its source text, this adaptation is projected as a series that, through the nature of its credit sequence, its marketing trailer, and its pilot episode invests to a more visible degree in the tropes of the crime genre than in experiential drama, even if what follows on from each is a story that deals more directly in the minutiae of the systems that impact on the lives of individuals caught up in them. However, in the *telling* of the tale, *The Night Of* mirrors its 'sister' text as an in-depth study of not only systems but of those whose life experiences are governed by them.

5.5   *The Night Of*: A Generic 'Makeover'

Both *Criminal Justice* and its remake are series characterised by their generic hybridity: each is affiliated with the generic markers of the crime drama, the courtroom drama and the prison drama; each follows in close up the harrowing journey of a young suspect through the complex labyrinth of custodial systems. Yet, despite their shared generic DNA and their shared narrative template, they differ somewhat in terms of their stylistic treatment of generic tropes and, as a consequence, not only the visualisation of the narrative but the construction of figures involved in that narrative are recalibrated in the transition to an American televisual context. As its credit sequence infers, *The Night Of* is affiliated with the traditions of American cinema's film noir; its dark and potentially dangerous New York city streets are established as the familiar territory of noir, and its colour and lighting palette emulate the expressionistic style of noir cinema, but both its marketing trailer and the treatment of story content within each episode are less directly influenced by a film noir-style aesthetic. From the outset, Zaillian's aim was to adopt a 'naturalistic' approach of a kind he associates with Italian neo-realism of the 1940s and early 1950s rather than the cinematic style of film noir with its highly stylised chiaroscuro lighting, its expressionistic camera work and its use of voiceover (Zaillian in Gills). The dangerous streets of New York city remain one of the narrative's backdrops, and certain scenes—the murder scene in particular—retain a darkly noiresque edge, but the noir elements of this series are more a reflection of its affiliation not with film noir but with TV noir. Glover and Bushman argue that 'on television, the noir ethos is identified not so much by stylistic considerations' but 'by such elements as tone, atmosphere, narrative patterns, recurring motifs, and character archetypes' (67), and in this sense, *The Night Of* remains a decidedly noiresque text, dealing in the kind of mystery that is invariably related to the investigation of a mysterious crime. Noir's capacity to reflect the societal and cultural concerns of its contemporary production climate is also part of its generic tradition; however, TV noir in particular presents 'societal order' as 'at best a myth' and constructs protagonists marooned in a narrative 'where truth shades into lie, righteousness into brutality, stability into confusion' (68). In this sense, both *Criminal Justice* and *The Night Of* engage with the overarching properties of TV noir, the protagonists of each placed in a similarly brutal, unstable and confusing environment in which a quest for some kind of truth unfolds and the solving of a mysterious crime provides narrative momentum. However, Moffat's series is rooted in the gritty social realist tradition of British crime and prison dramas, and though Zaillian seeks a similar realism, 'in the writing, the casting, the acting, directing, cinematography, production design, editing' (Zaillian in Gills), the series is informed not by the British social realist tradition but by a style of realism that aligns it with American TV noir in its earliest evolutionary form—one which is also characterised by its affiliation with the crime genre. Like the fifties ground-breaking television series *Dragnet* (1951–1959) with its 'particular brand of realism', of a kind 'hitherto only been found in European realist art', and its operational aesthetic 'partly inspired by noir film with a documentary style and feel' (Palmer 35–42), *The Night Of* attains a realistic portrayal that also embraces the tone and atmosphere of TV noir.

If, as Schickel contends, film noir is 'all about seductive women and seducible men' (36), Andrea Cornish emerges as one of the series' most clearly delineated and striking noir archetypes—the genre's 'agent of cruel fate' (Walker-Morrison 25) whose random act of entering Nasir Kahn's taxicab on the night of her death implicates him in her subsequent murder. The murder victim of Moffat's tale transitions from regular working-class girl to the more urbane, bohemian femme fatale of the HBO remake. Moreover, Andrea's life is shrouded in mystery: unlike Melanie Lloyd whose death is a consequence of unwittingly witnessing a murder on the Stockhill Estate, Andrea's death is precipitated by the complex web of her relationships with others prior to her murder. In *The Night Of*, Andrea's murder is about more than being in the wrong place at the wrong time, and the complicated backstory generated for the murder victim in this scenario takes this remake into the more complex police procedural territory of TV noir. The loaded line delivered by the murdered girl in each series is retained yet subtly amended to give a greater urgency to Andrea's statement as Melanie's line, 'I *don't* want to be alone tonight', transitions to 'I *can't*'. Similarly, while a certain sense of playfulness is retained in the construction of the relationship between Naz and Andrea, his fascination with her is far less romanticised than that of Ben Coulter whose encounter with Melanie involves flirtatious hand-holding moments, and the sharing of ice creams and flavoured milk before progressing to ecstasy pills, dangerous party games involving knives and consensual sex (1.1). From the outset, Andrea is constructed as a more enigmatic character: she appears out of nowhere, the camera initially providing only fragmented glimpses of her face and eyes, seen from Naz's point of view via the taxi cab's rear-view mirror. In this dimly lit interior scene, with its muted, grainy colour palette, Zaillian employs a noir style aesthetic to frame the strategic moment of first fatalistic encounter between this potentially dangerous, 'seductive' woman and 'seducible' Naz. There is minimal dialogue and little of the innocence that pervades the first meeting between suspect and victim in *Criminal Justice*: Naz buys beer for Andrea rather than ice cream and milk, and the extent of her drug habit becomes clear as the night's events unfold. While a naturalistic style aesthetic is the norm in *The Night Of*, moments between Naz and Andrea are characterised by a loaded noir aesthetic, both during their time together before her murder and in the flashbacks that haunt Naz in the aftermath.

Protagonist Nasir Kahn emerges as a complex noir archetype. His characterisation is much more layered than that of his *Criminal Justice* counterpart, Ben Coulter. The two share a similar fate and a seemingly innocent disposition beneath which secrets lie, but though both are placed in the 'irrational' territory of TV noir 'in which the individual has little or no control over his fate' (Glover and Bushman 68), it is Naz, reconfigured here as troubled noir archetype, who embodies both the 'dislocated sense of self' (Glover and Bushman 68) and the 'alienation, absurdity, meaninglessness, and nihilism' (Sanders 98) of the TV noir protagonist. His fractured identity is in part attributed to cultural and familial tensions—tensions that lead him to question his position within both his family and the Muslim community, and that inform this remake's darker narrative outcomes. Naz is not the boy his parents think he is: instead, he is a boy capable of taking his father's taxicab without permission, a boy capable of selling for profit his prescription drugs and, in his mother's estimation, possibly capable of murder. Like Ben, he is initially resistant to the prison system's survival regime which demands affiliation to a particular prison 'king-pin', but where Ben's initial refusal to adhere to the prison hierarchy is couched as stubborn intransigence, Naz's refusal is presented as a matter of principle and self-sufficiency; and though both Ben and Naz ultimately concede, for Naz it is about more than survival: it is about finding ways to belong, no matter how futile this noir protagonist's search for identity may be. Zaillian and Price introduce plot points that further serve to construct Naz as the noir protagonist 'compromised beyond redemption' (Sanders 105): though ultimately cleared of the murder of Andrea, he is culpable in the death of Petey, whom he could have 'saved' had he spoken sooner about Victor's paedophilic abuse of this young boy. While Ben Coulter, as a consequence of his experiences, ends up with an altered perception of the world around him, Naz ends up with an altered perception of himself. At the close of the series, Naz embraces the solitary fractured identity of the existentialist noir archetype, choosing the drug habit formed as a survival strategy during his prison term over any return to the familial or communal fold. The seemingly innocent and studious Muslim boy presented at the start of the narrative journeys to a point of nihilistic acceptance of his altered fate, despite his earlier attempts to survive above all else. Throughout this journey, Naz is, nevertheless, presented as the everyman character whose plight could as easily be that of any audience member. The writers of the series construct a character with whom we can continue to empathise and whose innocence we continue to invest in, despite the ongoing possibility that the suspect's inability to account for his actions during the time in which the act of murder is committed. There are no moments of nervous meltdown in the witness box, no scenes of ritualistic humiliation of the kind that are experienced by the more nervous and volatile Ben Coulter; Ben's angry courtroom outbursts reveal a potentially darker side to his nature, fuelling the ongoing possibility that he *may* be capable of murder, and his feud with prison hard-case Milroy culminates in his public shaming as a 'grass'. He is a far more exposed and potentially unstable individual than the increasingly prison-wise Naz whose physical transformation from reserved student nerd to the shaven-headed, tattooed member of Freddy Knight's gang underlines his capacity to adapt. Questions of guilt and innocence play out in both narratives as versions of 'truth' are steadily unveiled: each tale avoids the moral certainties of mainstream police dramas of the 1960s, 1970s and 1980s (Lane 138). Naz's more reserved, composed persona leaves room for the possibility of his guilt but in *The Night Of* there is a much greater emphasis on factors that speak to his innocence. There is, for instance, an accumulation of evidence that points to other possible suspects, and the singular knife wound that causes the death of Melanie Lloyd becomes, in *The Night Of*, a frenzied knife attack of the kind attributed to a crime of passion rather than of random opportunity. Ultimately, Naz is presented as the fatalistic victim of the noir genre rather than its devious murderer.

As with Nasir Kahn, the reconfiguration of Detective Dennis Box is dictated by generic considerations that in this instance are influenced not only by the series affiliation with American TV noir but with American TV crime drama. Though an inherently 'conservative' form, peopled by heroic law enforcers, and dealing in 'morality tales' where good ultimately prevails over evil (Nichols-Pethick TV Cops 3), the crime genre is viewed as one of television's most 'diverse and hybrid genres' (Turnbull 709), one capable of not only encompassing the sociocultural politics of its production climate but also engaging in acts of periodic renewal (Nichols-Pethick TV Cops 3). In its treatment of the crime genre, *Criminal Justice* belongs to one such period of renewal. From the early days of episodic series in which good prevails over evil and crimes are invariably solved, British crime drama has shifted to a narrative territory characterised not by the 'reassurance and moral certainty' offered in the 1960s, 1970s and 1980s but by the 'risk and moral ambiguity', and a new kind of 'cop culture' in which police corruption and criminal collusion play a part (Leishman and Mason 23). By the close of *Criminal Justice* Detective Box is revealed as one such law enforcer, ready to collude with criminals like Freddy Graham, and to circumvent the law and the orders of his superiors in pursuit of his own brand 'justice'. In *The Night Of*, Zaillian and Price construct a very different kind of lead detective working within a very different kind of police drama scenario. Here, Dennis Box is one of many hard-working law enforcers working within a system that is ostensibly seeking to do good, despite its many flaws and shortcomings. Price notes that:

> what you're seeing is a system under its best light. There aren't terrible people doing terrible things unjustly to [Naz],

> when we know what's going on. This is what it's like, under
> the best of circumstances (Price in Radish)

Box is recalibrated as an 'old-school' detective working with other officers who are going about their daily duties, and in keeping with the writers' intent to create a naturalistic narrative that deals in the minutiae of this murder case, the scenes prior to Naz being charged with Andrea's murder are expanded, providing the audience with a sense of the mundanity of procedures for both suspect and police. In this respect, *The Night Of* is more akin to one of America's earliest and most influential crime dramas; adapted for television in the fifties from a radio series, *Dragnet* (1951–59) is regarded as the police show that 'establish[ed] the conventions' that all subsequent police dramas build upon (Palmer 33). According to the series creator, Jack Webb, its protagonist, Sergeant Joe Friday, is 'a quiet, dedicated policeman who, as in real life, was just one cog in a great enforcement machine', an 'honest, decent, home-loving guy—the image of fifty thousand peace officers' (Webb qtd in Hayde, cited by Palmer 42). Box emerges as a law enforcer of this ilk. The opera-loving Box is referred to here as in *Criminal Justice* as 'a subtle beast', but the label in this instance is about his capacity to disarm suspects through strategies designed to encourage trust rather than an indicator of his capacity for underhand dealing. His storyline is expanded: his pending retirement forms a focal point around which the very ordinariness of his existence is presented, with running gags about the unappealing prospect of a post-retirement life filled with nothing but golf. He is also instrumental in persuading prosecutor Helen Weiss—another very ordinary individual working in an over-stretched system—to forego the opportunity to ask for a retrial of Nasir Kahn; instead, he persuades her to join him in his efforts to build a case against Andrea's financial adviser, Ray Halle, who is revealed as the murderer in the lead up to the series' close. In every respect, this is 'old-school' policing of the *Dragnet* variety rather than that of so many contemporary cop shows, peopled by anti-heroic officers of the Vic Mackay variety (*The Shield* 2002–2008) who are willing to compromise their principles in pursuit of a conviction.

Though the series affiliation with more formulaic shows like *Law and Order* (1990–2010) is volubly denied by Price (Price in Radish), there remains between the two a shared code of police conduct as well as a structural similarity in which the interplay between police and judicial systems forms part of the narrative arc. Unlike the anti-heroic leanings of contemporary cop shows in both a UK and an American context, in the seminal, long-running American police procedural *Law and Order* 'ideas of morality and justice still play the decisive role'; despite their innate cynicism, its law enforcers continue to 'fight the good fight' (Rapping 31–37). But it is 'the system itself that is the hero' in series like *Law and Order* rather than the individuals who people its weekly narratives (46). Even if construed as arbitrary and ambiguous concepts in *The Night Of*, questions of morality and justice remain central, and its law enforcers are similarly engaged in 'the good fight' against criminals, but the 'heroic system' heralded in *Law and Order* is presented by Zaillian and Price as decidedly unheroic and flawed. Rapping contends that *Law and Order* has evolved from the 'dark cynical' private eye stories penned by writers like Raymond Chandler and Dashiell Hammett, and from 'the classic crime dramas of the Golden Age of Hollywood' (30): despite its debt to *Criminal Justice* as its primary source text, *The Night Of* also owes a debt to such authorship, to American cinema's classic noir detective dramas, and to American TV series predecessors like *Dragnet* and *Law and Order*. In both *The Night Of* and *Criminal Justice*, a multiple structural framework is employed: as in *Law and Order* or the more complex contemporary French crime series *Spiral* (2005–), the investigative elements of the narrative are accompanied by courtroom scenes that intensify and complicate it, but the series also steps outside the formulaic boundaries of *Law and Order*, and the dictates of a French justice system in which criminal investigation and prosecution are constitutionally intertwined, to explore the prison context that is a consequence of each.

Dramatisation of matters related to the concept of justice is central to the courtroom drama in general and to *The Night Of* and *Criminal Justice* in particular, where questions of truth and justice remain central to narrative momentum and character development. The courtroom, with its clearly defined space and its even more clearly defined codes of conduct, provides a highly theatrical arena within which dialogue-driven battles can be stage-managed for maximum impact. In contrast to the physicality of each series' prison scenes, its courtroom moments are decidedly verbal, its narrative propelled through dialogue between lawyer and witness. The self-contained intimacy and intensity of the courtroom scenario provide a platform for the unravelling of complex plot points and moments of high drama engineered by lawyers as they strive to tell stories in pursuit of some kind of 'justice'. Presented as an 'ethical dilemma' that explores 'the tension between law and justice', the 'quest for justice' forms an integral part of this dramatic form (Greenfield and Osborne 251). As the name of Moffat's series implies, 'justice' lies at the heart of his narrative, and by inference that of the HBO remake; but where most traditional courtroom dramas revolve around the conventional battle between right and wrong, *Criminal Justice* and its remake are more concerned with the efficacy of systems that are dependent not upon 'truth' per se but versions of truth. As a trained lawyer Moffat has insight into the workings of the British legal system; there are, he argues:

> sets of facts, and you deal with them. But nobody is saying, what is the truth? There is no investigation by the court as to what happened. You're just telling different stories
> (Moffat in Galloway).

Fundamental questions of guilt and innocence are secondary to the believability of narratives presented as 'truth': within the courtroom scenarios constructed in both *The Night Of* and its sister text, the audience is lead to question the moral ethicacy of the judicial systems that underpin Western society. In each series, various lawyer archetypes are represented, all of whom (Stone included) seek not only to persuade the accused to collude in versions of truth, but to dissuade them from telling their own truth. As in *Criminal Justice*, on first meeting Stone orders the accused to 'shut it', advising him that due process within the judicial system is all a game-playing exercise in which they 'really, really don't want to be stuck with the truth' (*The Night Of*, ep. 1); rather, what is required is a version of truth that minimises impact and that a jury will believe. Stone simplifies the process for Naz, advising him that 'they (the prosecution) come up with their story, we come up with ours. The jury gets to decide which they like best' (ep. 2). Herein lies the dramatic crux of each series. The nature of the various 'truths' advocated varies; the more convoluted plea bargaining process undertaken in *Criminal Justice* is distilled into one moment in *The Night Of* when, in the tense atmosphere of the courtroom, Naz calmly chooses not to collude in lawyer Alison Crowe's version of events—a version which though likely to yield the best outcome for him in terms of prison sentence unfairly labels him a killer. Alison, who functions as the archetypally ambitious career-minded lawyer, who initially seizes the opportunity to further her reputation by successfully plea bargaining for the reduced sentence of a young Muslim man post-9/11, is replaced by idealistic lawyer 'rookie' Chandra

Kapoor whose naïve quest to tell Naz's truth in court backfires when, against Strong's street-wise advice, she calls him to testify. Each series presents a somewhat questionable gender politics: female defence lawyers are depicted as either Machiavellian types in the mould of contemporary lawyer figures like *Damages*' (2007–12) Patty Hewes, or gullible and romantically vulnerable novices. But in the guise of long-serving Helen Weiss, Zaillian and Price introduce a very different kind of female attorney for the prosecution: in a telling moment at the end of the trial, the camera focuses on Kapoor's stiletto-clad feet as she totters precariously out of court before shifting the focus to Weiss who removes her courtroom heels and dons a pair of timeworn trainers before striding out, her day's work completed. Weiss, like Box, is a throwback to an earlier kind of television narrative in which good at least attempts to prevail over evil, even when the system is not predisposed to such outcomes. When ultimately convinced of Naz's innocence Box influences an initially reluctant Weiss to drop the case against him; the close positions them as allies working outside the system to bring Andrea's murderer, Ray Halle, to trial. Ironically, the system saves Naz not by proving his innocence through a release realised by an agreed jury verdict of not guilty but by the system game-playing engineered by Weiss who, at the behest of Box, chooses not to ask for a retrial. Stone's earlier attempt to play the system by forcing a mistrial due to revelations of Kapoor's professional misconduct backfires. Instead of resulting in a mistrial, it leads to Stone's more prominent role in the closing stages of the trial, facilitating his dramatic closing speech—a speech which adds melodramatic weight to the narrative and that is denied to Moffat's Stone whose role as supporting defence lawyer is maintained throughout. Ultimately, there is a moral outcome of sorts since Naz is released from prison; however, the moral ambiguities of the justice system remain and the correctional system to which Naz has been exposed during the course of his quest for justice has already changed his own moral outlook and his capacity to be seen as 'innocent'—by his family, by his community, and by society at large—is forever compromised. The protagonist of Moffat's tale is initially found guilty of murder but is eventually released when the real killer is identified and brought to justice; Ben Coulter's innocence in the eyes of the law, of family and of society at large is restored, even if his prison experience has had a lasting impact on him. In *The Night Of*, Zaillian and Price choose to simplify Naz's journey through the judicial process but in so doing they also amplify the impact of the injustices he suffers at the hands of arbitrary systems. There is no guilty charge entered against Naz but there is also no neat resolution as Andrea's killer has yet to be indicted. Naz emerges as an isolated, drug-addicted loner whose role in the murder of Andrea Cornish remains unresolved.

Though some lawyers in TV narratives have attained iconic status as heroic defenders of the innocent, the lawyer hero is a rare species (Stark 256); John Stone emerges as *The Night Of*'s unconventional lawyer hero who, despite the inadequacies of the institutional systems he operates within, saves Nasir Kahn from a life of incarceration for a crime he has not committed. The TV lawyer hero plays a pivotal role in the drama enacted within the static, dialogue-driven parameters of the courtroom; however, he is also characterised by his involvement in matters that go beyond both his conventional and his lawful remit: he defends his client in court but, contrary to his designated role, he also serves as an investigator (Greenfield and Osborne 246). *Perry Mason* (1957–66) first established the figure of the lawyer hero during the early days of American television; he is the 'lawyer detective', TV's 'private eye masquerading as a lawyer' (Stark 250). Unlike the hard-boiled private eye archetype of cinema's film noir, Mason establishes a client–lawyer relationship built on trust and compassion; his clients are invariably white, middle class and innocent, his defence of them dependent not upon the dogged investigations of the lone private eye but on his reliable team—'girl Friday' Della Steele and upstanding detective Paul Drake—who help him track down and expose the real killer. Like Box, *The Night Of*'s Stone is, in part, a throwback to earlier TV archetypes: he is a pseudo-Perry Mason tasked with not only defending an innocent man but with identifying the real killer. Yet Stone is a much more complex subversion of that heroic lawyer archetype. He has more in common with the shady private eyes of film noir, and with 'rumpled, middle-aged shamuses' like Harry Orwell (*Harry O*, 1973–1976) and Jim Rockford (*The Rockford Files*, 1974–1980) who emerge in the seventies as 'knight errants' on a quest for justice, fuelled by their own unconventional 'code of honour' (Glover and Bushman 69), than with clean-cut defenders like Mason or Ben Matlock (*Matlock* 1986–1995). With a career built upon defending the guilty for petty crimes and his reputation for generating 'trade' via crass advertising signage, Stone is initially presented as more Saul Goodman (*Breaking Bad*, 2008–2013) than Perry Mason. In this instance, however, it is Stone's innate belief in a young Muslim boy's innocence that provides the story's overriding momentum. Stone's physical shortcomings and his emotional vulnerability are amplified here, making him a much more layered and compassionate character whose involvement with Naz, built across an eight-episode story arc, goes beyond the norms of the client–lawyer relationship. While his predecessor, Ralph Stone, is afflicted with a similar skin complaint and has a similarly 'rumpled' appearance, Ralph is not constructed as a system outsider with relationship issues. John Stone's storyline acquaints the audience with his deteriorating relationships, his attendance at group therapy sessions, his visits to prostitutes, doctors and Chinese herbalists, while his problematic relationship with lead defence lawyer Chandra Kapoor, and his growing relationships with Naz and the abandoned cat, serve to illustrate his compassion, the latter adding yet another quirky aspect to his characterisation. Moreover, Stone's role in the detection of the real killer is much more central to the narrative in this remake of Moffat's series. Moffat's Ralph Stone is in part restrained by the UK system: 'there is no investigation by the (UK) court as to what happened' (Moffat in Galloway), whereas John Stone's out of court investigations provide the main story threads in *The Night Of* and the dramatic momentum of events that unfold in the courtroom. There are many suspects and witnesses presented here as a consequence, taking the narrative on a much more procedural route than that of its sister text, *Criminal Justice*, and adding further plot twists that ensure Stone's prominence during the series' dramatic courtroom climax. Stone's attempts to serve justice through filing for a mistrial due to Kapoor's unprofessional conduct result in his own reluctant elevation to the role of lead defence lawyer, charged with the closing speech for the defence—a speech that is going to be instrumental in helping the jurors decide which 'story' they choose to believe in. He serves as the anchor for *The Night Of*'s complex hybridisation of the crime genre, the courtroom drama and TV noir, but it is in the closing courtroom scene—a scene that plays no part in Moffat's narrative—that, like all good TV lawyer heroes, Stone 'triumphs against adversity' (Greenfield and Osborne), having done enough to persuade at least some of the jurors that, even if the story presented by the defence does not clear Naz of the crime, it does leave room for reasonable doubt as to his guilt. In this final courtroom scene, Stone delivers an eloquent defence of his client, and of every American citizen's right to due judicial process:

> The night Naz was arrested, he lost a lot. He lost his freedom to return home to his family, to his school,

> to his night job that helps pay for that school. But what he didn't lose, what none of us can lose, were his constitutional rights to an attorney, to a fair and impartial trial by you, his peers, and the presumption of innocence beyond all reasonable doubt (ep. 8).

Though filtered through the lens of Naz's individual experience, Stone's speech returns us to Zaillian's overriding adaptive intention to explore notions of justice within 'the system itself' (Zaillian in Hughes).

As part of this exploration of the 'justice' afforded by institutional systems, Zaillian and Price follow Moffat's lead, creating a series that intermittently shifts the narrative into the generic arena of the prison drama presenting yet another critique of judicial systems. Prison films and TV narratives about prison experience are regarded as a significant means to revealing the lived experience within such institutions (Mason 2000; Wilson and O'Sullivan 2004); even if these constructed narratives remain a somewhat 'contested reality' (Wilson and O'Sullivan Images 11), they 'aler[t] the public to the failings of prison as an institution' (28) and provide for an audience who in the main has no experience of the system, a sense of what imprisonment entails. Zaillian and Price drew upon their research into life at New York's Rikers Island Prison Complex to present a realistic portrayal of the American prison experience (Zaillian in Ellis-Petersen); series' cast members also spent time interacting with inmates of Rikers Island as a means to understanding the lived prison experience, while prison scenes were shot on location at New York's Queens Detention Facility (Ellis-Petersen). Every effort was made to ensure the series is invested with a naturalistic realism. However, whether presented as fictional drama, reality TV show or quasi-documentary of the *Making a Murderer* variety, all prison narratives are to a certain extent creative constructs that seek to represent a life within a regime that lies outside mainstream experience, and all merge fiction and reality to come up with an approximation thereof in an effort to draw upon a public fascination with prisons and prisoners that dates back to the eighteenth century. The prison arena, like that of the courtroom, presents a confined space within which intense conflict-driven drama can unfold, providing the prison genre's 'trademark' appeal of 'an unfiltered, raw, and realistic perspective on criminality, systems of authority, and the socially marginal' (Wlodarz 66), even if that 'realistic experience' is filtered through the lens of creative storytelling of a fictional or documentary nature.

The TV prison series in general is not a popular form, particularly within an American context. Novek cites *Prison Break* (2005–) as the first 'sustained serial drama to appear' on US 'network television' (378), though HBO's *Oz* (1997–2003) appeared prior to this and can lay claim to being America's first hour-long TV prison series (Wlodarz 59). The current success of *Orange is the New Black* (2103–) points to a contemporary shift of American focus to narratives relating the lives of female inmates, a focus which has always prevailed in a British context with the hour-long prison TV series dominated by female prison narratives like *Bad Girls* (1999–2006) and imported product like the Australian prison drama *Prisoner* (1979–1986), its current remake *Wentworth* (2013–) and Netflix's *Orange is the New Black*. Nonetheless, *Porridge* (1974–1977) remains the seminal British prison drama: it is of a very different generic type that employs a half-hour sitcom format and presents a 'sanitized' portrayal of male prison experience (Wilson and O'Sullivan Images 7), with only *Buried* (2003) emerging as a serious treatment of the male prison drama on British broadcast TV in recent years. Wilson and O'Sullivan note that the popularity of prison movies that stay solely within the parameters of the prison genre has declined in recent times in favour of a more hybrid treatment that sees it form a constituent part of narratives with a wider reach, from 'cop-action-adventure movies, sci-fi prison movies', to 'gangsta-prison-hood movies and so forth' (Wilson and O'Sullivan Theoretical 486): a similar move to hybridity is in evidence in TV series like *Criminal Justice* and *The Night Of*, with their multistrand approach to narrative encompassing the generic tropes of crime, courtroom and prison drama, and both have more in common with uncompromising prison dramas like *Buried* and *Oz* than with the far more romanticised story treatment of a populist series like *Prison Break*, or the 'safe' prison narratives of *Porridge*. Nelson argues that *Oz* is a series that is 'primarily in a social realist tradition' of a kind 'untypical of American TV'; like *Homicide: Life on the Streets* (1993–1999), it has what he terms 'a hand-held documentary feel' (35). But the naturalism that characterises the televisual style employed in *The Night Of* has much more in common with the British social realist style signature of the TV series it adapts, and the more surreal moments found in *Oz* have no place in either.

Mason notes the clear 'correlation between prison, violence and masculinity' as a traditional trope of prison narratives (Prison 612), prison becoming what Wilson and O'Sullivan see as 'a testing ground for "cool masculinity"' of 'myth-making' proportions (Theoretical 486). In *Criminal Justice*, Freddie Graham is constructed as the genre's hyper-violent, hyper-masculine prison 'king-pin', interested only in maintaining control of the prison environment. Ben is just another new arrival cowered by and coerced into bending to the power of this menacing figure. The role of prison confidante falls here to prison veteran Hooch, The Listener, who serves as part social worker, part father confessor to vulnerable prisoners, but whose capacity to function in that role is also ultimately under the jurisdiction of Freddie. In line with the social realist style aesthetic of confrontingly violent British prison films like *McVicar* (1980), *Scum* (1983), and *In the Name of the Father* (1994), and TV series *Buried*, *Criminal Justice* presents harrowing images of prison violence in which displays of pack-driven masculinity lead to the intimidation and humiliation of the series' protagonist. 'Outed' as a 'grass' by prison bully Milroy, Ben is subjected to a painful, humiliating ritual, his naked body scalded, the burns covered in grass cuttings before being paraded in front of his fellow inmates. Wlodarz argues that HBO narratives 'privilege the masculine[e]' (65) and there are disturbingly violent moments in *The Night Of*'s prison scenes, but there is no ritualistic humiliation of its protagonist, and acts of violence perpetrated by its prison king-pin, Freddy Knight, are invariably constructed as acts of righteous retribution such as his killing of Victor whose sexual abuse of Petey leads to the latter's suicide. While American films of the late 1980s to mid-1990s present violent narratives where the prison arena is set up as a 'battlegroun[d] between warring gangs' (Wilson and O'Sullivan Images 17), in *The Night Of* Freddy's ascendancy remains unchallenged. Though equally menacing, equally controlling, and capable of shocking acts of violence, Freddy Knight, is constructed as one whose hyper-masculinity takes the form of benevolent father figure; he is on good terms with prison guards for reasons that go beyond intimidation and violence, and supportive of those prisoners who both work for him and who ask for his care and protection. Hooch is omitted, the compassionate elements of that figure becoming instead a part of Knight's characterisation. Just as Stone serves as the series' judicial 'knight errant', the aptly renamed Freddy Knight serves as knight protector of Naz within the prison context, presenting in the remake not only a different kind of relationship between prison 'king-pin' and the story's naïve protagonist, but a different tone to its treatment of the prison genre, even though its moments of on-screen violence are, in line with the traditions of the prison genre, 'decidedly' 'explicit' and 'scopophilic' (Mason Prison 615). In his previous role as Omar Little, the charismatic 'Robin Hood of the Projects' in Simon's *The Wire*, Michael Kenneth Williams attains a mythical status as the benevolent outlaw; the persona of Freddy Knight is thus similarly perceived from the outset, his role as prison patriarch built upon a '"cool masculinity"' of 'myth-making' proportions (Wilson and O'Sullivan Theoretical 486).

Prison films and TV series alike seek to 'humanize the offender' (Wilson and O'Sullivan Theoretical 473): American series like *Oz* and its British counterpart *Buried* provide not only 'visibi[lity]' for the prisoner but a greater understanding of the prisoner's plight (486), and both *Criminal Justice* and its remake build on this more compassionate representation of male prison experience through the vulnerable protagonist whose descent into the corrective system is charted from point of crime to arrest and trial, to the ongoing consequences thereof. The earlier attack upon Naz by one who initially purports to be his protector is less dramatic than that of Ben's 'outing' as a 'grass' and Naz's response is similarly more controlled. Where Ben remains vulnerable and non-violent throughout his prison term, Naz becomes increasingly aware of the prison system hierarchy: he actively seeks protection by aligning himself with Freddy, and a more violent side to his nature is revealed when he joins in the retributive beating of his attacker. Naz is constructed as one who, like Freddy, accepts the need to embrace a more hyper-masculine persona, donning tattoos, shaving his head, as a means to survival within the prison system; his 'cool masculinity' is amplified in this series, making him a character who, unlike Ben, is able to retain audience empathy as the everyman figure with whom we choose to identify rather than the victim with whom we merely sympathise. The genre's trope of the 'surrogate' prison family (Jarvis 163) remains an important generic marker of the series. Prison paterfamilias, Freddy, is attracted to Naz because of the innate innocence and tangible intellect that sets Naz apart from other inmates; he is that rare thing, a 'unicorn' (ep. 8) that Freddy chooses to protect and bring into the family fold as his companion. Moreover, though the prison genre is regarded as 'one of the most homoerotic genres in the history of cinema and television' (Wlodarz 66), this is one trope that plays little part in the narrative of *The Night Of* or its precursor text; the relationship between Naz and Freddy bears none of the hallmarks of the prison genre's homoerotic undertones. Scenes of a sexual nature are limited to disturbing moments in which Naz witnesses Petey's abuse at the hands of predatory Victor—an 'incestuous' abuse that constitutes an act of family betrayal. With family membership, however, comes an inevitable loss of innocence as Naz becomes increasingly involved in Freddy's drug-dealing enterprise in the role of both helper and client. Tellingly, where Ben is first introduced to drugs through the violent coercion of Freddie Graham, Naz is yet again constructed as one who makes this conscious choice of his own volition: he adopts the survivor mentality that Ben is never able to grasp, maintaining once more a façade of 'cool masculinity'.

The BBC's *Criminal Justice* functions as a short anthology series, retaining in its second season the same title and the same thematic preoccupation with matters of social justice, while presenting a different narrative peopled by different characters. Given the critical and commercial success of *The Night Of*, the production of further narratives based on the BBC series is likely, but whether HBO follows the British lead with an anthology-style format remake remains to be seen. Due to the more distinctive nature of the lead characters in *The Night Of*, there is a possibility that the existing remake narrative may instead provide a springboard for other stories revolving around its quirky lawyer John Stone, its 'old school' police detective Dennis Box, or its troubled post-release protagonist, Nasir Kahn, and this despite initial intentions of HBO and the series' writers to see it as a 'stand-alone' piece. Rumours abound as to the possibility of a second season and the shape and the focus of any further extension of the narrative has yet to be determined but like its precursor text, *The Night Of* is a series that presents 'infinite and endless possibilities' (Stam 64) for textual transformation.

Works Cited

Bazin, André. "Adaptation, or the Cinema as Digest." *Film Adaptation*. Ed. James Naremore. New Brunswick: Rutgers UP, 2000. 19–27. Print.

Bigsby, Christopher. *Viewing America: 21st Century Drama*. Cambridge and New York: Cambridge University Press, 2003. Print.

Birnbaum, Debra. "Writers' Rooms Vs. Solo Scribes: Where Does TV Creativity Flourish Best?" *Variety*, 8 June 2014. Web. 2 Nov. 2015.

Boozer, Jack. "Introduction." *Authorship in Film Adaptation*. Ed. Jack Boozer. Austin: University of Texas Press, 2008. 1–30. Print.
Braudy, Leo. "Afterword: Rethinking Remakes." *Play It Again Sam: Retakes on Remakes*. Eds. Andrew Horton and Stuart Y. McDougal. Berkeley, Los Angeles, and London: University of California Press, 1998. 328–333. Print.
Cardwell, Sarah. "Literature on the Small Screen: Television Adaptations." *Literature on Screen on Screen*. Eds. Deborah Cartmell and Imelda Whelehan. Cambridge: Cambridge University Press, 2007. 181–195. Print.
Chalaby, Jean K. "Drama without Drama: The Late Rise of Scripted TV Formats." *Television & New Media* 17.1 (2015): 1–18. Print.
Corcos, Christine C. "Legal Fictions: Irony, Storytelling, Truth, and Justice in the Modern Courtroom Drama." *UALR Law Review* 25 (2002–2003): 503–633. Print.
De Fino, Dean J. *The HBO Effect*. London and New York: Bloomsbury Academic, 2014. Print.
Ellis-Petersen, Hannah. "'It's Crazy, Scary': Drama *The Night Of* Exposes 'Predatory' US Justice System." *The Guardian* (Culture), 8 July 2016: Television. Print.
Galloway, Stephen. "How HBO's 'The Night Of' was Inspired By One Real-Life Lawyer's Encounters with Crime and Punishment." *Hollywood Reporter*, 30 July 2016. Web. 7 Aug. 2016.
Gil, Steven. "A Remake By Any Other Name: Use of a Premise Under a New Title." *Remake Television: Reboot, Re-use, Recycle*. Ed. C. Lavigne. Maryland: Lexington Books, 2014. 21–36. Print.
Gills, Melina. "Oscar-winner Steven Zaillian Makes His Hit TV Debut with HBO's *The Night Of*." *Tribeca* 7 April 2016. Web. 10 Aug. 2016.
Glover, Allen, and David Bushman. "Lights Out in the Wasteland: the TV Noir." *TV Quarterly* 37.1 2006: 67–75. Print.
Greenfield, Steve, and Guy Osborn. "Film Lawyers: Above and Beyond the Law." *Criminal Visions: Media Representations of Crime and Justice*. Ed. Paul Mason. London and New York: Routledge, 2003/2013: 238–253. Print.
Grindstaff, Laura. "A Pygmalion tale retold: Remaking *La Femme Nikita*." *Camera Obscura* 16.2, 47 (2001): 133–175. Print.
Hogg, Christopher. "Cracking the USA? Interpreting UK-to-US TV Drama Translations." *New Review of Film and Television Studies* 11.2 (2013): 111–132. Print.
Horton, Andrew. "Cinematic Makeovers and Cultural Border Crossing: Kusturica's *Time of the Gypsies* and Coppola's *Godfather* and *Godfather II*." *Play it Again Sam: Retakes on Remakes*. Eds. Andrew Horton and Stuart Y. McDougal. Berkeley, Los Angeles, and London: University of California Press, 1998. 172–190. Print.
Hughes, Sarah. "Richard Price: the Kingpin of Crime TV- and David Simon's Go-to-Guy." *The Guardian*, 1 September 2016: Television. Print.

Hutcheon, Linda. *A Theory of Adaptation*. London: Routledge, 2006. Print.
Idato, Michael. "A Gripping Takedown of American Justice, *The Night Of* is as great as *The Wire*." *The Sydney Morning Herald*, July 11 2016: TV & Radio. Print.
Jarvis, Brian. "The Violence of Images: Inside the Prison TV Drama Oz." *Captured by the Media: Prison Discourse in Popular Culture*. Ed. Paul Mason. Abingdon and New York: Routledge, 2013. 154–171. Print.
Klein, Amanda Ann, and R. Barton Palmer. Eds. *Cycles, Sequels, Spin-Offs, Remakes and Reboots: Multiplicities in Film and Television*. Austin: University of Texas Press, 2016. Print.
Lane, Philip J. "The Existential Condition of Television Crime Drama." *Journal of Popular Culture* 34.4 (2001): 137–151. Print.
Lavigne, Carlen, and Heather Marcovitch. (Eds.). *American Remakes of British Television: Transformations and Mistranslations*. Lanham, MD: Lexington Books. 2011. Print.
Leishman, Frank, and Paul Mason. "From *Dock Green* to Docusoap: Decline and Fall in TV Copland." *Criminal Justice Matters* 59.1 (2008): 22–23. Print.
Macauley, Stewart. "Images of Law in Everyday Life." *Law and Society Review* 21(1987): 185–218. Print.
Madger, Ted. "The End of Reality TV 101: Reality Programs, Formats, and the New Business of Television." *Reality TV: Remaking Television Culture*. Eds. Susan Murray and Laurie Ouellette. New York: New York University Press, 2004. 137–156. Print.
Martin, Brett. "Inside the *Breaking Bad* Writers' Room: How Vince Gilligan Runs the Show." *The Guardian*, 9 September 2103: Television. Print.
Mason, Paul. "Prison Decayed: Cinematic Penal Discourse and Populism 1995–2005." *Social Semiotics* 16.4 (2006): 607–626. Print.
McCabe, Janet. "HBO Aesthetics: Quality TV and Boardwalk Empire." *TV Aesthetics and Style*. Eds. Steven Peacock and Jason Jacobs. New York and London: Bloomsbury, 2013. 199–209. Print.
Mittell, Jason. *Complex TV: The Poetics of Contemporary Television Storytelling*. New York and London: New York University Press, 2015. Print.
Moran, Albert. "Makeover on the Move: Global TV and Programme Formats." *Journal of Media and Cultural Studies* 22.4 (2008): 459–469. Print.
———. "Global TV Formats: Genesis and Growth." *Critical Studies in TV: The International Journal of TV Studies* 8.2 (2013): 1–19. Print.
———. "Americanisation, Hollywoodization, or English-language Market Variation? Comparing British and American versions of Cracker." *American Remakes of British Television: Transformations and Mistranslations*. Eds. Carlen Lavigne and Heather Markovitch. Plymouth: Lexington Books, 2011. 35–54. Print.
Murray, Simone. *The Adaptation Industry: The Cultural Economy of Contemporary Literary Adaptation*. London, New York: Routledge: 2012. Print.

Nelson, Robin. "HBO PREMIUM: Channelling Distinction Through TVIII." *New Review of Film and Television Studies* 5.1 (2007): 25–40. Print.
Newman, Michael Z, and Elana Levine. *Legitimating Television Media Convergence and Cultural Studies*. New York and Abingdon: Routledge, 2012. Print.
Nichols-Pethick, Jonathan. *TV Cops: The Contemporary American Television Police Drama*. New York: Routledge, 2012. Print.
———. "Nobody with a Good Script Needs to be Justified." *Cinema Journal* 50.2 (2011): 153–166. Print.
Okeowo, Alexis. "Riz Ahmed's Tragic Transformation on 'The Night Of'." *The New Yorker* 30 Aug. 2016. Web. 10 Sept. 2016.
O'Regan, Tom, and Sue Ward. "Defining a National Brand: Australian Television Drama and the Global Television Market." *Journal of Australian Studies* 35.1 (2011): 33–34. Print.
Ousborne, Jeff. "Policing the Crime Drama: Radio Noir, *Dragnet*, and Jack Webb's Maladjusted Text." *CLUES: A Journal of Detection* 34.2 (2016): 32–42. Print.
Palmer, R. Barton. "*Dragnet*, film noir and postwar realism." *The Philosophy of TV Noir (Philosophy of Popular Culture)*. Eds. Steven M. Sanders and Aeon J. Skoble. Kentucky: University of Kentucky Press, 2008. 33–48. Print.
Palmieri, Lea. "Queue and A: What Images Never Made it into 'The Night Of' Opening Credits?" *Decider* 18 July 2016. Web. 10 Sept. 2016.
Perkins, Claire. "Translating the Television 'Treatment' Genre: *Be'Tipul* and *In Treatment*." *Continuum* 29.5 (2015): 781–794. Print.
Poniewozik, James. "*True Detective*, *Louie*, and the Limits of TV Auteurism." *Time*, 11 Aug. 2015. Web. 11 Sept. 2016.
Radish, Christina. "Steven Zaillian, Richard Price, Riz Ahmed and Michael K. Williams Talk 'The Night Of'." *Collider*, 21 Aug. 2016. Web. 11 Sept. 2016.
Rapping, Elayne. *Law and Justice as Seen on TV*. New York and London: New York University Press, 2003. Print.
Robson, Peter. "Lawyers and the Legal System on TV: the British Experience." *International Journal of Law in Context* 2.4 (2007): 333–362. Print.
Sanders, Steven M. "Noir et Blanc in Color: Existentialism and Miami Vice." *The Philosophy of TV Noir (Philosophy of Popular Culture)*. Eds. Steven M. Sanders and Aeon J. Skoble. Kentucky: University of Kentucky Press, 2008. 95–114. Print.
Sanders, Steven, and Aeon J. Skoble. (Eds.). *The Philosophy of TV Noir (Philosophy of Popular Culture)*. Kentucky: University of Kentucky Press, 2008. Print.
Schickel, Richard. "Rerunning Film Noir." *The Wilson Quarterly* 31.3 (2007): 36–43. Print.
Stam, Robert. "Beyond Fidelity: the Dialogics of Adaptation." *Film Adaptation*. Ed. James Naremore. London: Athlone, 2000. 54–76. Print.

Stanhope, Kate. "'The Night Of' Executive Producer: 'We're Talking About' a Possible Second Season." *Hollywood Reporter*, 30 July 2016. Web. 11 Sept. 2016.
Stark, Steven D. "Perry Mason *Meets Sonny Crockett: The History of Lawyers and the Police as Television Heroes*." *University of Miami Law Review* 249 (1987): 229–280. Print.
Steemers, Jeanette. "British Television in the American Market Place." *American Remakes of British Television: Transformations and Mistranslations*. Eds. Carlen Lavigne and Heather Markovitch. Plymouth: Lexington Books, 2011. 1–16. Print.
Tate, Gabriel. "How Noah Hawley became TV's most wanted writer." *iNews* 17 Feb. 2017. Web. 21 Feb. 2017.
Travers, Ben. "The Night Of Season 2: Riz Ahmed, John Turturro, and Steven Zaillian explain what it would take to make more seasons." *IndieWire* April 7 2017. Web. May 10 2017.
Turnbull, Sue. "Trafficking in TV Crime: Remaking Broadchurch." *Continuum* 29.5 (2015): 706–717. Print.
Walker-Morrison, Deborah. "Sex, Ratio, Socio-sexuality, and the Emergence of the Femme Fatale in Classic French and American Film Noir." *Film & History* 45.1 (2015): 25–37. Print.
Wells-Lassagne, Shannon. *Television and Serial Adaptation*. New York and Abingdon, 2017. Print.
Wilson, David, and Sean O'Sullivan. *Images of Incarceration: Representations of Prison Film and Television Drama*. Winchester: Waterside Press, 2004. Print.
———. "Re-theorizing the Penal Reform Functions of the Prison Film: Revelation, Humanization, Empathy and Benchmarking." *Theoretical Criminology* 9.4 (2005): 471–491. Print.
Wlodarz, Joe. "Maximum Insecurity: Genre Trouble and Closet Erotics in and out of HBO's *Oz*." *Camera Obscura* 20(1:58) (2005): 59–105. Print.
Yousman, Bill. "Inside Oz: Hyperviolence, Race and Class Nightmares, and the Engrossing Spectacle of Terror." *Communication and Critical/Cultural Studies* 6:3 (2009): 265–284. Print.
Zeitchik, Steven. "HBO's Topical Crime Drama 'The Night Of' is More of a Character Study than a Procedural." *Los Angeles Time*, 8 July 2016. Web. 11 Sept. 2016.

Screenography

Television

Bad Girls (1999–2006, UK: ITV).
Be Tipul (2005-Israel: HOT3).
Breaking Bad (2008–2013, US: AMC).

Broadchurch (2013–2017, UK: ITV).
Buried (2003, UK: BBC).
Cambridge Spies (2003, UK: BBC).
Cracker (1993–2006, UK: ITV).
Criminal Justice (2009–2010, UK: BBC).
Dragnet (1951–1959, US: NBC).
Gracepoint (2014–, US: FOX).
Harry O (1973–1976, US: ABC).
Hatufim (2009–2012, Israel: Channel 2).
Homeland (2011–, US: Showtime).
Homicide: Life on the Streets (1993–1999, US: NBC).
House of Cards (2013–, US: Netflix).
In Treatment (2008–2010, US: HBO).
Law and Order (1990–2010, US: NBC).
Life on Mars (2006–2007, UK: BBC).
Making a Murderer (2015–, US: Netflix).
Matlock (1986–1995, US: NBC).
North Square (2001, UK: Channel 4).
Oz (1997–2003, US: HBO).
Orange is the New Black (2103–, US: Netflix).
Penny Dreadful (2014–2016, US: Showtime).
Porridge (1974–1977, UK: BBC).
Prisoner (1979–1986, Australia: Network Ten).
Prime Suspect (1991–2006, UK: ITV).
Prison Break (2005–2017, US: FOX).
Sanford and Son (1972–1977, US: NBC).
She's Gotta Have it (2017–, US: Netflix).
Steptoe and Son (1962–1967, UK: BBC).
Top of the Lake (2013–, UK/Auatralia/US: BBC/BBCUKTV/ Sundance).
ShakespeaREtold (2005, UK: BBC).
Silk (2011–2014, UK: BBC).
Soupçon (2004, France: Canal+).
Spiral (2005–, France: Canal+).
The Jinx: the Life and Death of Robert Durst (2015, US: HBO).
The Office (2001–2003, UK: BBC).
The Office (2005–2013, US: NBC).
The People v O. J. Simpson (2016, US:FX).
The Rockford Files (1974–1980, US: NBC).
The Shield (2002–2008, US: FX).
The Sopranos (1999–2007, US: HBO).
The Strain (2014–2017, US: FX).
The Wire (2002–2008, US: HBO.

The Village (2013, UK: BBC).
Wentworth (2013–, Australia: SoHo).

Film

Fargo. Dirs. Joel, and Ethan Coen. 1996.
American Gangster. Dir. Ridley Scott. 2007.
Clockers. Dir. Spike Lee. 1995.
Gangs of New York. Dir. Martin Scorsese. 2002.
In the Name of the Father. Dir. Jim Sheridan. 1994.
McVicar. Dir. Tom Clegg. 1980.
Schindler's List. Dir. Steven Spielberg. 1993.
Scum. Dir. Alan Clarke. 1983.
The Color of Money. Dir. Martin Scorsese. 1986.

Podcast

Serial (2014–2016, US: iTunes).

Afterword: One More 'Turn'....

This study was never intended to be the definitive word on TV and adaptation. Rather, my intention has been to encourage further discourse around this particularly fertile and yet to date relatively uncharted area of adaptations scholarship, by exploring the adaptive processes at work in the re-visioning of pre-existing stories into long-form serial narratives within the media-specific parameters of television production. What emerges is an understanding that the creative and industrial processes that shape these serialized adaptations present *new* ways of engaging in the re-presentation of not only pre-existing stories but of pre-existing style aesthetics. Moreover, they emerge as intertextually complex constructs, connected to *networks* of both medium-specific and culturally-specific genre practices that inform their inception, their reception, and their consumption.

In a TV medium acutely aware of the financial rewards of appealing to an existing fan-base, the adaptation of pre-loved stories is becoming a favoured mode of story design. The strength of these serialized adaptations lies in their capacity to become what Palmer terms 'gestures of continuation' (76): by expanding story worlds within the time-rich structures of the long-form narrative, TV adapters are able to create innovative riffs on what has gone before. The adaptive opportunities presented by serial adaptation are boundless: story design becomes a complex interplay between the existing tale and the newly conceived diegesis in which the thematic layers embedded in a precursor text can be unravelled across not just seasonal story arcs but an entire series. Series like

Penny Dreadful and *Orange is the New Black* illustrate the myriad ways in which TV serial adaptation enacts expansion of existing story worlds in pursuit of densely stratified narratives that provide opportunities to draw ever more layered character studies, and ever more nuanced explorations of issues that connect with matters related to the contemporary era of production as well as the contemporary scene of the precursor text. The study heralds a growing tendency towards the production of adaptations that, like *Orange is the New Black*, are from point of inception envisioned as stories that will play out across multiple seasons. The popularity of series like *The Handmaid's Tale* (2017–) and *Twelve Monkeys* (2015–), now in their respective second and fourth seasons, demonstrates the potential longevity of existing narratives that within the context of TV production can play out ad infinitum, despite the more limited narrative scope of the texts they spin out from. Narrative continuity is wired into the story mainframe in ways that exceed the boundaries of their story origins.

Matters of authorship and ownership of narrative remain central to scholarly discourse in the field of adaptation studies but when coupled here with television studies what emerges is an understanding that, even though the quest for authorial integrity now forms part of a quest for prestige brand identity in what is the highly competitive TVIII marketplace, there are signs that the *sharing* of an authorial signature is an accepted and acceptable part of textual transformation when narratives transition to the platform of TV serialisation. *Fargo* is a series that has a potential for adaptive continuity that differs from that of series where story remains one of the key signifiers of appropriation. Taking not story but style aesthetic as its overriding point of adaptive transition, the series has the capacity to play out across multiple anthologized seasons that add their own mark to the Coen brothers' pre-existing style signature. In this highly innovative and equally rich approach to adaptation, Hawley models an alternative way of engaging with a prior text or body of texts that, given the ongoing success of the series, has the potential to become an accepted mode of adaptive industry practice worthy of further study.

What also emerges during the course of this study is that in design, production and consumption, the act of adaptation is one that is considered without prejudice. In the paratextually rich environs of TV production the relationship between prior texts and serial adaptations is invariably debated as a point of interest rather than as a site of contested ownership as demonstrated by the positive reception of *The Night Of.*

The recycling of narrative forms is an established mode of production embraced by the television industry as profitable industry practice employed on an increasingly global scale, and the remake that successfully transitions to its new geographical and cultural locale can establish an identity that is independent of its relationship with any former story. In the current 'golden age' of serialised television drama, the practice of adaptation constitutes an evolutionary rather than an interventionist act: an act that entails but one *more* 'turn' (Stam 81) in a story's journey to an endlessly yet unidentifiable destination point. This study is another such 'turn', designed to generate further discourse around TV serial adaptation as an increasingly dominant mode of creative expression.

WORKS CITED

Palmer, R. Barton. "Continuation, Adaptation Studies, and the Never-Finished Text." *Adaptation in Visual Culture: Images, Texts, and Their Multiple Worlds*. Eds. Julie Grossman and R. Barton Palmer. Houndsmill: Palgrave Macmillan, 2017. 73–100. Print.

Stam, Robert. "Beyond Fidelity: The Dialogics of Adaptation." *Film Adaptation*. Ed. James Naremore. New Brunswick: Rutgers University Press, 2000. 54–78. Print.

Screenography

Fargo (2014–, US: FX).
Orange is the New Black (2103–, US: Netflix).
Penny Dreadful (2014–2016, US: SHOWTIME).
The Handmaid's Tale (2016–, US: HULU).
The Night Of (2016, US: HBO).
Twelve Monkeys (2015–, US: Syfy).

Index

A
Adaptation, 1, 2, 4–10, 13–20, 22, 23, 25, 27, 42–44, 46, 48, 49, 52, 55, 56, 59, 67–72, 85, 86, 105, 106, 111, 139, 144–146, 152–154, 156, 157, 161–164, 167, 172, 195
Anthology series, 4, 5, 9, 10, 38, 67–72, 75–78, 80, 84–87, 91, 92, 97, 100, 187
Appropriation, 5, 9, 13–15, 22, 26, 35, 38, 42, 47, 50, 51, 58, 59, 71, 72, 77, 78, 89, 140, 196

B
Branding, 2, 6–8, 54, 159

C
Canon/canonical, 4–7, 9, 13–17, 19, 20, 22–25, 27, 28, 33, 38, 42–44, 46–52, 55, 56, 58, 59
Coen, Joel and Ethan, 5, 7, 9, 18, 67–80, 82, 84–100, 196
Comedy, 37, 70, 75, 76, 88, 105, 106, 111, 115, 116, 117–119, 122, 123, 131, 132, 134–138, 143, 144, 156
Costume drama, 9, 13–23, 24, 36, 37, 39, 51, 55–58
Courtroom drama, 151, 164, 172, 178, 179, 182, 184
Crime drama, 151, 154–156, 164, 166, 167, 169, 170, 172, 173, 176–178, 184
Criminal Justice, 151, 161–164, 166, 167, 169, 170, 172–174, 176–179, 182, 184–187

D
Detective genre, 20, 21, 178
Dracula, 13, 17, 23, 26, 27, 29, 35, 36, 42, 44, 46–49
Dramedy, 105, 111, 116, 132, 143

F
Fargo (film), 67–69, 71–74, 78, 80, 84, 85, 90–92, 94, 97, 196
Fargo (TV), 4, 5, 7, 9, 10, 68–73, 75, 77, 79, 92, 95, 100, 160

Film noir, 99, 170, 172, 173, 181
Frankenstein, Or the Modern Myth of Prometheus/Frankenstein, 13, 17, 20, 23, 27, 30–34, 36, 39, 40, 42, 44–48, 51, 55–57
FX, 1–3, 7, 38, 49, 70, 71, 154, 156, 160

G

Gender, 15, 21, 26, 76, 117, 131, 132, 180
Genre, 6, 7, 9, 14, 15, 17, 19, 21–28, 31, 32, 34, 36–40, 42, 52, 57, 59, 68, 73, 87, 105, 106, 109, 111–117, 119, 120, 122, 123, 125, 130–134, 136, 137, 139, 143, 160, 168–173, 176, 182–187, 195
Golden Age of TV, 1, 38, 59, 67, 146, 151, 152, 154, 156, 164, 194, 197
Gothic, 6, 13, 14, 16, 21–30, 32, 34–42, 47, 49, 52, 53, 55, 57, 58
Gray, Jonathan, 6, 50, 51, 117, 139

H

Hammer horror, 6, 39, 44, 46–48, 52
Hawley, Noah, 5, 9, 67–83, 85–88, 90–93, 95–100, 160, 196
HBO, 1–3, 7, 8, 10, 18, 49, 151, 152, 154, 156, 158, 159, 161–164, 166, 167, 173, 179, 184, 185, 187
Horror genre, 7, 23, 28, 31, 36–40, 57, 134, 143
Hutcheon, Linda, 7, 42, 55, 152, 155, 157

I

Intertextuality, 5, 6, 9, 20, 24, 35, 44, 47, 50, 67–69, 71, 72, 80, 81, 94, 96, 100, 105, 111–113, 116, 117, 130, 131, 134, 139, 140, 151, 166, 167

K

Kerman, Piper, 5, 105–108, 110, 112–117, 119–123, 126, 127, 129–135, 140, 143–145
Kohan, Jenji, 5, 8, 10, 105–127, 130–137, 139–142, 145
Kohlke, Marie-Luise, 14

L

Logan, John, 5, 15–17, 19–24, 26–36, 39–49, 51–56, 58, 145
Lotz, Amanda D., 7, 50, 58, 117, 132, 139

M

Marketing, 6, 7, 20, 50–54, 58, 140, 143, 146, 152, 154, 156, 158, 171, 172
Melodrama, 10, 39, 111, 115, 119–122, 124–130, 143, 180
Memoir, 5, 10, 105–110, 112–117, 119, 121, 124, 127, 129–133, 135, 139–141, 143–146
Mittell, Jason, 3–6, 8, 14, 44, 45, 50, 54, 111, 119, 142, 157, 158, 160, 163
Moffat, Peter, 164, 169, 179, 180, 182, 183
Moran, Albert, 153, 154
Myth/mythology, 9, 16, 22, 31, 35, 36, 40, 42–44, 46–50, 68, 71, 72, 74, 77–86, 100, 106, 153, 173, 185, 186

N

Neo-Victorian, 6, 9, 13–17, 21–26, 28, 30, 33, 34, 38, 42, 44, 59

Netflix, 1–3, 7, 18, 105, 112, 140–143, 154, 156, 159, 184
The Night Of, 2, 5, 7, 10, 151, 152, 155, 160–174, 176–182, 184–187, 196

O
Orange is the New Black (book), 105, 106, 108, 130, 135, 136, 139, 144, 145, 196
Orange is the New Black (TV series), 2, 7, 10, 106, 108, 109, 111, 113–117, 119–122, 127, 129, 131, 132, 136–140, 142, 143, 166, 184, 196
Original, 3, 7, 8, 10, 15, 45, 48, 57, 59, 90, 105, 142, 151–158, 162, 164

P
Palmer, R. Barton, 9, 20, 68, 89–91, 153, 173, 177, 195
Paratext/paratextuality, 2, 6, 7, 22, 49–51, 58, 105, 139, 140, 142, 143, 196
Penny Dreadful, 2, 5–7, 9, 10, 13–22, 24, 25, 27, 30, 33, 35–59, 146, 196
The Picture of Dorian Gray/Dorian Gray, 23, 26, 27, 40, 42, 44, 46, 49, 51, 55–57
Popular culture, 36, 54, 81, 100, 112
Prequel, 1, 10, 33, 54, 67, 68
Prestige quality/TV, 14, 120, 146, 154, 163
Price, Richard, 160–169, 175–178, 180, 183
Prison drama, 151, 164, 172, 173, 183, 184

Production context, 2, 4, 8, 17, 41, 91, 106, 139, 152, 153, 157, 159–161

R
Reboot, 1, 67, 69
Remake, 1, 5, 7, 10, 67–69, 113, 151–157, 161, 162, 164, 166–168, 170, 172–174, 179, 182, 184–187, 197

S
Sequel, 1, 10, 33, 54, 67
Serial/seriality, 1–10, 14, 18–21, 27, 41, 44, 45, 49, 51, 55, 71, 110, 120, 127, 133, 142, 145, 184, 195–197
Series, 2, 4–10, 13–15, 17–28, 30–46, 48–59, 67–76, 78–88, 90–95, 97–100, 105–120, 122–137, 139–146, 151–180, 182–187, 195, 196
Sex and the City, 108, 117–119, 132, 135–137, 143
Showrunner, 8, 157–161
Showtime, 1–3, 17, 18, 22, 36, 49–54, 58, 146, 154, 156, 159
Soap, 120
Stam, Robert, 7, 9, 42, 59, 68, 139, 153, 187, 197
The Strange Case of Dr Jekyll and Mr Hyde, 42, 49

T
Transgender, 107, 118, 119, 140, 141
TV auteur, 6, 8, 9, 145, 158–160
TV noir, 170, 172–174, 176, 182

W

The Wire, 120–122, 127, 129, 130, 158, 160, 163, 186

Women-in-Prison genre, 105, 106, 109, 111–117, 119, 130–132, 136–139

Z

Zaillian, Steven, 161, 162, 164, 165, 167–169, 172–176, 178, 180, 183

Zaillian in Travers, 165

Lightning Source UK Ltd.
Milton Keynes UK
UKHW02n0629310718
326547UK00019B/416/P